THE WILDERNESS OF ZIN

THE WILDERNESS OF ZIN

ARCHAEOLOGICAL REPORT

First published by Order of the Committee
PALESTINE EXPLORATION FUND
in
ANNUAL
1914 – 1915
DOUBLE VOLUME

This edition published 2003
Stacey International
128 Kensington Church Street
London W8 4BH
Tel: 020 7221 7166 Fax: 020 7792 9288
E-mail: stacey-inter@btconnect.com

© Palestine Exploration Fund 2003

ISBN: 1 900988 291

Printed and bound by Oriental Press

British Library Cataloguing-in-Publication Data
A catalogue record for this publication is available from the British Library

Half-title picture: Carchemish Excavations, Spring, 1913
Detail showing T E Lawrence and C Leonard Woolley
Department of The Ancient Near East, British Museum, Neg. No. Carchemish 645
(Courtesy of the Trustees of the British Museum)

PALESTINE EXPLORATION FUND

THE WILDERNESS OF ZIN

C. Leonard Woolley
and
T. E. Lawrence

REVISED EDITION

Preface by **Jonathan Tubb**
Introduction by **T. Sam N. Moorhead**

STACEY INTERNATIONAL

CONTENTS

ILLUSTRATIONS IN THE TEXT

Preface to the Third Edition by Jonathan Tubb, Chairman of the Palestine Exploration Fund

The Wilderness of Zin was first published by the Palestine Exploration Fund in autumn 1915 as its Annual for 1914-5. This re-publication has not been precipitated by a momentous event as was the case with its predecessor – the 1936 edition, published by Jonathan Cape, was produced in direct response to the death of T. E. Lawrence in 1935.

The Fund has decided that it is time to present this important work to a new public. Such is the stature of this pioneering survey that it is still able to stand alone as a remarkable piece of scholarship despite its age. However, it has been deemed appropriate to alter the format slightly whilst retaining all the content of previous editions, and to provide some extra unpublished information from the P.E.F.'s archives. During a recent reorganisation and study of the Wilderness of Zin material in the Fund's archives, much new information has been uncovered which casts additional light on the pursuit of the survey. The Fund is indebted to Jeremy Wilson who conducted the bulk of this work whilst researching for his biography of T. E. Lawrence, a book which includes the most comprehensive account of the survey (Wilson 1989, 135-154).

The work of co-ordinating and editing the new contributions has been undertaken by Sam Moorhead whose dedication to the project of re-publishing the Wilderness of Zin is clear from his own chapter; in itself, a work of outstanding scholarship which provides new insights into the background to, and execution of, the survey, and paves the way for further research on the archaeological collections from Zin, housed at the Fund.

Sam Moorhead has also sorted further archival material with the assistance of Felicity Cobbing, the Curator at the Palestine Exploration Fund, and it is she also who has, with great skill and sensitivity, re-imaged the original photographs, the majority of which have seriously faded and detiorated since the Cape edition in 1936. A selection of letters relating to the survey is appended, notable being those by C. Leonard Woolley, T. E. Lawrence, Stewart F. Newcombe and Frederic G. Kenyon. An extra map, reprinted from the comprehensive article by Rupert Chapman and Shimon Gibson on the photography undertaken during the survey (Gibson and Chapman 1996, 94-102), a select bibliography, and a selection of reviews of the 1936 edition are also provided. The purpose of these additions is to enable the reader to understand more clearly the background to the survey, its publication and reception by the public, as well as illuminating the dramatis personae behind the romantic facade of this expedition on the eve of the First World War.

Introduction to the Third Edition by T. Sam N. Moorhead, Keeper of Archives, Palestine Exploration Fund

It is not the intention of this third edition to reappraise the archaeological work and conclusions of Woolley and Lawrence. Such an undertaking requires a volume of its own as the survey covered numerous sites dating from the prehistoric to modern eras. However, it is intended that such a work will be prepared and published under the auspices of the Fund within a few years. To learn more about the history and archaeology of the region, readers are directed in the first instance to *The New Encyclopedia of Archaeological Excavations in the Holy Land* (1993). However, at this stage, it is appropriate to discuss the background of the survey in greater detail than was done in the original publication, primarily through reference to the Fund's extensive archive, a listing of which is provided in Appendix 2. The following account, 'The Genesis, Conduct and Publication of The Survey' is intended to supplement *The Wilderness of Zin* by establishing a more comprehensive context for the reader.

The author is grateful to a large number of people who have helped bring this re-publication to completion. Numerous scholars have provided generous assistance: Sean Kingsley and Peter Clayton at *Minerva*; Peter Metcalfe, secretary of the T. E. Lawrence Society; Henrietta McCall and Paul Dove at the British Museum; several committee members at the Fund: Denys Pringle, David Jacobson, Ashley Jones and the Chairman, Jonathan Tubb. Throughout the work, Rupert Chapman, Executive Secretary of the Fund, has been a constant source of information; I am grateful to him and Shimon Gibson for being able to reproduce the map from their article on the photography of the expedition (Chapman and Gibson 1996); Felicity Cobbing, the Fund's Curator must be credited with many days of work scanning and cleaning the images, some photographs requiring three hours work. Like many of our projects, this has been a team effort in the best traditions of the Palestine Exploration Fund.

The PEF is most grateful to C. V. Carey and the Trustees of the Seven Pillars of Wisdom Trust for allowing the publication of various excerpts from T. E. Lawrence's letters, and to Christopher Leaver at Moorhead-James for advice about other copyright issues. The Fund is also deeply grateful to Max Scott and Kitty Carruthers at Stacey International for seeing the work through publication and bringing this book to light again.

I must state how deeply indebted I am to two scholars whose research and publications have been invaluable in the writing of the piece that follows: Jeremy Wilson is the authority on T. E. Lawrence (1988 and 1989); Victor Winstone has written excellent volumes on the Near East, Leonard Woolley and Gertrude Bell (1982, 1990 and 1993). Despite this, I take full responsibility for any errors.

Finally, on a personal note, I would like to thank the Bedu community of Segev Shalom in the Negev for their kind hospitality in 1994 and 1995. It was with them that I visited the Wilderness of Zin, along with James W. Flecker, the nephew of James Elroy Flecker to whom Lawrence wrote about his travel in the region (Garnett 1938, 171-177, no. 72). I did not know about this link then - serendipity was at play. I must also thank my wife, Fiona, who has supported me throughout this project and who has an uncanny knack for spotting works on T. E. Lawrence in second-hand book shops!

'The Genesis, Conduct and Publication of the Wilderness of Zin Survey'
T. Sam N. Moorhead

The Dark Clouds of War

In 1913, war with Germany was looming. Although it cannot be proven explicitly by the Palestine Exploration Fund's (hereafter also P.E.F. and the Fund) archival material, the imminence of war would seem to explain the election of Colonel W. Coote Hedley to the Committee of the Fund on October 21st, 1913 (PEF/EC/7, 89 and 92). Hedley was in the Geographical Section of the General Staff at the War Office (M.O.4), a unit that was actively procuring information required for the conduct of war not only against Germany, but also against the Ottoman Empire. Before Hedley's appointment, a survey of southern Palestine had already been mooted in a confidential letter from the Director of Military Operations to the Under Secretary of State for Foreign Affairs on 19th September, 1913 (Appendix 3, Zin 1). This letter refers to earlier correspondence in April and May 1913 and then proceeds to support the need for a survey:

'The proposed survey is very desirable from a military point of view, and is essential for the proper study of the problem presented by defence of the north-eastern frontier of Egypt.'

This copy of the letter was submitted by Colonel Hedley to the Committee of the Palestine Exploration Fund on November 4th,

1913, the date on which the Committee apparently agreed to the survey (PEF/EC/7, 93-4).

The Turkish authorities had not been supportive of the project, but on September 25th the Secretary of State at the Foreign Office surmised that with the end of the Balkan War the presentation of a survey proposal under the auspices of the Palestine Exploration Fund would find the Turks more amenable. His speculation was swiftly realised when the British Ambassador in Constantinople, Sir Louis du P. Mallet, wrote on September 29th that the:

'Turkish Government have decided to allow "Survey of Palestine Exploration Committee" to be completed up to the Egyptian frontier....'

(FO 371/1812; PEF, Zin 3)

On October 30th, soon after his election to the Committee (PEF/EC/7, 7.10.13 and 21.10.13, pp. 90 and 92), Colonel Hedley wrote from the War Office to the Fund's chairman, Sir Charles Watson, K.C.M.G., C.B. (Appendix 3, Zin 5). He confirmed that the Fund had granted permission for the survey, but added that 'the whole of the work must be carried out under the auspices of the P.E.C. [P. E. F.] but we will supply two officers and pay all their expenses - you will perhaps want to send an archaeologist.' Indeed, it is now clear that the entire archaeological venture was a smokescreen for a military survey, a fact confirmed by a letter from the War Office to the Under Secretary of State for Foreign Affairs (4.11.13; Appendix 3, Zin 8), which states that Sir Charles Watson, chairman of the P.E.F. 'would be glad if the services of Captain S. F. Newcombe, R.E., could be lent for this survey.....Sir Charles also hopes that it may be possible to secure the services of an archaeologist.' The letter then includes the draft of a telegram to be sent to General Lord Kitchener with the request for Newcombe, who was at that time already surveying further south in Sinai, to lead the expedition. In his *Fifty Years' Work*, Watson actually states 'the War Office allowed Captain S. F. Newcombe .... to carry out the survey'

(Watson 1915, 148). Furthermore, in his *marginalia* to the typescript of Liddell Hart's *'T. E. Lawrence': in Arabia and After*, (1934), Lawrence wrote that the survey was used as 'whitewash' by Kitchener, 'the only begetter of the survey' (Garnett 1938, p. 181). Jeremy Wilson concurs with this view, stating that the expedition 'was to be disguised as an archaeological venture' (Wilson 1988, 30). Below, the military nature of the survey will become all the more apparent. However, it should be noted here that Kitchener, himself, as a junior officer, had also surveyed for the P.E.F. in Palestine, on the Survey of Western Palestine in the 1870s and on the Wadi Arabah Survey in the 1880s, and would have been fully aware of the need to map the missing section that had not been covered (Zin 14/1; Tubb and Chapman 1990, 20-23 and 25-26; Wilson 1989, 136).

Captain Stewart F. Newcombe, known as 'skinface' because his skin peeled in the sun (Winstone 1990, 50), was soon instructed by Kitchener to lead the survey, as we know he was at Gaza by November 30th (Zin 20/1). Furthermore, on December 2nd the Fund's Committee learnt that he was to be accompanied by three other soldiers, also from the Royal Engineers: Lieutenant J. P. S. Greig, Corporal J. Rimmer and Lance Corporal W. W. McDiarmid (Zin 16). The Fund was also fortunate in receiving financial support in the shape of a £100 grant from the Royal Geographical Society (PEF/EC/7, 16.12.13, p. 103; Zin 14 and 17). However, they still needed an archaeologist. Their first choice, the Egyptologist T. E. Peet, was unavailable, so they had to cast their net wider.

Watson had already been in contact with Sir Frederic Kenyon, Director of the British Museum, in the pursuit of an archaeologist (Winstone 1990, 49). Kenyon was an expert on manuscripts, notably papyri and early biblical texts (Wilson 1988, 42). After consultation with D. G. Hogarth at the Ashmolean Museum, who had known Lawrence since 1909, Kenyon wrote to Watson on 21st November suggesting that C. Leonard Woolley and T. E. Lawrence, presently working at Carchemish, might be the men for the archaeological survey. He wrote that Woolley was the senior man and that Lawrence was good with the Arabs but very shy with the 'instincts of an explorer' (Appendix 3, Zin 12). For those interested in Lawrence's subsequent career, these are prophetic words indeed.

Both men agreed to undertake the survey although it was emphasised that their work at Jerablus (Carchemish) must take overall priority. They were prepared to spare two months on the survey and accepted the pay of £1 a day (Zin 15 and 18). Wilson explains how this venture saved the British Museum from paying half-pay during January and February; however, this was not to please the two men as they felt exploited (Wilson 1989, 137-8, 139). The P.E.F. received confirmation from Kenyon that the two men would survey in a letter dated December 11th (Zin 18). It is noteworthy that although both were archaeologists working in the region, they were not well qualified for a survey of southern Palestine. Indeed, Lawrence's Introduction to the Wilderness of Zin (hereafter WOZ) starts with the apology that neither he nor Woolley were Semite [sic] specialists. Also, the Introduction explains that they were not aware of previous research in the Negeb, especially by the likes of Edward Palmer, Charles Tyrwhitt Drake, Huntington and the French Fathers. However, the P.E.F. were hardly in a position to be selective; the subsequent expedition and publication were to prove that Woolley and Lawrence were certainly up to the task, although some have criticised the survey as lacking in archaeological rigour (Winstone 1982, 109).

With this matter concluded, Sir Charles Watson sent a detailed set of instructions, drawn up by the Executive Committee of the P.E.F., to Woolley (December 16th; Appendix 3, Zin 23). The document summarised the geographical parameters of the survey and clarified that Captain Newcombe was in overall command of the expedition. Woolley and Lawrence were told to plan archaeological sites, to take photographs of buildings and other points of interest, to record inscriptions, to collect geological specimens and lithic implements, and to record all place-names in use. However, the Committee was aware that it could not make definite instructions and it was trusted that the archaeologists would "understand the spirit of what is required". The sum of £100 was to be deposited with Thomas Cook in Jerusalem and the two men were to rendezvous with Newcombe at Gaza. The Committee also recommended that Yusuf Canaan, who had served under R. A. S. Macalister at Gezer and under Duncan Mackenzie at Beth-Shemesh, join the survey team. Finally, the P.E.F. requested that an article and some photographs should be submitted for publication in the Quarterly Statement for April 1914.

Woolley received this letter in Aleppo on January 1st, 1914, and sent an immediate reply to Watson (Zin 32). The next day, he and Lawrence were to set off by rail for Beirut where they boarded a steamer for Jaffa, arriving there on January 4th. They took Dahoum, one of their senior assistants at Carchemish, whom they would use to help with photography and squeeze work (Zin 32 and M. R. Lawrence 1954, 279-80) He was to be paid 1/9d, or 12 piastres, a day. Woolley was not inclined to take up the offer of using Yusuf Canaan, although in the end he was ultimately to accompany the party and to prove of great assistance (Zin 32; WOZ, p. 3).

Lawrence's first reference to the scheduled survey occurs in a letter to Florence Messham, dated December 20th (Garnett 1938, 161-2, no. 66). A much-quoted letter to Mrs. Reider written on December 26th, refers jokingly to 'horrible political complots' (Garnett 1938, 162-4, no. 67). Ironically, he seemed unaware how much truth lay in this statement of jest. As has been stated earlier, the archaeological team of Woolley and Lawrence was simply a smokescreen for Newcombe's military survey. However, any suggestion that Lawrence and Woolley had been officially informed about the real objective of the survey must remain unsubstantiated. In a letter, written on board the steamer from Beirut, Lawrence states that they were 'ignorant of our supposed work as we were at first' although he did speculate, 'We are obviously only meant as red herrings, to give an archaeological colour to a political job.' (M. R. Lawrence 1954, 279-80). Many years later, in 1953, Newcombe specifically emphasises their innocence in a letter:

'... but to suggest that either of them were secretly working for Military Intelligence before that date is to me, ridiculous.'

(Knightly and Simpson 1969, 41)

The Survey Starts

Meanwhile, Newcombe had been busy arranging the logistics for the expedition. In a letter dated January 3rd, he informed the P.E.F. that he had arrived in Gaza on December 6th and had encountered great difficulty obtaining camels (Zin 33). The survey started, without Woolley and Lawrence, on Christmas Day 1913; Yusuf Canaan was to investigate various remains, including the Bronze and Iron Age site of Tell Abu Hareira; however, most sites visited dated to the Byzantine period. In another letter to the War Office, started on the 7th and completed on the10th of January, Newcombe complained about the delay and slow progress of the survey. This letter, and the previous one, do give a sense of what it was like to survey in an inhospitable terrain, and even with sub-standard equipment - Newcombe is scathing about the new theodolytes his men have to use (Appendix 3, Zin 37). The selected survey area had to dovetail geographically into three earlier surveys: Captain Conder's to the north; Major Kitchener's to the east; the Egyptian-Turkish Boundary Commission on the west. This delineated an area of about 4,500 square miles to be covered. Mount Hor, near Petra, was chosen to be a crucial landmark for the survey; being painted white, the tomb of Aaron was visible up to 50 miles away (Ibid).

Woolley, Lawrence and Dahoum arrived at Gaza on January 5th, 1914. From here, they surveyed up to Beersheba: an undulating treeless plain, across which were scattered villages strewn with Byzantine pottery, olive presses and crumbling cisterns.

On January 7th, they arrived at Beersheba, and on the 9th, Woolley and Lawrence met up with Newcombe. In his 'Personal Reminiscences' (1935, 110), Newcombe wrote that he expected to meet "two eminent scientists", but when he "found two young and very bright people" realised that his correspondence to them had been "too polite" and that "undue deference ceased forthwith". Newcombe actually noted that the two men "looked about twenty-four and eighteen years of age respectively" (Newcombe 1935, 162). With time, however, the archaeologists earned Newcombe's respect and they become close friends.

If they were not sure of the main objective behind the survey, this meeting with Newcombe must have made it quite clear to them. Woolley was to write '... Moses' footsteps, of course, led us outside the Egyptian frontier into the Turkish part of Sinai, and the expedition we were joining was headed by a sapper officer who, with his assistant, was making a military map of Turkish Sinai, and we were playing the part of red herrings.' (Woolley 1962, 88).

Woolley's first letter back from the field to the P.E.F. on January 10th complained that he had been under the impression that they were joining a fully equipped expedition, a point that he reiterated many years later (Zin 38; Woolley 1962, 88). As this was not to be the case, it was fortunate that he and Lawrence had brought a camera, some notebooks and squeeze-paper with them. They were greatly assisted by the British Consular Agent at Gaza, Mr. Knesivitch (sometimes Knesevich), but it was unfortunate that the £100 was not deposited with Thomas Cook in Jaffa rather than Jerusalem; Woolley did not have the time to get to Jerusalem. Despite all of this, Woolley and Lawrence lost no time getting down to work and had copied 18 Byzantine inscriptions at Beersheba and also visited Tell Abu Irgeig (WOZ, pp. 3-4).

On January 11th, they moved on to Khalasa (also known as

Elusa on the Madaba Map; Donner 1992, 72, no. 104) where they stayed for four days. En route, they had already noticed evidence for substantial agricultural activity in the Negev's past, at a time when diligent collection and storage of water enabled the landscape to blossom. As the survey progressed, they became increasingly appreciative of how careful hydraulic engineering had resulted in extensive agricultural exploitation of the region in the Byzantine period. It was this management of water, they claimed, not climatic change that accounted for the settlements in late antiquity (WOZ, 20-23 and 97-98); as such they pioneered awareness of a subject which remains an area of intense study today. Woolley and Lawrence were also the first archaeologists to attempt to draw a plan of Khalasa, where they also found an important Nabataean inscription recording King Aretas (probably Aretas IV; WOZ, p.189, Fig. 59). From Khalasa, they visited Raheiba (modern Rehovath-in-the-Negev) and Saadi. On the road to Saadi, they recorded several Greek funerary inscriptions from the 6th century, and at Raheiba a large Byzantine reservoir, photographed by Lawrence, using Dahoum as a scale (WOZ, 182-185 and Pl. XXVIII, 2).

On January 16th, the team moved south to Esbeita (also known as Sobata and Shivta). Here the two men conducted the most accurate survey initiated to date, planning the site and photographing the most important features: the south, central and north churches. They also studied private housing, a Byzantine terrace wall and a reservoir for run-off water (WOZ 97-120). From Esbeita, they visited Mishrafa (Mizpe Shivta) which they identified, almost certainly correctly, as a Byzantine monastery or *laura* (WOZ 120-123). Although they failed to identify certain features as reservoirs for water at this site, their overall success in recording low-status archaeological features (and not just standing architecture) was a major achievement, methodologically well in advance of their day and even much subsequent fieldwork until the 1970s.

They left Esbeita for El Auja (Nessana) on January 24th, the day on which Lawrence wrote to E. T. Leeds from 'a little lost Gov[ernment] station on the frontier line of Egypt and Syria' in a somewhat irritable mood, 'over the consequences of much riding of camels I draw thick veils: but take it as a summing up that we are very unhappy: Woolley is the more uncomfortable, since he is a flesh-potter: I can travel on a thistle, and sleep in a cloak on the ground. Woolley can't, or at least, is only learning to, quite slowly.' (Brown 1991, 56-7). This is interesting because other sources suggest that Lawrence would only walk in the desert and an earlier letter suggests that he might not have relished the idea of riding a camel (M. R. Lawrence 1954, 279-8; Aldington 1955, 102; Asher 1998, 176). Lawrence goes on to inform Leeds about Woolley's frustrations with a cook who could not speak English; not that there was much to eat other than Turkish delight, 'foul stuff: I don't want much more of it.' This letter does make it clear, however, that the two men were probably already beginning to sense that in looking for the Children of Israel they might be chasing a mirage:

'Not a sign or smell of Israelites wandering about here: only on the old road from Gaza to Akaba did we find the little scraps of early pottery; we are doing the P.E.F. in the eye. Fancy our transforming a hill fort of the Amorites into a Byzantine monastery! Sounds almost impious, doesn't it.' (Brown, *ibid*)

El Auja was another site occupied between the Nabataean and Byzantine periods. Significantly, the surveyors' results indicate that two churches noted by Huntingdon in 1909 had been largely obliterated by Turkish works (*WOZ*, 155-159). However, Woolley and Lawrence surveyed the ruins and the remaining church, and also noted that the site had been fortified in the late-Roman / Byzantine period. In this regard it proved similar to Abda and Kurnub which would be visited later. From El Auja, they also visited Tell es-Seram where they excavated some cairns, establishing that one of the burials was Islamic because the skeleton lay facing Mecca; pottery finds suggested others were Byzantine. They also noted flints amongst Byzantine pottery, suggesting contemporaneity and cited ethnographic parallels from their work in Syria (*WOZ*, 24-25; 30-32). In one of his letters to the Fund, Woolley also noted that "pre-historic" and "stone-age" were not necessarily synonymous terms (Zin 45/46).

On January 27th, Woolley and Lawrence left El Auja for 'Ain Kadeis. However, they missed their baggage animals along the way and instead were compelled to travel on foot to 'Ain Kadeis over a barren mountain landscape, using footpaths inaccessible to camels. They were finally re-united with their party at the Egyptian Government station, at Kossaima, at 5pm on January 28th. This was too late to have prevented Newcombe sending out the Egyptian Police Camel Corps as a search party and notifying the Turkish authorities of the men's disappearance. Michael Asher, a veteran of travel in the desert, has explained that Lawrence realised how simple it was to avoid detection in the desert. Lawrence, himself, wrote from Kossaima the next day, 'It shows how easy it is in an absolutely deserted country to defy a government.' (M. R. Lawrence 1954, 284-5; Asher 1998, 116; Wilson 1989, 138-9).

At Kossaima, they investigated Bronze Age burials before moving on to the valley and springs of 'Ain Kadeis (*WOZ*, 29-30). This was the region about which the subscribers and committee of the P.E.F. would be most interested; Lawrence and Woolley seem to be almost apologetic when dealing with later, non-Biblical, periods (Appendix 3, Zin 48/9; M. R. Lawrence 1954, 56-7; PEF/LL 2). Was 'Ain Kadeis indeed the Kadesh Barnea of the Bible where Moses and the Israelites stayed for 40 years in the Wilderness? (see *Genesis* 14.7 and *Numbers* 13-14, 20 & 25). In his letter of January 29th from Kossaima, Lawrence had already stated 'Ain Kadeis is a very poor place: it cannot possibly be Kadesh-Barnea. At the same time the country around may be.' (M. R. Lawrence 1954, 285). In a letter from Ain el-Guderat, dated Feburary 3rd, Woolley curiously by-passed the topic (Zin 45/46). In this letter, however, he did enclose his report for the *Palestine Exploration Quarterly* with six negatives

(Woolley 1914, 58-66). Logistical problems still remained with Woolley having to sort out financial matters with Knesivitch, to whom Woolley had advanced an additional £100 of his own funds. Further, Woolley and Lawrence had been delayed at 'Ain Kadeis for five days while fresh photographic supplies arrived from Cairo.

Lawrence was near 'Ain Kadeis when he wrote to E. T. Leeds a few days later, from "An Oasis" in the Wilderness of Sin [Lawrence's spelling], on February 6th (Garnett 1938, 164-5, no. 68). He described the natural beauty of the terrain and lists the varied foodstuffs available to the survey (beans, lentils, rice, potatoes, onions, Turkish delight, figs, raisins, eggs and marmalade, with bread); he was certainly more enthusiastic about available food supplies than he had been on an excavation with Flinders Petrie in Egypt (Garnett 1938, 132-6, nos. 46-47; Drower 1995, 319-320). Overall, the letter is a good deal more upbeat than his previous one written from Kossaima (see above; Brown 1991, 56-7) and Lawrence even commented that 'all is rosy'. He was writing from near the presumed location of Kadesh-Barnea (Ain Kadeis) and jokes "the Israelites grumbled. I hear Moses led 'em here, and all once more was peace. In fact they stayed forty years, and we are so sad that we cannot do so too." He now seemed much more at ease in the desert.

In a letter of Feburary 17th, Woolley reported more detail about the Kadesh Barnea region (Appendix 3, Zin 48/49). He explained how they had investigated the small fort in Ain el-Guderat from which they removed a number of potsherds (some of which are be in the PEF collections). He continued by referring to Byzantine remains, arguing 'I know of course that Byzantine sites are late for the interests of the society, but the fact is that there are very few places where traces of earlier occupation exist; .... the cities of Joshua XV etc. either lay north of our boundary or were largely mythical...' He makes it clear that the region is really only suitable for nomads, and that it is "so bad" that even the Bedouin move north in the summer. Woolley noted that he had not yet seen

Trumbull's book *Kadesh Barnea* (1884) - Newcombe had it at Aqaba - but stated 'if the rest of it is on a par with his description of Ain Kadeis quoted in "Thirty Years Work" [Palestine Exploration Fund 1895, 70-3], it is the most egregious farrago of lies. It speaks wonders for the Children of Israel that they left Moses alive after he brought them to a place like that.' Lawrence mocks Trumbull's description of an oasis in which Arabs jumped into bathe by stating, 'Our guide also washed his feet in it.' (Hart 1934, 32). Woolley's and Lawrence's conclusion was that the Israelites could not have survived for forty years at Ain Kadeis and that Kadesh-Barnea in fact represented 'the country of Ain el-Guderat, Muweilleh, Kossaima and 'Ain Kadeis.' (WOZ, 91). Interestingly enough, Rudolf Cohen stated in 1993 that this was still the generally accepted view (Cohen 1993, 843). Only in very recent publications has the veracity of this episode of the Exodus story been seriously reappraised from an archaeological point of view (Finkelstein and Silbermann 2001, 63).

On February 8th, Woolley and Lawrence parted ways. Woolley stayed in the Negev, moving northwards to Kurnub, south-east of Beersheba. He travelled with Yusuf Canaan along Wadi Khoraisha to the cistern at Ras el-Aziz, which supplied water to the area. Woolley also noted how the Bedouin re-used caverns in the area as grain stores (WOZ 7).

He then travelled further north along Wady Ramliya to Abda (Oboda and Avdat) where he arrived on February 9th. This important Nabataean and Byzantine city had already been surveyed by scholars of the École Biblique in 1904. Woolley laments that had he known about this report, it would have saved him a great deal of time taking photographs, planning, sketching and recording inscriptions. At the site, he failed to identify some features that they had found, including a large Nabataean camp (WOZ, 125-128).

On February 15th Woolley left Abda and continued north to Bir Rakhama, aiming at Kurnub (Mampsis and Mamshit) on the 16th. Woolley was able to add a little more archaeological information to earlier survey work conducted by A. Musil in 1901 (1901, 25-8) about this Nabataean-to-Byzantine period town, which appears on the Madaba Map (Donner 1992, p. 69, no. 93). He identified watchtowers and recorded dams in the wady (WOZ 160-168). From Kurnub, Woolley wrote another update to the P.E.F. on February 17th (Appendix 3, Zin 48/49; cited above) in which he emphasised the predominance of Byzantine remains in the area: 'A great deal of our work is concerned with Byzantine things simply because they exist, and as we are to examine the archaeology of the country they cannot be omitted.' Such a pluralistic approach to Near Eastern archaeological landscapes can still be considered progressive by modern standards!

From Kurnub, Woolley headed north-west towards Beersheba on February 19th. He based himself at Tell es-Seba from where he visited several other tell sites discussed in Chapter 3 of *The Wilderness of Zin*. On February 22nd, Woolley left Beersheba for Gaza and Aleppo. In a letter from Jaffa, dated February 26th, he informed the P.E.F. that he had now finished the archaeological survey, and also stated that Lawrence was still in the Arabah (Zin 52).

Lawrence, meanwhile, had accompanied Newcombe on the "old road" along the Wadi Lussan through Kuntilla to Aqaba, where the survey was to encounter unexpected difficulties.

On February 15th, Newcombe wrote to the P.E.F. from Aqaba, explaining that work had come to a halt as the Kaimmakam [local Governor] at Aqaba had no knowledge of the survey (Zin 47). Lawrence had just arrived and was about to have a famous stand-off with the Turkish authorities. In his 'Personal Reminiscences', Newcombe tells us how 'Lawrence was all for ignoring the Turkish governor and was quite surprised and even hurt that I curtailed my mapping.' The following day Kitchener ordered Newcombe not to survey or map in places unauthorised by the Turks (Newcombe 1935, 112). Colonel Hedley informed the P.E.F. of the problems with surveying in the Aqaba region in a letter of March 10th and stated that the survey would be restricted to the province of Gaza, but was sure 'that Newcombe will make it extend as far south as possible.' (Appendix 3, Zin 56)

Newcombe's letter of the 15th (Appendix 3, Zin 47, see above) also noted that he had sent his report for the P. E.Q. to the Army of Occupation in Cairo, from where he hoped it would be forwarded to the Fund. Hedley's letter of March 10th (*ibid*; see above) also informed the P.E.F. that Newcombe's report for the P.E.Q. had been marked "SECRET" and could not be published. Therefore, only Woolley's report reached the subscribers (Woolley 1914). We can assume that Newcombe's report would have contained much information already included in his letters to the Fund. It is possible that the report was in fact forwarded as a typescript by W.C. Hedley to the P.E.F. (see Addenda, Zin 37)

Lawrence found little of interest in the region of Akaba, but when barred by the Turkish authorities the use of a boat to cross to see the castle on Gesiret Farun (Faraun Island; Pharaoh's Island; Île de Graye), used some of Newcombe's 10 gallon water cans to paddle over on instead. Lawrence was subsequently escorted out of the area by a Turkish police officer, but managed to slip away near Petra. Lawrence tells the story in two letters and obviously told it to Woolley who recounted his partner's account. Lawence's version, which is also cited by Wilson, talks of an escort of a lieutenant and half a company of soldiers (Garnett, 165-9, nos. 69 and 70; Zin 55; Wilson 1989, 141). Newcombe, on the other hand, gives a less fantastic account in which he notes that Lawrence was accompanied by just the single policeman! However, he was to add that no one was to know how Lawrence's antics would presage the campaign of 1917 (Newcombe 1935, 112). It does seem that Lawrence could embellish a story, a trait that has been recently explored by John Rodenbeck in a discussion of the Dera'a incident (2001).

What is clear is that once away from Woolley, Lawrence did become more the 'explorer' whom Kenyon had perceived in his letter to Watson (Zin 13). Richard Aldington wrote that at

Carchemish Lawrence 'got on well enough with Woolley, who did all the real intellectual work of the expedition while allowing Lawrence to do much as he wished, yet without excluding him from such work as pottering with the ceramics and photography which really interested him.' (Aldington 1955, 97). Lawrence's activity in the latter part of the survey does seem to substantiate Aldington's view. However, it would be unfair to write off Lawrence as an archaeologist. Flinders Petrie had recommended that Lawrence should excavate on Bahrein Island to find links between Mesopotamia and Egypt, and even offered £700 towards the project, an unprecendented act in Petrie's career (Garnett 1938, 136-7, no. 49; Wilson 1989, 99-100; Chapman 1991, 28; Drower 1995, 320). Furthermore, Lawrence was to write later to Dick Knowles that the war "cut short that development of me into a sort of Hogarth: a travelled, archaeological sort of man, with geography and a pen as his two standbys.' (Garnett 1938, 553-5. no. 329).

Woolley tells us that Lawrence found no evidence for settlement or agriculture in the Wadi Arabah (Zin 55). Furthermore, when Lawrence wrote to a friend about Petra, he did not marvel at the archaeology: 'Petra [name omitted] is the most wonderful place in the world, not for the sake of its ruins, which are quite a secondary affair, but for the colours of its rocks, all red and black and grey with streaks of green and blue, in little wriggly lines ...' (Garnett 1938, 165-7, no. 69; also see Wilson 1988, p. 45, no. 75). Wilson explains how Lawrence was to learn a great deal about geology from the survey team, and this knowledge was to be put to good use in his topographical descriptions in his *Seven Pillars of Wisdom* (Wilson 1989, 140-1).

However, to suggest that Lawrence was not interested in the archaeology of Petra is to do him a disservice. We know he was there on February 25th when he wrote home from the site. He described the tombs as being of Greek and Egyptian style, but states, 'There is also no fine work: the beauty of the place lies in the contrast between the green oleander and the red of the sandstone, and in the queer way in which without plan the tombs are dotted over the cliffs of the valleys.' (M. R. Lawrence 1954, 286-7). This letter was written rather prematurely because in another letter written home, this time from Damascus, he writes, 'but the finest building and the most beautiful piece of gorge was on the way out - or in, as you like it - and it was I think the best thing I have seen in all my goings about.' (M. R. Lawrence 1954, 288). Here, he obviously refers to the Siq and the Khazneh (Treasury) which confirms that he entered via Mount Hor to the south. It also seems likely that he did not see the ed-Deir (Monastery), the other splendid monument at Petra, which lies up the rocky Wadi Kharareeb to the north-west.

By now, Lawrence was short of money; he explains that the post arrangements had broken down. He recounts in a letter home, written on February 28th from Damascus, how he had borrowed money from Newcombe, his policeman and even the British Consul in Damascus. But he also tells us how he had to borrow from two English ladies, Lady Evelyn Cobbold and Lady J. Legge, to pay his fare on the Hedjaz line back to Syria (*ibid*, 287 and 292; Garnett, p. 167). Before he caught the train north, he claimed that he had arrested three policeman at Ma'an so as to secure his camels, another skirmish that would prepare him well for later work in the region! (Garnett 1938, 165-67, no. 69). He complains in another letter how he was forced to wait two days for a train at Ma'an. In this same letter he states that he has no idea of the whereabouts of Woolley. (M. R. Lawrence 1954, 287-8). The two aforementioned letters do tell us that Lawrence had completed his part of the survey by February 28th, when he was in Damascus.

Here it is appropriate to discuss Victor Winstone's suggestion that Lawrence might have met Gertrude Bell whilst she was with the Howeitat at Tor al Tubaiq in Northern Arabia. Bell was en route for Hail, possibly on a spying mission for the British, to observe unrest caused by a dispute between pro and anti-Saudi factions in the northern Arabian region. It has been suggested that

Lawrence appears in native woman's dress in a photograph taken by Bell of Howeitat women (Winstone 1993, xvi-xviii and pl. 19; also see 1982, 111; 1990, 53). One cannot deny that one of the women bears a tremendous likeness to Lawrence. The problem is trying to reconcile the dates of the two people's journeys. Bell had been at two places in modern Jordan, Bair on January 21st and 22nd, and at Jabal Tubaiq from January 26th to the 30th (Winstone 1982, 108, Map 7); she camped outside Hail on February 24th (Winstone 1993, 137). Lawrence separated from Woolley at Muweilla in the Negeb on February 8th and was back in Syria at the very end of the month; he would only have been within striking distance of Jabal Tubaiq in mid to late February. In the light of this, it seems quite impossible that Lawrence could have been in the Jabal Tubaiq region when Bell was there in late January. This requires us to return to the picture (Winstone 1993, p. 19). A comparison of this image with others of Lawrence, especially ones taken at Carchemish in 1912 and 1913 does suggest to the author that it is not in fact Lawrence dressed as a Howeitat woman (Wilson 1988, 38, no. 64; Chapman and Gibson 1996, 95, Fig. 1; this volume, p. xxx). In this matter, I must concur with Jeremy Wilson (1989, 999, note 2).

Lawrence was re-united with Woolley at Aleppo on March 2nd. Woolley subsequently wrote to the P. E. F. from Aleppo on March 7th, discussing the accounts for the survey and Lawrence's activities from Aqaba to Petra (Zin 55). In another letter home, Lawrence tells us that half of the text for the survey's publication was written up at Jerablus (Carchemish), but that 'It will be very dull ... We neither of us found anything.' Not knowing that the outbreak of war was going to change his life, Lawrence wrote that he expected to stay in England for six weeks that summer, finishing 'Sinai'. (M. R. Lawrence 1954, 292). However, it does seem that there was still a great deal of work to do on the survey for Woolley writes at the end of his letter: ' you will probably be in no great hurry for our material and it certainly would be better to defer it until we can have something in the nature of a map on which to enter such discoveries as we have made and the places we have visited.' (Zin 55).

Meanwhile, Newcombe continued the survey in the Arabah region, which was completed around mid-May 1914, and he and Lieutenant Grieg went north to meet Woolley and Lawrence at Jerablus on May 19th (Zin 67). It is now apparent that Woolley had learnt about the need for intelligence in the region. Initially, Kitchener would not allow Newcombe to visit Carchemish, but reversed his decision when Woolley suggested that it would provide an opportunity to find out more about the construction of the German railway in the region (Woolley 1962, 88-89). Newcombe wrote to Sir Charles Watson from Jerablus on May 21st, stating that he and Grieg would be returning home, and that the maps were safely in Cairo and should reach London in time for the P.E.F. meeting on June 16th (Zin 67). However, there is no evidence from the P.E.F. Minute Book that any maps were presented at the Fund, even when Woolley and Lawrence attended on July 7th, 1914 (PEF/EC/7, 1911-1922, pp. 130-1).

The first official piece of writing concerning the survey to come from Lawrence's pen was on June 1st, in the form of a receipt for £66 as payment for his work on the survey, written at Jerablus (Appendix 3, Zin 68). Although he now had a substantial amount of money, it still did not stop Lawrence leaving his bill unpaid at The Baron Hotel in Aleppo on June 8th (Dalrymple 1997, 133). Newcombe was to write to Woolley from Constantinople saying that he had failed to get sufficient military information about the German railway through the Taurus mountains and asked if Woolley and Lawrence could return by that route. The two men obliged and Woolley tells the story of "their only piece of spying" before the war in a most jocular manner (Woolley 1962, 88-93).

It was only after Woolley and Lawrence had returned to England in June that Lawrence wrote a lengthy letter to the poet James Elroy Flecker who was dying in a sanatorium in Switzerland which mostly described the work at Carchemish (Garnett 1938, p. 172, no. 71). However, at the end Lawrence tells Flecker about the Zin survey:

'Do you know that in January & February Woolley & I explored the desert of the exodus, looking for the foot-prints of the children of Israel. And now we have to write the next annual of the Palestine Exploration Fund to describe our non-success. The Fund inform us that the tone of the annual is usually slightly devotional, so prepare yourself for something hotter than *Alsander*.' [*The King of Alsander*, a novel by J. E. Flecker]

This reference to the survey as a failure does prepare us for several disparaging remarks that Lawrence was to make about the final publication over the following months.

Publishing the Survey

Both men were involved in the publication of the survey, although the outbreak of war on August 4th was to disrupt the process somewhat as we shall learn. In July, Woolley expressed concern about finding a scholar to work on the Byzantine inscriptions (Zin 69), and the P.E.F. approached Mr. F. W. Hasluck at the British School of Archaeology in Athens (PEF/EC/7, 1911-1921, p. 133). It was not until October that Hasluck recommended Mr. Marcus N. Tod of Oriel College to publish them (*ibid*, pp. 135-6). Lawrence also managed to secure the services of Dr. A. Cowley (Sub-Librarian, later to be Librarian, at the Bodleian) to work on the Aramaic [Nabataean] inscription and Prof. D. S. Margoliouth on the Arabic one (PEF/Lawrence Letters [hereafter PEF/LL] 4, October 29th/30th; WOZ, 188-190).

Between July and October, our sources for progress on *the Wilderness of Zin* publication are sparse. The survey map was produced jointly at the Royal Geographical Society in Kensington by the Secretary, Arthur Hincks, and the Honorary Head of the Map Room, Douglas Carruthers. They worked with Dr. H. N. Dickson of Admirality Intelligence in an attempt to get the map completed. Turkey then entered the war at the end of October.

The Geographical Section of the General Staff (M.O.4), under Colonel Hedley, was also closely involved in the preparation of the master maps (Winstone 1990, 60). However, the two smaller maps, and at least one of the plans, used in the final publication of *The Wilderness of Zin* were prepared by Mr. B. V. Darbishire for Lawrence (PEF/LL 1 and 6; Wilson 1988, p. 43, no. 73; WOZ, Maps I and II).

Kitchener was determined to have the survey published as soon as possible and by the end of September Woolley and Lawrence had completed their respective parts (Wilson 1989, 152). Watson's Prefatory Note at the beginning of *The Wilderness of Zin* explains who wrote which sections of the work. Chapter I described the route of the survey, Woolley writing most of the first half and Lawrence the second half. Chapter II gives a general account of the Southern Desert, providing an outline of their work on stone age and prehistoric sites. Lawrence wrote the early part, but Woolley seems to be responsible for the bulk of the section. Chapter III included Lawrence's work on Darb esh-Shur, the old road running to Egypt, and Woolley's work on the northern tells. In Chapter IV, Lawrence discusses the Kadesh Barnea issue. Woolley writes about the Byzantine towns in Chapter V, Lawrence only providing the last part on Aqaba. Mr. M. N. Tod published the inscriptions in Chapter VI. Chapman and Gibson have written the definitive account on which photographs were taken by each of the two men (1996, 94-102).

By now, we know that both men wanted a job with Military Intelligence (Garnett 1938, p. 181), but we also know that Woolley joined the Territorial Army on September 23rd, 1914 and then gained a commission in the Royal Field Artillery on October 14th. On October 6th, The P.E.F Minute Book records that two letters from Lawrence (dated September 24th and October 2nd) were laid in front of the P.E.F. Committee. The minute tells us that Lawrence had agreed to collate the final publication now that Woolley was in the army (PEF/EC/7, 1911-1922, pp. 135-6). Sadly, these letters have not survived in the

P.E.F. archive and this does support the impression that more letters from Lawrence were originally sent to the Fund which have not survived (see Appendix 2).

The nine Lawrence letters that do survive in the P.E.F. cover the period between October and December, when he was making final touches to the publication. He was originally based in Oxford, but moved to London in October to be closer to the Royal Geographical Society; he was to receive a post in M.O.4. under Colonel Hedley on October 19th; he was commissioned as a second lieutenant on October 26th. It does seem that Lawrence attended the P.E.F. Committee meeting on October 20th, 1914, when it was decided that the length of the publication would require the work to be published as the Annual for both 1914 and 1915. In a letter, apparently written later that day, Lawrence speaks of how he had cut parts of the text, presumably at the request of the Committee. Prejudices against the Byzantine period are laid bare: '[Chap.] V deals only with the Christian Greek, which has been all done before nearly as well, and I think that 40 or 50 pages of its 120 could come out. This would relieve you of about 10,000 words.... and so few people like Byzantine things. Also, these are bad Byzantine!' (Appendix 3, PEF/LL 2). Lawrence was to continue working on proofs whilst maintaining a hectic schedule at the War Office (PEF/LL 3). This was made worse after the entry of Turkey into the war on October 29th, 1914, for Lawrence was ordered to prepare a road-report on Sinai. This resulted in Lawrence's second work on the region, *Military Report on the Sinai Peninsula*.

Woolley wrote from his Artillery barracks to the P.E.F. on November 4th, asking to see the final manuscript after Lawrence had checked it (PEF/LL 5). He was soon also to move to a post in M.O.4. On November 21st, Lawrence wrote to the P.E.F. saying that he would be leaving the country for Egypt in a week (PEF/LL 7), but would pass the manuscript on to Mr. Hogarth before he went. This letter led the Committee, on December 1st, to ask Hogarth to see the publication through press (PEF/EC/7, 1911-

1922, pp. 143-4). Lawrence sent the final manuscript to J.D. Crace, Honorary Secretary at the P.E.F., on December 3rd 1914 (Appendix 3, PEF/LL 9 / Garnett 1938, no. 76), after Woolley had just completed a final edit. On the same day, Lawrence wrote to James Elroy Flecker, stating that all his Sinai and Syria work was completed, the 'little grind....is all over' (Brown 1991, 67-8). Flecker was to die of consumption the following year.

Lawrence then left with Newcombe for Egypt on December 9th and Woolley followed on December 12th. It is clear that both men were forced to let go of the manuscript due to external pressures - the war - for Lawrence says, 'we could go tinkering on it for months.' (Appendix 3, PEF/LL 9; Garnett 1938, 188-8, no. 76). Also, Lawrence was aware of the irony that he might have to 'confiscate' *The Wilderness of Zin* given his new post in Military Intelligence! (Garnett 187-8, no. 75). However, we know that Lawrence's Sinai Map was shown at the fund on December 15th (PEF/EC/7, 1911-22, pp.145-6).

However, there is a twist in the tail. Woolley wrote an undated letter, which seems to date to late November or early December, to Hogarth in which he made a few comments about the manuscript. Jeremy Wilson dates the letter to '?October 1914' (Wilson 1988, p. 46, no. 78), but Hogarth only took responsibility for seeing the work through publication in November and the formal decision was made on December 1st. Woolley writes, 'I put L's [Lawrence] name on the title page, which he hadn't done, but of course it ought to be there.' (Appendix 3, PEF/LL11). However, Lawrence saw this letter. It has to be assumed that this letter was delivered to him with the manuscript by Woolley in late November. This gave Lawrence the chance to write a footnote in red ink objecting to Woolley's alteration, 'I must object to this: it wasn't in any respect my book and I would very much rather that name was not on the title page. TEL' Interestingly enough, the original frontisepiece without Lawrence's name survives in the PEF archives (Zin Addenda 3). That Lawrence did not want his name on the book is made even clearer in a letter that he sent to Hogarth from Cairo: 'Please don't put my name on the thing - the book that is - Darbishire should sign the map.' (Garnett 1938, 190-1, no.78). In this letter might lie a clue to Lawrence's motives. Although he urged that Crace should publish the volume in January or February 1915, he was concerned about the quality of the work: 'It certainly was the filthiest manuscript made.'

In another letter of October 29th, 1914, to Dr. A. Cowley, the Oxford scholar who translated the Nabataean inscription, another tantalising reason emerges: 'Parts of the book are frivolous, so don't call it a "serious contribution"...' (Brown 1991, 66; Zin 84, typed transcript). He wanted them to 'rush it out', but was he concerned that his reputation might suffer if it was received poorly? Did he feel that it was really sub-standard? Or, was his innate shyness, to be so evident after the War, the major reason? Whatever the truth, he was concerned that Darbishire sign the maps, which indeed he did (Garnett 1938, 190-1, no.78 & WOZ, Maps I & II). It is also evident from this letter that Crace wanted to pay Lawrence and Woolley for their work on the volume. Lawrence was not keen on this and preferred that the money be spent on the publication: 'to put a colour on the map, or something.' Whatever Lawrence's genuine motives, he does seem to have been deliberately distancing himself from the project. In his Seven Pillars of Wisdom, he does not refer to the survey directly, although when crossing the Arabah, his group 'were steering only on my three-year-old memories of Newcombe's map.' (Lawrence 1935, Chap. XC, p. 513)

If Lawrence had possible misgivings about elements of the survey and its publication, Woolley's complete silence about the survey in his three general books on archaeology and exploration, Dead Towns and Living Men (1920), Digging up the Past (1930), and Spadework (1953) might be highly revealing. It seems that only once does he refer to the survey in a later work, and that is a very short reference in his somewhat frivolous *As I Seem to Remember* (Woolley 1962, 88). Personal reasons for Woolley's apparent silence about this particular project episode are not easily explained. He might have believed that their work was largely a repetition of earlier research conducted by other scholars and that their publication was not particularly original.

By April 20th, Hogarth had finished his work on the final manuscript and the Committee instructed the printers to produce 1000 copies (PEF/EC/7, 1911-1921, p. 158). However, the map was not to be published during the war:

'The map ... cannot yet be issued to subscribers for evident reasons connected with the war, in which Turkey, contrary to her own interests, has been compelled to join with the enemies of England, thus causing much distress to the inhabitants of Palestine.' (Watson 1915, 154)

The Committee raised and deferred the issue of an honorarium for Woolley and Lawrence on January 4th, 1916 (PEF/EC/7, p. 178). In 1915, just before the 1914-15 Annual was published, Sir Charles Watson wrote:

'When the work of the Palestine Exploration Fund is resumed after the termination of the war, it may, perhaps, be under even more favourable conditions than in past years.' (Watson 1915, 154)

These were prophetic words indeed, as the British Mandate in Palestine was a direct result of General Allenby's and Lawrence's advance to Damascus. During these campaigns, Newcombe was to play a major part in the Arab Revolt, Lawrence telling us in his *Seven Pillars of Wisdom*, 'Newcombe is like fire ... he burns friend and enemy'. Furthermore, he also tired out Feisal's camels because 'as a surveyor, he could not resist a look from each high hill over the country he crossed.' (Lawrence 1935, Chap. 41, p. 246). Woolley's war ended earlier; he spent two years in a Turkish prisoner-of-war camp after his spy-ship *Zaida* sank in August 1916 (Winstone 1990, 80).

After the War, the Minute Book (PEF/EC/7, 8th May, 1919,

p. 296) records that the P.E.F. wrote to Colonel Lawrence inviting him to the Annual General Meeting. No reply was received and the Committee assumed that he must have been *en route* to the East from England. This is the last mention of Lawrence in the P.E.F. archives before his death in 1935. Finally, in September 1920, the Thomas Cook and Son account at Jerusalem was wound up, and a month later Colonel Hedley retired from the Committee, having left the War Office (PEF/EC/7, p. 348; p. 355). On May 18th, 1921, Colonel S.F. Newcombe, 'Who showed them "the way wherein they must walk, and the work that they must do"' and Sir Charles Close, Treasurer of the Fund, presented the complete 1914 Negeb map to the Committee (*ibid*, p. 366; PEF/M/ Zin *Addenda* 8; Wilson 1988, p. 46, no. 77). Woolley and Lawrence were not present. Nor could the 'begetter of the survey' be there; Kitchener had drowned when H.M.S. Hampshire sunk in 1916. It is easy for us, with the benefit of a nostalgic, or even romantic hindsight to eulogise about Newcombe's survey, but the words of Sir Charles Watson about the mapping were written only a year later, and he was not a man to proffer false praise:

'Considering the large area and the difficulties met with, the completion of the survey in so short a time was a remarkable piece of work, and the greatest credit is due to Captain Newcombe and his assistants for the manner in which it was carried out.' (Watson 1915, 150)

After the war, Woolley did return to Carchemish before going on to lead a distinguished career as an archaeologist, notably at Ur in southern Mesopotamia. Lawrence, after his blast of fame in the Arab Revolt, intentionally slipped out of the limelight under assumed names, John Hume Ross and T. E. Shaw. Nevertheless, he was to remain a close friend of Hogarth (Wilson 1988, 31).

Lawrence's Death and the Re-publication, 1935-6

However, it was Lawrence's death on May 13th, 1935, that precipitated the republication of the *Wilderness of Zin*. At the P.E.F. Committee meeting, prior to the Annual General Meeting, on June 27th, 1935, Colonel Newcombe, by now Treasurer of the Fund, suggested that they should publish a new and cheaper edition of *The Wilderness of Zin*. Newcombe, who was a pall-bearer at Lawrence's funeral, would have wanted this to have been a further tribute to a friend; Lawrence was even godfather to one of his children (*Huddersfield Examiner* 22.5.1935, Zin Addenda 7.2.4). However, as Treasurer of the Fund, the commercial benefits of republication at such a time would surely not have been lost on Newcombe, nor, for that matter, the committee. A decision was deferred, but the existing stock of the original publication (in sheets) was to be bound and sold immediately. [These copies were sold at 30/-, a discount of 15/- from the original price of 45/-.] During the subsequent Annual General Meeting, the Honorary Secretary recorded the loss of Mr. T. E. Lawrence (PEF/EC/8, pp. 395-6 & 398). It is also recorded that a copy of the *Wilderness of Zin* was presented to Mr. A. W. Lawrence by the committee at the end of the year (PEF/EC/9, 5.12.1935, p. 6).

At the Committee meeting on July 27th, 1935, Colonel Newcombe reported about the sale of the remaining stock of the *Wilderness of Zin* and it was agreed to republish in octavo. If no one submitted a better financial estimate than Jonathan Cape's offer of July 16th, they would go with them. Jonathan Cape had just published Liddell Hart's *'T. E. Lawrence', in Arabia and After* in 1934. It was also agreed to ask Sir Frederic Kenyon if he would write an introduction to the new work (PEF/EC/8, pp. 400-1). This duly occurred: Jonathan Cape's edition appeared at a price of 15/- on March 13th, 1936, with Kenyon's introduction (PEF/EC/9, 26.3.1936, p. 14).

The work was advertised widely and was received with great acclaim across the world. The P.E.F. Archive contains a listing of

110 local, national and international newspapers (Zin 2, 114). To this can be added 13 extra publications from which we have cuttings of announcements and reviews. In total, the Archive houses 28 reviews and announcements, ranging from *The London Guardian* to the *Egyptian Gazette* and the *Montreal Gazette* to the *Natal Advertiser*. Appendix 4 reproduces reviews from the above-mentioned papers. It can be argued that these evaluations of the re-publication of *The Wilderness of Zin* are still valid today; indeed, they are more eloquent than this introduction. One review, by C. S. Jarvis for the *Egyptian Gazette* (Alexandria), does surmise over the military nature of the expedition, concluding that 'only those "in the know" can tell' the truth of the matter (see Appendix 4. The work was also to be published in French the following year as *Le Desert de Sin* (Woolley and Lawrence 1937).

It has not been the objective of this article to judge the success of the survey. As we have seen, Sir Charles Watson had already praised the mapping carried out by Newcombe's team (Watson 1915, 154). Although Woolley and Lawrence were to become aware that they were repeating work carried out by earlier scholars, the *The Wilderness of Zin* does provide an invaluable overall synthesis. Furthermore, they did record unpublished inscriptions, and made important new surveys of sites like Mishrafa, Esbeita and Tell el-'Ain-el Guderat. Moreover, their conclusions about 'Ain Kadeis and Kadesh-Barnea were to become accepted by the academic world. Along the way, they were to make important observations about the dating of stone tools and they were to make an important contribution to our understanding of the climate and use of water in the Negeb in the Byzantine period. All of this was the result of a mere six weeks in the field and a hurried publication which was impeded by the onset of war.

This does make *The Wilderness of Zin* a remarkable work. Perhaps better than any other single publication of its period, it encapsulates the nature and romance of archaeology of the early

20th century - we see gentleman scholars pitting themselves against a harsh environment with a sense of adventure and determination, using innate common sense and basic survey techniques to the best of their ability. Finally, as noted by the reviewer for *The Egyptian Gazette* (Appendix 4), the report is beautifully written - it is as accessible today as it was in 1915, another reason behind the P.E.F.'s decision to republish the work again. It should be a lesson to us today, living in an age when so many archaeological reports are written with increasingly impenetrable language.

Having provided the reader with this introduction to the third edition of *The Wilderness of Zin*, it can be said that retrospect is a wonderful benefit because it provides the modern reader with the critical distance to reappraise an archaeological project in its historical and political context. The Committee's presentation of this book, with new archival material, to the public is a humbling experience. It reminds us of eminent archaeological exploration undertaken by the Woolley and Lawrence generation, whose pioneering scientific work the Fund strives to emulate. They have "shown us the way!"

T. Sam N. Moorhead,
Keeper of the Archives,
The Palestine Exploration Fund.

BIBLIOGRAPHY
FOR NEW MATERIAL IN THIS REVISED EDITION

Editions of Zin:

C. Leonard Woolley and T. E. Lawrence (with a chapter on Greek Inscriptions by M. N. Tod), *The Wilderness of Zin (Archaeological Report)* (Palestine Exploration Fund Annual 3, 1914-15: London)

C. Leonard Woolley and T. E. Lawrence (with a chapter on Greek Inscriptions by M. N. Tod and an Introduction by Sir Frederic Kenyon), *The Wilderness of Zin* (Jonathan Cape 1936: London)

C. L. Woolley et T. E. Lawrence, *Le Desert de Sin* (trans. Charles Mauron) (Payot, 1937: Paris)

Other Works
Aldington, R., 1955 *Lawrence of Arabia* (Collins, London)
Asher, M., 1998 *Lawrence, The Uncrowned King of Arabia* (Viking, London)
Brown, M. (ed.) 1991 *The Letters of T. E. Lawrence* (Oxford University Press)
Chapman, R. L. C. III, 1991 'Lawrence as Archaeologist', *The Journal of the T. E. Lawrence Society*, Vol. I, No. 1, 21-29
Chapman, R. L. C. III and Gibson, S., 1996. 'A Note on T. E. Lawrence as Photographer in the Wilderness of Zin', *Palestine Exploration Fund Quarterly Statement* (128th year), 94-102
Cohen, R., 1993. 'Kadesh Barnea, The Israelite Fortress', *The New Encyclopedia of Archaeological Excavations in the Holy Land*, (The Israel Exploration Society and Carta, The Israel Map and Publishing Company Ltd., Israel), Vol. 3, 843-7
Dalrymple, W., 1997 *From the Holy Mountain* (Flamingo/Harper Collins, London)
Donner, H., 1992 *The Mosaic Map of Madaba* (Palaestina Antiqua 7; Pharos, Kampen)

Finkelstein, I and Silbermann, N., 2001 *The Bible Unearthed* (Free Press, Simon & Schuster, New York)

Garnett, D. (ed.), 1938. *The Letters T. E. Lawrence* (London)

Hart, B. H. Liddell 1934. *'T. E. Lawrence', in Arabia and After* (Jonathan Cape, London)

Knightly, P. and Simpson, C., 1969 *The Secret Lives of Lawrence of Arabia* (Nelson, London)

Lawrence, A. W. (ed.), 1937. *Lawrence by his Friends* (Jonathan Cape, London)

Lawrence, A. W. (ed.), 1939. *Oriental Assembly by T. E. Lawrence* (Williams & Norgate, London)

Lawrence, M. R. (ed.), 1954. *The Home Letters of T. E. Lawrence and his brothers* (Basil Blackwell, Oxford)

Lawrence, T. E. 1935 *Seven Pillars of Wisdom* (Jonathan Cape, London)

Magnus, P., 1964. *Kitchener: Portrait of an Imperialist* (John Murray, London)

Musil, A., 1907-8. *Arabia Petraea, vol. 2 Edom* (Kaiserliche Akademie der Wissenschaften, Vienna)

The New Encyclopedia of Archaeological Excavations in the Holy Land (4 Vols.) (The Israel Exploration Society and Carta, The Israel Map and Publishing Company Ltd., Israel, 1993)

Newcombe, S. F., 1935. 'T. E. Lawrence: Personal Reminiscence', *Palestine Exploration Fund Quarterly Statement,* (67th year) 110-13, 162-64

Palestine Exploration Fund, 1895. *Thirty Years Work in the Holy Land* [ed. W.B. = Walter Besant] (London)

Pringle, [R.] D., 1992. 'T. E. Lawrence As Photographer', in L. Grant (ed.), *Along the Golden Road to Samarkand: Photographs of Monuments in the Middle East by T. E. Lawrence, A. W. Lawrence and Robert Byron* (London), 13-14

Rodenbeck, J., 2001. 'Deraa Revisited', *Desert Travellers* (J. Starkey and O. El Daly, eds., Astene, Durham), 257-292

Trumbull, H. C., 1884. *Kadesh Barnea* (Charles Scribner's Sons, New York)

Tubb, J. N. and Chapman, R. L. C. III, 1990 *Archaeology and The Bible* (British Museum Press, London)

Watson, C. M., 1915, *Fifty Years' Work in the Holy Land*, 1865-1915 (P.E.F, London)

Wilson, J., 1988. *T. E. Lawrence* (National Portrait Gallery, London)

Wilson, J., 1989. *Lawrence of Arabia: The Authorised Biography of T. E. Lawrence* (Collier/Macmillan, London)

Winstone, H. V. F., 1982 *The Illicit Adventure* (Jonathan Cape, London)

Winstone, H. V. F., 1993 *Gertrude Bell* (Constable, London)

Winstone, H. V. F., 1990 *Woolley of Ur* (Secker and Warburg, London)

Woolley, C. L., 1914. 'The Desert of the Wanderings', *Palestine Exploration Fund Quarterly Statement*, (46th year) 58-66

Woolley, C. L. 1920 *Dead Towns and Living Men, being Pages from an Antiquary's Notebook* (London: Lutterworth)

Woolley, C. L., 1930 *Digging up the Past* (Penguin, London)

Woolley, C. L., 1953 *Spadework* (Lutterworth, London)

Woolley, C. L., 1962 *As I seem to remember* (George Allen and Unwin, London)

Introduction to the Second Edition
by Sir Frederic Kenyon

In the autumn of 1913 two young English archaeologists, C. L. Woolley and T. E. Lawrence, were conducting excavations on behalf of the British Museum at Jerablus on the upper Euphrates, the site of the ancient Hittite capital, Carchemish. These excavations had been undertaken on the recommendation and under the advice of the late Mr. D. G. Hogarth, and it was he who had chosen Woolley and Lawrence for the work. Lawrence (then only 22 years of age) had been employed on it since its beginning in March, 1911; Woolley had succeeded Campbell Thompson in charge of it in 1912. Operations were conducted in two seasons of each year, spring and autumn. It was Lawrence's habit to remain out in the East during the intervals between digging seasons, acquiring that intimate knowledge of the native populations of which he was afterwards to make such good use; but at the end of the autumn season of 1913 the Director of the British Museum was asked whether the services of both scholars could be made available for an archaeological survey which the Palestine Exploration Fund desired to undertake in southern Palestine. Both were willing to undertake it; the Museum made the necessary arrangements for their remaining in the East instead of returning to England or going off on their own devices; and at the end of the year they left Carchemish to join Captain (now Colonel) S. F. Newcombe, who was in general charge of the Survey.

The Wilderness of Zin is shown in Bible atlases as the narrow valley of the Arabah northwards from Akaba towards the southern end of the Dead Sea. To the east of it, and separated by a line of hills, lay the land of Edom; to the west, the Wilderness of Paran, and to the west again of this, as far as the Mediterranean coast, the Wilderness of Shur; while south of the two last-named sections, and separating them from the mountainous region of Sinai, lay the Wilderness of El-Tih. The term 'wilderness' does not necessarily mean an uninhabitable waste; rather it means a country such as nomads may inhabit, with oases and wadies where crops may be reared. The Wilderness of El-Tih is indeed described by Palmer as an arid and almost waterless waste; but the northern areas between it and Palestine, though far from hospitable, are suitable for a nomad population. From the narrative of the wanderings of the Israelites one would gather that the most habitable area was that known as Kadesh-Barnea, which according to the earliest portions of the Pentateuch narrative was the headquarters of the Israelites during those forty years Its location has been a matter of much controversy. The books of reference now generally identify it with Ain Kadeis, on the strength of the flowery description of its beauties given by Mr. H. C. Trumbull in 1882; but Lawrence deals very caustically with this description, and is emphatic as to the complete inadequacy of the spring of Ain Kadeis to be the headquarters of a wandering tribe. If Kadesh-Barnea is to be connected with Ain Kadeis at all, as suggested in the concluding section of Chapter IV (not written by Lawrence), it can only be by extending the term to cover the whole adjoining district of Kossaima. This lies to the west of the Wilderness of Zin in the narrower sense described above; and when Kadesh-Barnea is said to be in that Wilderness (as it is in Num. xx. 1), the name must be extended (if Ain Kadeis and Kossaima are to be part of it) to include what is elsewhere called the Wildernesses of Paran and Shur. It is in this wider sense that the title of the present volume must be understood; for the survey extended over a great part of the area south of the line Gaza-Beersheba, through country which is cut diagonally by the Egyptian frontier from Rafa SSW. to Akaba.

The time available for the expedition was not much more than six weeks, in January and February, 1914. In that time the two travellers made their way from Gaza to Ain Kadeis, where they parted, Woolley working northwards by Abda, Kurnub, and the neighbourhood of Beersheba, while Lawrence continued south to Akaba, thence northwards up the Arabah to the watershed near Petra, and thence across to Maan, thus making acquaintance with some of the country which a year or two later, under very different conditions, became his happy hunting-ground.

During this short time, however, the two travellers were able to obtain a general knowledge of an area which, except for the few centuries of settled Byzantine government, can have changed little since the days of Moses. The description of it will be found in the following pages, of which perhaps the most valuable features are the account of the central area of Ain Kadeis, the discussion of the climatic conditions in the past, the elucidation of the routes from Palestine to Egypt in biblical times, and the exposition of the way in which the Byzantine government, in spite of the most unfavourable circumstances of soil and climate, was able to spread over the whole district a veneer of settled civilization, of which the remains are everywhere discoverable to-day. But more than this, the reader will, I think, feel that he has gained a clear general idea of the nature of this almost unknown country, for which he is indebted to the keen eyes, the alert intelligence, the trained observation, and the vivid literary gift of the two travellers.[1]

The war added not a little to the geographical knowledge of which the foundations were thus laid, especially in the regions of Beersheba and the Arabah. Since the war archaeological research has been pushed southwards into this area, particularly by the excavations conducted by Mr. H. Dunscombe Colt and Mr. T. J.

---

[1] Some personal reminiscences by Col. Newcombe, published in the *Quarterly Statement* of the Palestine Exploration Fund for July, 1935, add a livelier colour of first-hand knowledge than is at my command. I could have wished that Col. Newcombe would have written this Introduction himself.

Colin Baly at Esbeita. Mr. Baly, in some notes which he has kindly sent me, expresses great admiration of the work done by Woolley and Lawrence in so short a time. Further acquaintance with the Azazma Arabs has given him a more favourable opinion than is expressed by Lawrence and Kinglake. At Esbeita the excavations show that it was not finally deserted in the seventh century, but was occupied until the twelfth and possibly the fourteenth century. Traces of rebuilding are frequent, and the desertion seems to have been gradual. It would not appear to be true that the Byzantine churches in southern Palestine habitually have three apses. According to Mr. Baly, only two triapsidal churches can be traced outside the Negeb. It is also misleading to speak of 'the usual dog-tooth ornament'; what is meant is probably the chevron ornament which is common. At Abda the so-called Greek sherds appear rather to be Nabatean, a class of pottery which has only recently been identified. To the account of Auga it may be added that the church described by Woolley and Lawrence was destroyed during the war, but the same operations brought to light a new church north of the Serai, which it is hoped to investigate shortly.

These, however, are small details, which are added only for completeness sake.

Some further opinions of interest, formed by the two travellers as the result of their exploration, are recorded by Col. Newcombe from his recollection of conversations with them. It was Lawrence's view, with which Woolley concurs, that the roads from Akaba to the Mediterranean were used, instead of the route from Suez to Pelusium, in Solomon's time (when his fleet had its harbour at the head of the Gulf of Akaba), and also later whenever Egypt was at war with Palestine or when its tariff on goods in transit became too high. Hence the wealth of Gerar, Beth Pelet, and the seaport near Gaza, which has been disclosed by the recent excavations of Sir Flinders Petrie; and hence also the somewhat surprising prosperity of Khalasa. Ultimately the Nabateans became the great carrying merchants; but Lawrence contended that it is a mistake to suppose that Petra was ever their trading centre, for it was never on the line of their goods traffic. Rather it was a religious and residential centre, where wealthy merchants could live in comfort and civilization, sufficiently near to but above the very uncomfortable highway from Akaba to Gaza.

The Wilderness of Zin was first published as the Annual of the Palestine Exploration Fund for 1914-15. In view, however, of the subsequent careers of its two authors, and of the literary merit which adds charm to the description of a country of no little biblical and historical interest, it seems to deserve a wider publicity than the proceedings of a learned society.

F. G. Kenyon
November 1935

Note

The Committee of the Palestine Exploration Fund feel it necessary to state that both the principal authors having been called to Egypt, for Special Military Service, before the end of the year 1914, Mr. D. G. Hogarth kindly undertook to see this volume through the press. He wishes it to be understood that he has written none of it except a paragraph on the Hora pottery (p. 66); that the transliteration of Arabic names and words, and the arrangement of the matter are the authors' own; and that he has not been able to assign with complete confidence their places in the text to the following illustrations, Figs. 1; 2; 26 c, d, f, g; 31; 43; 45; 46.

The book (except Chapter vi) has been produced jointly by the authors; but the following parts of the text are more the work of one than of the other. Mr. Woolley is chiefly responsible for the first half of Chapter I; the sections on stone implements and monuments, climate, and the Byzantine period in Chapter II; the account of the Northern Tells in Chapter III; and all Chapter V, except the concluding section.

Mr. Lawrence is chiefly responsible for the second half of Chapter I (on Akaba); the first part of Chapter II; the account of the Darb el Shur in Chapter III; most of Chapter IV;-and the concluding section only (Akaba) of Chapter V.

The maps in the book were compiled by Mr. Lawrence from the Survey Materials and drawn out by Mr. B. V. Darbishire. The Plates are from photographs taken by both authors. The plans and drawings reproduced in the text are, almost without exception, the work of Mr. Woolley, who drew them to scale on the spot.

The Committee feel deeply indebted to Mr. Hogarth for the care and labour devoted to the production of the work, for which task none could be better equipped by knowledge and experience.

C. M. Watson
Chairman of the Executive Committee
The Palestine Exploration Fund.

PALESTINE EXPLORATION FUND.

ANNUAL

1914-1915.

DOUBLE VOLUME.

PUBLISHED BY ORDER OF THE COMMITTEE,

AND SOLD AT

THE OFFICES OF THE FUND, 2, HINDE STREET, MANCHESTER SQUARE, W.

PALESTINE EXPLORATION FUND,

1914.

THE WILDERNESS OF ZIN

(ARCHÆOLOGICAL REPORT.)

By

C. LEONARD WOOLLEY

and

T. E. LAWRENCE.

With a Chapter on the Greek Inscriptions by M. N. TOD.

PUBLISHED BY ORDER OF THE COMMITTEE

AND SOLD AT

THE OFFICES OF THE FUND, 2, HINDE STREET, MANCHESTER SQUARE, W.

HARRISON AND SONS,
PRINTERS IN ORDINARY TO HIS MAJESTY,
ST. MARTIN'S LANE, LONDON

THE PALESTINE EXPLORATION FUND.

a 2

To Captain S. F. Newcombe, R.E.

Who showed them " the way wherein they must walk, and the work that they must do."

(*Exodus* 18 : 20)

PREFATORY NOTE.

The Committee of the Palestine Exploration Fund feel it necessary to state that both the principal authors having been called to Egypt, for Special Military Service, before the end of the year 1914, Mr. D. G. Hogarth kindly undertook to see this volume through the Press. He wishes it to be understood that he has written none of it except a paragraph on the Hora pottery (p. 48); that the transliteration of Arabic names and words, and the arrangement of the matter are the authors' own; and that he has not been able to assign with complete confidence their places in the text to the following illustrations, Figs. 1; 2; 26 *c, d, f, g*; 29; 31; 43; 45; 46.

The book (except Chapter VI) has been produced jointly by the authors; but the following parts of the text are more the work of one than of the other. Mr. Woolley is chiefly responsible for the first half of Chapter I; the sections on stone implements and monuments, climate, and the Byzantine period in Chapter II; the account of the Northern Tells in Chapter III; and all Chapter V, except the concluding section.

Mr. Lawrence is chiefly responsible for the second half of Chapter I (on Akaba); the first part of Chapter II; the account of the Darb el Shur in Chapter III; most of Chapter IV; and the concluding section only (Akaba) of Chapter V.

The maps in the book were compiled by Mr. Lawrence from the Survey materials and drawn out by Mr. B. V. Darbishire. The plates are from photographs taken by both authors. The plans and drawings reproduced in the text are, almost without exception, the work of Mr. Woolley, who drew them to scale on the spot.

The Committee feel deeply indebted to Mr. Hogarth for the care and labour devoted to the production of the work, for which task none could be better equipped by knowledge and experience.

C. M. WATSON,
Chairman of the Executive Committee.

February, 1915.

INTRODUCTION

We must begin with apologies. Mr. Woolley and I are not Semitic specialists, and our hurried flight across the country did not give us either time or opportunity to collect place-names. We therefore deal simply with the archaeological remains in the desert, and even on these, from pressure of work elsewhere in Syria, we could only spend six weeks. When we went to Sinai we learnt for the first time the names of former travellers; and in our ignorance of how much they had done, we repeated a great deal of their work, especially on the later sites. French, German, American and English travellers had recorded all these before us. What certain of those travellers have published is usually more than sufficient, and the limited public interested in Byzantine matters will naturally refer to their special articles. As a rule, we have avoided making infinitesimal corrections in their plans or notes, and have put forward only fresh information or criticisms which we think pertinent. If these latter are sometimes drastic, we must plead that our knowledge of pottery, acquired during some years of excavation in the neighbouring countries, and our experience of the allied remains in Egypt and Syria have enabled us to take a wider comparative view of the civilization of the Negeb than most of our predecessors could. We both speak Arabic easily.

Our Forerunners

On the whole, the work done by the French fathers in this country and published by them from time to time in the *Revue Biblique*, seems to us at once very sane, very interesting, and very exact. Their notes on Abda, so far as they go, are admirable. Their description of their ride from Nakhl to Kadeis and through Wady Jerafi to Petra could not be improved upon; and on more particular points, as in their description of Graye (Geziret Faraun), or in their historical and anthropological notes on the Arab tribes, they show the learning of specialists tempered with mercy. Musil, their Austrian competitor, has made wonderful collections of Arab songs, mostly from the Kerak district, and he has been over the whole country, surveying and photographing; but his field notes are sometimes both vague and heavy.

In English there is occasional work, of very varied quality, in the *Quarterly Statements of the Palestine Exploration Fund*. The field notes of Mr. Holland are of interest between the Canal and Jebel Muweilleh, and he was a keen observer; but his excursions into archaeology are not successful. The really great man is Professor Edward Palmer, who, aided by Tyrwhitt Drake, made a journey in the Tih and Negeb in 1869 and 1870. His book is a very carefully written, very lively and very complete summing up of the features of the country. Palmer was a great linguist, and therefore particularly interested in place-names. His zest for these sometimes led him astray. If he had had an archaeological instinct or training, our visit to the Desert would have been waste of time. As it was, he was afraid to be too definite in his judgments, and so laid himself open to misuse or misquotation by champions of private and particular theories upon the country and its occupation. His book should be read in conjunction with our own, for we have avoided, where possible, allusion to things which he has done once and for all.

Where we have had occasion to criticise his work or attack his theories we have done it vigorously; but we hope that people will not read into our attitude anything more than the respect due to a powerful opponent; for Palmer himself and for the journey that he and Tyrwhitt Drake, under great difficulties, made so vivid and fruitful for us, we have nothing but unqualified admiration.

The main objects that we had in view were four: to get some idea of the character of the country in successive periods; to trace the Darb el Shur, the old inland route of caravans from central Palestine to Egypt; to identify sites mentioned in the Bible and other historical writings; and, though this lay outside the limits of the new survey, to study the neighbourhood of Ain Kadeis, supposed to be the Kadesh-Barnea of the Israelite wanderings. In all these endeavours, except, perhaps, the third, we had some measure of success. If a disproportionate amount of our results is devoted to Byzantine instead of to earlier and more interesting remains, it is because we were obliged to deal with the actual rather than with the desirable. The identification of old sites of the Bible, so frequent in the former survey of Palestine, was there made possible by the careful collection of place-names. In our haste we could not enter upon this work. It has been very completely done, however, by the actual surveyors, and it is their opinion that in this desert country, subjected to the fluctuating waves of nomad invasions, old names are little likely to survive. Places are usually called after some temporary and recent inhabitant, or after some prominent but not always permanent natural feature.

The Attitude of the Arabs

In the beginnings of our journey, we were aided (in common with the other surveyors) by Erfan Bey, Kaimmakam of Beersheba. He was free from the widespread suspicion of map-makers, and was very friendly. With the Arabs we had the best relations throughout. Of course, each tribe has a vile opinion of the virtues and morals of its neighbours; but Captain Newcombe began work in the country by getting to know the chiefs, and so secured for himself and the other members of the survey – without paying blackmail or giving presents – a toleration that became cordiality at times. The tribesmen we met were naturally inquisitive and sometimes distrustful, since we did not always follow the lines of the survey parties. But they were all very good-tempered, quite ready to act as guides or emergency helpers (of course, expecting a reward – a frame of mind not unknown in Europe), very hospitable, and most scrupulously honest. Near Ain Kadeis, where our riding camels strayed away, the Arabs brought them in, unasked, to the station at Kossaima. It will be obvious from this that we had no dragoman with us.

We must beg from our critics (if there are any critics in these busy days) more mercy than we ourselves have shown. The original scheme of this book has suffered many things in execution. It was to have been rounded off by some chapters from Captain Newcombe, to treat of place-names and of the histories of Arab tribes, and to explain the triangulation of the actual survey and its results. None of these chapters was written, but all were in preparation when the outbreak of war changed Captain Newcombe's plans, and hurried him into France in the first days of the campaign.

As there is none of Captain Newcombe's independent work in the following pages, I think we shall be justified in saying a few words about his leadership of our party. We were sent down in the midst of his work (which was being done against time) to bother him on a subject that furthered his own studies in no way. We had with us only a scratch outfit raked up in Gaza. Yet he welcomed us, stripped himself of what he called his 'luxuries' for us (and he was already living in the barest way), got us camels, and in Khalasa fed us till our stores arrived. Living with him we got a clear insight into his methods. He had five parties under him, and yet in this unmapped wilderness always knew exactly where each party was, and how its work was going on. He established a regular post, and supply caravans from El Arish, Gaza, and Beersheba, to feed his men and animals. He was ambassador for all of us to Arab tribes and to Turkish officials, and managed both, leaving behind him a reputation which will smooth the way of any future English traveller in the desert. This labour of organization would have been enough for most men, living as roughly and uncomfortably as Newcombe did: yet in addition he contrived to map a larger district than any of his assistants. Off by dawn with guides and instruments, he would return to camp at dark, and work perhaps till midnight, arranging and calculating and recording for the benefit of the other parties. He was the prime begetter of the Survey, and thanks to his elaborate camel-contract, his skilful handling of his transport and supply columns, and the Spartan simplicity of life to which he also converted his subordinates, the expedition, in economy of money and time, beat all records of similar surveys in the East.

This book as it stands, therefore, is the work only of Mr. C. L. Woolley and myself. Mr. Woolley had written of the Byzantine towns, the Northern tells, and the journey, when the war sent him also into the Army, and forced him to transfer his materials to me, These included parts of the historical chapter, and parts of that on the Darb el Shur. It is, however, impossible for either of us to take sole responsibility for any part. Some of the book is a transcript of field notes, hammered out between us in the evening in the tents. Some of it was written in collaboration at Carchemish, before the excavatious there began in the spring. In Mr. Woolley's absence I have revised parts of his work where I was competent to do so, and have left it untouched elsewhere.

Dr. A. E. Cowley, of Magdalen College, Oxford, worked out such Hebrew and Nabatean fragments as we brought back. He is responsible here for the Nabatean inscription from Khalasa, printed in Chapter VI. Mr. M. N. Tod. of Oriel College, has done the Greek inscriptions, and has prepared for publication all those given in Chapter VI, and Professor D. S. Margoliouth, of Oxford, has translated the Arabic stone from the Nagb of Akaba given in the same chapter. I owe thanks also to Mr. D. G. Hogarth, who read the text, and improved it in many details, and to Professor A. S. Hunt, of Oxford.

T. E.L.

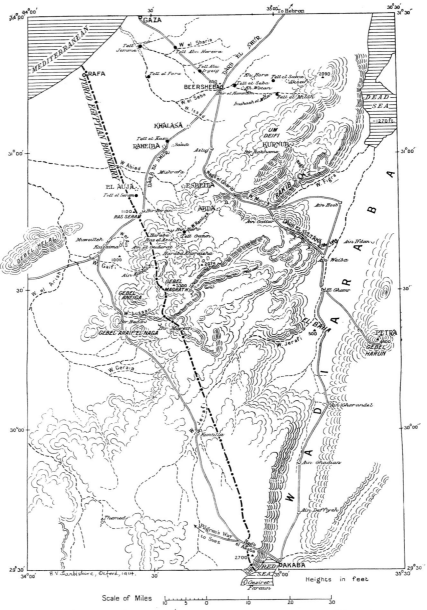

Scale of Miles

Ruined towns ∴ other ruins ∴ Police posts ♂ Mounds ● Wells, springs & cisterns ∪ Main roads ══════

Heights in feet

B.V. Darbishire, Oxford, 1914.

CHAPTER I

OUR ROUTE IN THE DESERT

If ye go thyder, ye must consider,
When ye have lust to dine,
There shall no meat be for to gete
Nether bere, ale, ne wine,
Ne shetès clean, to lie between.

('The Nut-Brown maid' anonymous, 15th Century, lines 193-197 from
A. Quiller-Couch (ed.)
1919 *The Oxford Book of English Verse; 1250-1900*)

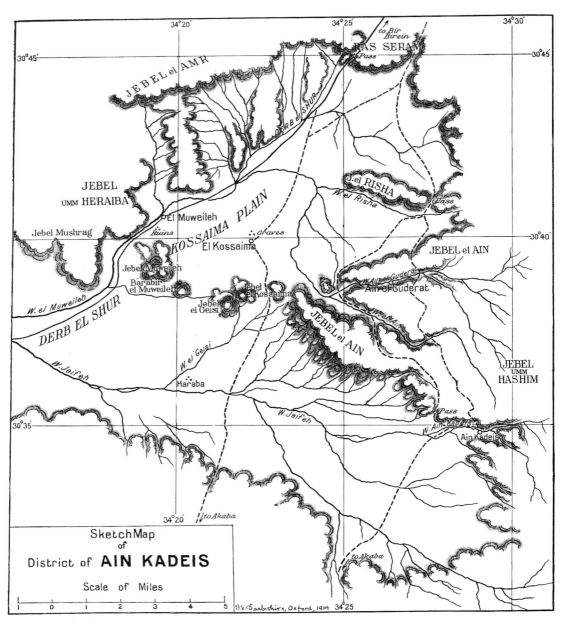

Sketch Map
of
District of **AIN KADEIS**

Scale of Miles

B V Darbishire, Oxford, 1914

ERRATA.—Derb el Shur should be Darb el Shur.
Muweileh should be Muweilleh.

Gaza: Beersheba: Khalasa: Esbeita: Auja: Ain Kadeis: Ain el Guderat. We divide: Khoraisha: Abda: Kurnub: Northern Tells: Gaza. Ain el Guderat to Kuntilla: The Nagb of Akaba: Wady Araba: Ain Ghadian: Gharandel: Wady Musa and Maan.

We left Carchemish in the last days of 1913, hurrying southwards to join Captain Newcombe, the director of the Survey, who had already been for some time in the field. We brought with us from Carchemish one of our own followers, Dahoum, an Arab boy accustomed to the work of photography, squeeze-making, etc., and we had also the services of Yusuf Canaan, an old foreman of the Palestine Exploration Fund's field work.[1] We reached Gaza early in January, 1914, and found ourselves obliged, owing to circumstances we could not control, to provide ourselves there with the outfit necessary for the trip. Gaza today is not exactly an emporium, and for helping us in our necessities we owe a deep debt of gratitude to the Rev. Dr. Sterling, and to Mr. A. A. Knesevich (British Consular Agent) and his son Emil. Both gave us hospitality and active aid. Mr. Knesevich and his son acted as agents for us, found us servants and stores and tents, and throughout our expedition were of the greatest possible help.[2] Thanks to these gentlemen we were able to leave Gaza on January 7th, the day after our arrival there, for Beersheba, where Captain Newcombe had arranged to meet us.

Our Preparations

From Gaza the track to Beersheba passes through a wide undulating plain of deep, rich soil; there are no trees, and virtually no houses to be seen, but everywhere there are visible the traces of an older and more settled civilization – village sites strewn with

The Start

---

[1] Yusuf actually joined us at El Auja, and proved very useful.
[2] The words of Antoninus of Placentia (§ 33, *Corp. Script. Eccl. Lat.*, vol. 38, p.211) – 'Gaza autem civitas splendida deliciosa homines honestissimi omni liberalitate decori amatores peregrinorum' – apply only to the staff or buildings of the C.M.S. Hospital and the British Consular Agency. Elsewhere Gaza shows a falling off.

Byzantine pottery, olive presses built of marble and cement, and broken water-cisterns. A little way from the road, on the west bank of the Wady Sharia, rises Tell abu Hareira, a splendid mound, partly natural and partly artificial, now crowned by a shrine of the saint, and covered with Arab graves. Further to the south Tells Fara and Jemme can be seen in the distance, and nearer to Beersheba, on the bank of the Wady abu Irgeig, a small double tell close to the roadside bears witness to the early occupation of these fertile lowlands. At Beersheba we spent three days, and then, on January 11th, moved to Khalasa. South of Beersheba the country changes, and the rolling plain gives place to barren hills and ridges of soft limestone, overlaid with loose gravel and flint; some of the wider valleys are cultivated for catch crops, but the general effect of the country is desolate, though the broken terrace walls in even the narrowest wadies are evidence of a more industrious husbandry in the past. As one approaches Khalasa (Plates I, 1, 2, and II, 1), the stony hills are exchanged for wide sand-dunes dotted with scrub, the country becomes flatter and less broken, and near the ruins of the town stretches a wide plain of light but good soil, a considerable part of which is tilled by the Arabs, whose cluster of tents stands near the well. At Khalasa we stopped four days, visiting in that time Raheiba and Saadi, and also making an excursion back towards the north to examine some of the cairns that top most of the stony hills between the sand-dunes and the Beersheba plain. On January 16th we moved our camp to Esbeita. After following the Saadi road for about half its length, we turned southwards, and, passing over a fairly wide plain, came to a great belt of drift-sand, whose long, regular ridges, from forty to fifty feet high, we had to cross at right-angles, Here cultivation was impossible – only a few tamarisk bushes pushed up through the sand. From this we passed to a country not less barren – rough limestone hills, banded with flinty strata, which rose gradually on either side of the little valley up which we rode, until at the top of the watershed the ground fell away suddenly before our feet, and we stood looking over the great Wady Migrih. To our right the

Khalasa

walls of Mishrafa crowned the highest hill-top on the west side of the valley; on its east side, in the distance, the ruins of Esbeita could just be distinguished. The valley was wild and barren: red ridges of flint rose between stretches of scrub-dotted sand; below Mishrafa a few patches of poorly cultivated soil but threw into relief the hopeless character of the surrounding desert. By the evening we reached Esbeita, and pitched our camp close to the northern church. The planning of the ruins and a visit to Mishrafa occupied us until January 24th, when we shifted camp to El Auja. The road took us across the flint mounds of the valley, and up the Wady Abiad, a fairly wide plain of sandy, but good soil, once all cultivated, through which the torrent has cut many winding channels with steep banks, and stony, scrub-covered beds. In the middle of the valley was a group of walled gardens, together with the ruins of some five or six stone towers. Then the hills closed in on either side and, by the time we had ridden for seven miles, rose almost directly out of the stream bed. On the hills, long saddles or cone-shaped mounds of flint-strewn limestone, were to be seen numerous cairns and stone piles. The valley widened again, and between the low shelves of rock that now edged it patches of cultivation reappeared, the salvage of the prevailing sand-dunes. In the rock face was cut a large Christian tomb. We left the wady and rode west-south-west over flat land which, though sand-covered, was plainly fit for tillage, then crossed a wady and, cutting across the Darb el Shur, climbed a long, steep ridge of limestone that shut off this plain from the Wady Hafir. Soon a steep descent took us down into the Wady Hafir, a broad valley once fertile but now given over for the most part to scrub and drift sand, on the further side of which were the ruins of El Auja and the modern Government station – the only buildings to be found between Beersheba and Akaba.

Esbeita

Auja

We spent two days planning the town buildings and examining some stone cairns upon Tell el Seram, an isolated hill which rises up boldly in the middle of the wady some three miles south of El Auja. Then, on January 27th, sending our baggage camels on ahead, by the direct route for Ain Kadeis, we struck eastwards, and hitting the Darb el Shur, where we had crossed it two days before, followed it southwards to Bir Birein, where we found an early building on the hill-top, and thence on to Ras Seram, a stony pass looking over the plain across which runs the Kossaima road. Going straight on, we missed our baggage animals (which had taken the Kossaima road) and had to spend the night in the open; on the next day we secured a guide and went straight for Ain Kadeis. The fact that our two camels had bolted in the night proved to be rather an advantage, for the tracks which we followed were almost impossible for camels. We climbed up and down steep scree-covered hills rising about a thousand feet above narrow wadies; nowhere was there any cultivation, nor the possibility of any; it was the most impressive mountain landscape, and the most barren that we had seen since leaving Gaza. Only in one place did we find a group of five Arab tents close to a water-hole dug in the wady bottom; elsewhere there were no signs of any inhabitants. We crossed the upper reaches of the Wady Guderat and the Wady el Ain, reached Ain Kadeis at about 1.30 p.m., and finding that our tents were not there turned northwards, and passing along the broken foothills that skirt the Ain Kadeis plain reached, about 5 p.m., the Egyptian Government station of Kossaima. From Kossaima we visited Muweilleh and Ain Kadeis; and then moved our camp to the pleasant Ain Guderat valley. Here we spent some days, examining the ruins on the little tell, some graves in the wady, and the main features of the surrounding country. On February 8th we separated, Mr. Lawrence to go south to Akaba and thence up the Wady Araba, I to return north. My road led me up the Wady Guderat and then over a ridge up another small wady called Wady el Ain but really a north-eastern branch of the main valley of that name. This was a narrow flat wady, carefully terraced; about the middle of it stood the ruins of a small Byzantine hamlet, about a dozen houses, close to a big rock-cut cistern now blocked with stones and rubbish. The cultivation continued to the watershed, the high tableland that

Ain Kadeis

flanks the Wady Khoraisha; on a low hill-top close to the path were some twenty large cairns. The Wady Khoraisha where I crossed it is fairly wide, and the flat banks show signs of former cultivation; higher up steep slopes and rocky cliffs close in on it, broken by the mouths of tributary valleys in which occasionally fair-sized trees can be seen clinging precariously to the stones. In the cliff sides are caverns roughly walled up and used by the Arabs as corn stores. Further up, the wady passes close to the bare sides of Jebel um Hashim; then a climb over a steep rocky path, worn almost as smooth as glass by the feet of camels, leads one to the *haraba*, a large rock-cut cistern which is one of the few water supplies available in the barren wilderness of the Negeb (Plate XXIII, 1). Half a mile away, in a tiny wady, is a patch of once cultivated land, with the ruins of a rather large Byzantine building, perhaps a khan used by the travellers on this inhospitable road. On this occasion, however, I turned northwards down the wady, and after some five miles passed a little settlement of half a dozen Arab tents; the wady then opened out into a fairly broad plain, parts of which are ploughed by these Arabs, and I camped for the night close to the *haraba* Ras el Aziz, on which they depend for their water. On the next day, turning eastwards, I passed one or two ridges and struck the Wady Hafir, here a broad level plain, once all under cultivation, and crossing it diagonally reached the Bir el Hafir, a shallow stone-lined well in the middle of the stream bed. More stony ridges led to the Wady el Gatun, a complex of small torrent beds of which one was more conspicuous than the rest; in this, and in some of the other wadies, where there was a patch of level ground, terrace walls had been built and the land tilled. On a slight mound (Tell Gatun) were the ruins of three or four Byzantine farms; farther on, another larger building of the same date looked down over the main wady, and on the south side of our road were two or three other houses of the same uncut rubble construction and a few contemporary graves. After more stony ridges I came out on the watershed, a wide plateau of arable soil, from which the road led down a cultivated wady running almost due north,

Khoraisha

7

perhaps two miles long, and on the average fifty yards wide. This brought us to the Wady Ramliya. Though broken terraces spoke of former cultivation, the soil was practically pure sand, through which torrent waters had cut a deep bed. It was curious to see here, reproduced on a small scale, the phenomenon remarked by Sir Aurel Stein in Chinese Turkestan: many fragments of walls are left standing on isolated tongues or islands of sand some six feet high, while around them the light soil, not solidified by any superimposed weight, has all been carried away by the flood. At one point on the west bank stood the ruins of a large farmhouse with caves behind it cut in the lofty cliff; fragments of Syrian *terra sigillata* showed that the building dated back fairly early in the Roman period. For some two miles below this the valley is still cultivated; hedges cross it at frequent intervals, and there are even three or four old trees. Lower still the modern cultivation stops, but the signs of the old are more striking: carefully built terrace walls of ashlar masonry six feet high border the torrent bed, and cross walls run at all angles to disperse the flood-water. Cutting across a high shoulder of the west bank, I came out on rolling

Abda

country, and looking across a fresh bend of the Wady Ramliya saw the hill of Abda pockmarked with the black mouths of its ruined cave dwellings.

I left Abda on February 15th, and crossing Wady Ramliya close to the town climbed down and up the sides of Wady Murra, a wonderful gorge, its barren sides cut by torrents into a huddle of isolated rocky pinnacles and narrow sloped arêtes through which it was difficult to thread one's way. From this the road ran across a broad table-land stretching away to Nagb el Gharib; to the east, across the Araba, could be seen the mountains of Kerak, very far away. The whole plain showed traces of ancient cultivation; this continued down the wady along which the track led us to Bir Rakhama, a shallow stone-lined well in the wady bed. Near the well were some Arab tents, and a considerable amount of the land was under cultivation. The only ancient remains were some Byzantine potsherds which strewed a little knoll (probably the debris of old tent dwellings, for there were no buildings), and a few ring-graves of the same period. The so-called Tell Rakhama was a natural limestone hill. On the next day I went about two miles along the wady; though there had been no rain for a twelvemonth, water was obviously close to the surface – indeed, in one place a woman was filling her pitchers at a hole less than two feet deep which she had dug in the sandy bed of the stream. Masses of small flowers covered the ground. Leaving the wady the road ran across the district of Um Deifi, a wide stretch of rolling hills, half of it covered with scrub and half of it cultivated; but since there had been no rain, it was only in the hollows that a film of green relieved the brown of the ploughlands. By eleven o'clock the camels reached the long line of hills that shut in the plain to the north, and crossing a low neck came out on another plain watered by several wadies. The main stream, the Wady el Sidd, sweeps eastwards in a great curve under the high southern hills up to Tell Kurnub, when it breaks through them by a precipitous gorge, and runs on to the Dead Sea.

Kurnub

I left Kurnub on February 19th for Tell el Seba, and from there visited Tell el Sawa, Khirbet Wotan, Bir el Hammam, Tell el Milah, and Khirbet el Imshash; then on February 22nd I left for Gaza and the north.

In the meantime Lawrence had struck southwards from Kossaima along the old road by Wady Lussan and Kuntilla towards Akaba. All cultivation ceases south of the plain of Ain Kadeis, save for a couple of small fields banked out of the water-courses in Wady Mezra and Wady Lussan. And naturally when cultivation fails, all traces of fixed habitation fail also. Beduins have passed over the country and buried their dead there; travellers have gone up and down the great roads; but the only ancient one to build a house was a solitary Byzantine in Wady Lussan, and then perhaps it was rather for a road station than for a dwelling-place. By the wayside is one ring cairn of early date, piled together on a rocky outcrop half a day's journey below

Wady Lussan

Kuntilla,[1] the new frontier-post of the Sinai Government; and there is a modern ring cairn just above Kuntilla. On the other hand there is everywhere clear-marked the great road, running straight over the low country, and twisting cunningly among the hills; a road of from ten to forty single tracks, all of which are worn down an inch or two into the flint-covered limestone, and polished by the pads of camels till they glitter white in the sun.

The Limestone Plateau

The landscape is only an exaggeration of the northern country. There are the same great stretches of flaky limestone, so overlaid with brown flints, sand-polished, that the whiteness only shows through on slopes too steep to hold the flint; and rising out of these flats and bounding them are ridges and mounds of the same limestone, capped with a harder layer, as smooth as a table-top and strewn with the everlasting flints (Plate XXXIII, 2). The straightness and regularity of these formations are curious. For instance, at a point five hours below Kossaima the plain is crossed directly from east to west by a sharp wall of hill, like a colossal embankment, two hundred feet high, broken just in the middle by a deep gully through which as by a door the old road passes. To one coming from the south this gateway is the point from which he first sees the plain of Ain Kadeis, while the Kossaima plain is hidden behind its hills: Ain Kadeis is therefore the more notable point, and might attach its name to the district.[2]

To Kuntilla

To the east of the road the prospect is always mountainous. At the first on leaving the Kadeis plain are Jebel Um Hashim and Jebel Aneiga; later on Jebel Araif el Naga, isolated (Plate II, 2); and south of it the mountains of Arabia, which form the further bank of Wady Araba. On the west side are some hills, but for the greater part the country is almost flat into the distance. Wady Mezra is the first great wady, Wady Lussan the second, Wady Mayein the third;

---

[1] Which is not Contellet Garaiyeh.
[2] P.75 ff.

and the last running down from the huge cone of Araif el Naga spreads out into a plain (Wady Geraia), many miles in width, of sand thinly covering a bed of flints. At times, however, there are low mounds and undulations rolling enough to hide the many wavering lines of brushwood which mark the almost imperceptible wady-beds. The water-holes Beda, Agrud, and Kuntilla all lie a little off the road, as do the wells of Mayein. Kuntilla is the Government post, made up of three or four stone houses on steep ridges, lying a couple of miles east of the great road. The well is in a wady before the houses, and is new; but an older one, now dry, lies farther down the torrent bed.

After Kuntilla the layer of flint that hid the limestone is replaced by nearly clean sand and the scrub of mingled *rimth* and tamarisk that is characteristic of much of North Sinai. A day to the south the granite and sandstone country begins in an abrupt row of knotted peaks, red or brown in colour and very hard and sharp in outline. The main road enters the middle of the wall of these hills by a narrow pass, and beyond them finds again open country – a white dusty plain with a floor of hard mud, in patches wind-swept clean of the sand. From this plain one comes quite suddenly to the edge of the plateau, the pilgrim way from Suez falls in on the right, and the united roads turn sharply down a little valley that is the beginning of the Nagb or pass of Akaba (Plate III, 1).

The way down is very splendid. In the hill-sides all sorts of rocks are mingled in confusion;[1] grey-green limestone cliffs run down sheer for hundreds of feet, in tremendous ravines whose faces are a medley of colours wherever crags of black porphyry and diorite jut out, or where soft sandstone, washed down, has left long pink and red smudges on the lighter colours. The confusion of materials makes the road laying curiously uneven. The surface

The Nagb of Akaba

[1] *Cf.* Weill, 'La Presqu'île du Sinai', for the geology of Akaba.

11

is in very few cases made up; wherever possible the road was cut to rock, with little labour, since the stone is always brittle and in thin, flat layers. So the masons had at once ready to their hand masses of squared blocks for parapets or retaining walls. Yet this same facility of the stone has been disastrous to the abandoned road, since the rains of a few seasons chisel the softer parts into an irregular giant staircase; while in the limestone the torrent has taken the road-cutting as a convenient course, and left it deep buried under a sliding mass of water-worn pebbles.

The gradients are steep, as is necessary in such precipitous country if great road-works are not to be undertaken: yet not so steep as to be impossible for wagons. A light cart could be taken up the road as it is today, though only as an experience, and not habitually. In the time of Ibrahim Pasha, who took guns over, it was doubtless in better repair. Here and there the rock-walls have been blasted. This is probably his work, and the lime and ashlar bridge at the foot of the great descent might be of his period also. It would be idle on such a road to look for very early traces. Macrizi says that Faik, about the time of Ahmed ibn Touloun (868 – 884) first made the road practicable for baggage animals, and that Bedr, governor for Haroun ibn Koumarouwaih and afterwards Mohammed ibn Kelaoun, repaired his work. Lying a few hundred feet above the bridge on the road-side are the broken pieces of an Arabic inscription of Kansuh el Ghuri, one of the last Mameluke Sultans, who also seems to claim the road.[1] The many stone huts on the ridges at each side were some of them sentry-boxes, others workmen's huts of the time of the road's prosperity, and there are many graves of Arabian pilgrims.

The great descent takes about an hour and a half on foot from the plateau to the bridge in Wady el Masri; and from there to the

---

[1] Translation by Professor Margoliouth on p. 189.

beach in Wady Araba is another hour and a half of easy road across the buttresses and soft foothills of the cliffs, down wadies and over ridges. The crests of some of these are cut through to ease the gradient, but it is only petty work.

The road finally reaches sea level on the extreme north-west beach of the Gulf of Akaba, and runs over the sand of the shore and through the old site of Aila between the palm-gardens into the modern village. It thus has to traverse the whole width of Wady Araba, a perfectly flat sandy expanse, very salt, with a few dom palms and many date palms and a little scrub to disguise its ugliness. Sweet water, or at least water not very brackish, is to be found by digging a hole a few feet deep anywhere near the beach. *Akaba*

Proceeding northwards from Akaba the sand becomes cleaner, and there are few water holes; but past Ain Deffiyeh and till Wady Ghadian the Araba has in spring an almost park-like air in comparison with the desert plateaux on each side of it. The tamarisks and small scrub found everywhere in wady beds here become very thick and green, stretching over the flat floor of the plain in long lines like hedges, and every now and then great woody acacias stand out free of these, singly or in small groves. The surface soil is generally bad, much of it with the hard smoothness of never-broken ground; there are no old sites or ruins in the main valley, and no roads, though indeed these latter are unnecessary where the whole surface is indifferently flat and easy. Every few hours' journey a greener patch marks a stagnant hole of water, which is always nasty to drink, in part from its own sedgy taste, and in part from the mixed flavours added to it by Arabs and their camels. *The Araba*

The Wady Araba has ever been a road from north to south, and of late years theorists in biblical geography have exercised their fancy in building ancient towns by the roadside. Thus Robinson identifies Ain Ghadian, a point a day's journey for a pack camel north of the Gulf, as a possible site not only for the Roman station of Ad Dianam (which might pass) but also for Ezion-Geber, and suggests that the sea may well have come up so far. It is true that *Ghadian*

Ain Ghadian seems to be the solitary spot in the southern Araba, not on the sea coast, which has any traces of settled occupation.[1] Two little rooms of mud and stones show that a Turkish patrol was posted there at the time of the delimitation of the frontiers, and behind the rooms is a very low mound about fifty yards square, which is probably the remains of an earlier building. There is just enough Byzantine pottery on the site to make possible the suggestion that in late classical time a policeman was stationed here to guard the wells; and, of course, there is no proof that there was not a similar inhabitant in Jewish times. Yet Solomon's great seaport must surely have measured more than fifty yards each way, and it would strain the Indian Ocean to bring it two hundred feet uphill. Ghadian today is not attractive: there are eight smelly pits in which water collects a few feet down, and the land about is a bush-covered, salty, sandy waste, fit for camels.

Ain Gharandel

North of this point the valley becomes entirely sterile as far as Wady Gharandel (Plate IV, 1). It is all filled with waves of shifting sand, very deep and soft, in which grow colocynths, and in harder hollows tamarisk. Ain Gharandel wells out in a narrow cliff-edged valley of green trees on the east side of Wady Araba, but the water, though sweet, is not very plentiful. Wady Gharandel is a roadway to the eastern table-land, and at its side are two ruined buildings.[2] Geographically it is a useful point, since from it northwards the Araba becomes nearly free of sand, but mounts up in a long stony slope, very barren, to the watershed a few miles south of Jebel Harun. Also, from Gharandel northwards the western range breaks down; and in place of the riot of hills around the Nagb is a soft country of white limestone-like chalk, very passable, though tedious, since it has worn away into numberless little folds and ridges. Still, it is a distinction that from Gharandel to Wady Musa

---

[1]There are ruins in the side valleys of Wady Gharandel (Musil, *Edom*, ii, pp. 194 – 196) and Wady el Meneiaieh (Musil, *Edom*, ii, pp. 187 – 189).

[2]Sufficiently planned by Musil in his *Edom*, Part ii, p. 196.

on the Sinai side the Araba is not an impassable ditch, but a depression.

Jebel Harun is visible from just before the watershed, and thereafter the look of the valley changes. Its slopes are cultivated in places, broader, at any rate at first, without trees or tall scrub, and with ring graves and cairns, occurring not uncommonly on the lower foothills.

Lawrence went no further up the Araba than this, however, but passed by a steep route over the shoulder of Jebel Harun into Wady Musa, and thence to Maan and the Hedjaz railway.

CHAPTER II

THE HISTORY OF THE SOUTHERN DESERT

'A blank, my lord.'

(*Twelfth Night*, act 2, scene 4, line 109)

Physical characteristics: An inhospitable desert: The stones of it: The hills and valleys: Floods: Shrubs: Climate: Lack of written records: Permanence of material remains: Flint implements: Stone circles and cairns: Many varieties: Their classification and chronology: at Kossaima: at Ain el Guderat: on Tell el Seram: at Muweilleh. Dwelling-house ruins: at Muweilleh: Guderat: Raheiba: Bir Birein: Akaba. The Nabatean period: Abda: Khalasa. The Byzantine period: Increase of population: Wealth: Trade routes: Fortresses: The religious elements: Churches: Monasteries: Agriculture: Rainfall: not more than to day, judging from the state of early remains, lack of timber, and lime mortar in Byzantine houses, cisterns, and corn stores, wells at Khalasa, Raheiba, Auja, tamarisk-hedges, and extent of plough-land. The fall of Byzantine civilization. Sinai during the Crusades and today.

The sketch of our route in the foregoing chapter will give an idea of the physical characteristics of the country. The wearing monotony of senseless rounded hills and unmeaning valleys makes this southern desert of Syria one of the most inhospitable of all deserts – one which, since the Mohammedan invasion, has been an unenvied resort of defeated tribes too weak to face the strenuous life of the greater deserts. The names of its tribes, the Tiyaha, the Alawin, the Terabin, the Azazma, are unknown beyond its limits, and their men are few in number, poor in body, and miserable in their manner of life, 'very small, very spare, and sadly shrivelled – poor over-roasted snipe – mere cinders of men.'[1]

A Poor Country

[1]Kinglake, *Eothen.*

Stones

The surface of the desert is, for the most part, a limestone so soft that it offers little resistance to the erosion of wind and rain. Quarrying produces a hard shelly stone, much in use at Abda, an equally hard semi-crystalline limestone that is used in the lower parts of town buildings of the Byzantine period – the stone of the boulders of all the watercourses about Ain Kadeis – and a soft honey-coloured chalky limestone used by Byzantine masons for the upper parts of walls, and for vaults and arches. In the extreme south and east, along the Araba and above Akaba, the limestone disappears, and diorites, porphyries, and sandstones take its place. In the extreme north, east of Beersheba, the hills are covered with, and in part formed of, a kind of flinty conglomerate. The softest stone, the chalk-like limestone, is everywhere seamed and laminated with strata of red flint. As the limestone crumbles these flints are washed out by the rain, and cover the whole surface for miles and miles with a layer so thick that the white powdered stone scarcely shows through between. Into this surface the feet of men and camels sink a little every step, except where well-worn tracks have pressed hard the ground beneath. When there is a wind (and nearly always there is a great wind) a fine blast of sand drags over these hills, polishing the surface of the flints to a deep brown-yellow that reflects the sun's rays, shining as though the stones were wet with dew. Most of the map is filled with petty hills and small shallow valleys; there are many barren table-lands and a few deep hollows and wide valleys

Water Courses

drowned from bank to bank under the great billows of moving sand-dunes, and overgrown with colocynth, which emphasizes their incurable desolation. In rare places the narrow torrent beds spread out into broad, smooth plains, whose floors of original sand have been laced with plant roots and cemented by water into a hard soil worthy of cultivation. The brief winter rains generally bring some measure of fertility to these lands; but the water either drains quickly through the light soil and is lost in the stones beneath, or is dried up by the heat. More often than not the thin veil of green that February drew over the ploughed valleys of the

Beduins disappears before the suns of March, leaving the face of the country as bare and hopeless as before. The harvest depends chiefly on the latter rains of early spring, and so fickle are these that the crops seldom ripen to maturity oftener than once in three or four years.[1] Even the scanty soil itself, which the Arab ploughs less in hope than by habit, is sometimes lost to him, carried away by a torrent that sweeps down the wady, and leaves in its track bare white boulders and a tangle of uprooted shrubs. The water of the flood made the field in the first instance by depositing its alluvial earth; and it is as ready on a second occasion to remove it to a new place, or to dissipate it among the stones. From these destructive floods the local eras are reckoned, and it is seldom that two have descended the same valley in the memory of an ordinary man.

Only in one place in all this country is there a stream of real running water that can serve for irrigation – in the little valley of Ain el Guderat, where for two or three miles fields of corn and spreading trees refresh the eyes wearied by the glare of the sun on white ground and polished flints, and by the uniform grey scrub on bare hill-sides and in grey-brown valleys. The unaided vegetation of the Negeb hills is *rimth*[2] a wizened cankerous scrub of stiff twigs, unpleasantly adorned with colonies of white snail shells. The snails for some reason climb up the *rimth* shoots, and spend the summer hanging there dried up; it may be that the parasite growth all over the plant affords them a little nourishment. On the hills is some juniper, on the plains much white broom, and everywhere the beautiful feathery tamarisk in abundance along each dried-up watercourse. Sometimes the tamarisk is almost a tree, growing to a height of fifteen feet or more, but generally the Arabs cut it down and use it for firewood

Running Water

Trees

---

[1] W. E. Jennings-Bramley, in *P.E.F: Quarterly* for Jan., 1914.

[2] *Anabasis.*

before it reaches its maturity. Thanks to the tamarisk and broom, travellers in Sinai in the winter season can always have a fire at night to keep warm their camps. There are also *ethyl* and *butmeh*[1] trees: they are no use for anything.

Climate

The climate of Sinai is a trying one. In summer, of course, it is blisteringly hot, and in the winter cold with the unbridled cold of an abandoned country over which the wind can rage in unchecked fury. Snow is rare, but frost not uncommon. In winter there is much rain; in spring it blows both cold and hot, and there are occasional storms of rain and sleet, and sometimes days of a steady downpour, in which the Beduins rejoice. After such there will be a splendid harvest; all the better, no doubt, from the enforced fallows of the barren years; but such success is too rare and too uncertain to attract the professional farmer. We shall have something to say later on, when dealing with the Byzantine period, about the vexed theory of a greater rainfall in antiquity; but we may state here our emphatic belief that at no time since man first settled in this land has the rainfall been appreciably greater or more regular than it is now. All our evidence points to the antiquity of present conditions: to a state in which water was most precious, and the tilling of the soil at once laborious and ill-repaid. If the reverse were the case it would not make of this desert a fruitful field, for the most abundant rains can do but little to fertilize limestone and flint. It is emphatically a country either for nomads whose camels and goats may contrive to exist upon the scanty pasturage of the stunted scrub, or else for a very clever and frugal agricultural people who can husband such little water as there is, and, by a system of dry-farming, overcome the niggardliness of nature. In no respect is it a land for a large population, and the considerable towns whose ruins now surprise

[1] *Butmeh* is terebinth.

us in the waste all obviously owed their existence to extraneous forces. It is, we think, both natural and correct to assume that at all periods in man's history the southern desert has been very much the desert that it is today.

In writing the history of Northern Sinai we are at once met by a great difficulty, the absence of significant references to the country in early records. This, of course, in its not very satisfactory way, gives an exact indication of the importance of the country in that time. It was a roadway at best, and a very unpleasant one. Travellers passing from Egypt to Syria by land all had to traverse it, and they went, as they do today, by the El Arish road if the governments were favourable, and by the Hebron – Beersheba – Muweilleh roads in other cases. The Egyptians, the Patriarchs, the Jews, the Romans, the Crusaders and the Arabs all passed over these tracks, and they have given us place-names and no more. Probably in their eyes the country was too detestable to merit further reference, and by their default our notes on the history of the desert have to be compiled from the remains of occupation preserved in the country itself. By good fortune Sinai lends itself to such research, for everything that has ever been made in the desert is kept for ever for all to see. The careless traveller who piles up four stones in a heap by the roadside here erects an eternal monument to himself.

No Written Records

In the books of our predecessors the prehistoric age is the most fertile in material remains in the Negeb. They make constant reference to flint implements, and to cairns and graves and dwelling-houses of the Stone Age. Palmer even saw in the stone-heaps of Muweilleh a great city of the prehistoric period, and has no hesitation in describing as neolithic the stone circles of Ras Seram and other places. Holland traced ancient roads across the desert by the heaps of flint arrow-heads lying on either side.[1] Only Lord

[1]Holland, *P.E.F. Quarterly,* 1879, p. 62.

Flint
Implements

Kitchener thought that some of the cairns must be of comparatively recent and Arab origin.[1]

Now we have searched for stone implements over the whole face of the country, and have found very few. We brought away the four or five we found, and also a representative collection of flints so chipped that they might well be mistaken for results of human industry, while, in fact, they were found in circumstances which made any but a natural origin ludicrous. The land is a land of flints: on all hill-slopes the exposed edges of the limestone have been eaten away by the wind, and the flints of the alternate layers have slipped forward until the slopes are red with them. The nodules in these strata are usually cracked into numberless pieces that still cling together; others have been splintered and scattered before the stone formed around them. On every yard of ground, and even out of the broken nodules that still hold together in their matrices, one can pick up what might well pass as worked flints. We chose our selected pieces carefully from such impossible places, and in England have succeeded in deceiving with them several good authorities on flints by presenting these, so to speak, without context.[2] Were these genuine, a little patience only would be required to collect from any one hill-side such an array of primitive weapons as would sink a battleship. It was this abundance of nature, rather than the extravagance of primitive man, which made ancient roads so easy for Mr. Holland to follow. Of the four or five real stone implements which we found, one came from Wady Ain el Guderat near the threshing floor, and all the others from Tell el Seram, a conspicuous natural hill in the middle of a wady south of Auja. We have no means of dating the Guderat flint, but those from Tell el Seram were found in and about the drift-sand which

---

[1] Hull, *Mount Seir*, Appendix, p. 204. The other members of the expedition were not of his opinion, but he adduced good reason on his part.

[2] Sir Arthur Evans was not deceived.

filled stone hut-ruins on the hill-top, together with quantities of broken pottery of the Byzantine period. Everything points to the potsherds and the flints being contemporary. The peasants of the Byzantine Age were presumably as resourceful as those of today, and today throughout all Syria flint instruments are freely used. The teeth of chaff-cutting instruments are always small pointed flakes of flint properly struck from a core. Oval 'scrapers' are used by shepherd-boys to shear the sheep, ousting, in many cases, the iron shears to which European commerce gave a brief vogue, and straight heavy knives, often a foot or more in length, are made in any emergency for hacking to pieces a dead animal. Zeyd, Mr. Holland's guide, knapped a flint when he wanted to trim his toe nails, and sometimes a flint razor is still used for shaving the head. In all cases the implement is used upon the one occasion and then thrown away. To date such castaways is difficult, for the brown patina of Sinai takes only a few years to produce; flints lying on modern Arab graves are a beautiful brown on the exposed side and quite white underneath. Any man at any period may knap and use a flint, especially when there is such profusion of raw material, and one cannot from the casual product of his industry argue a Stone Age in the exclusive sense of the term. In our opinion all flint evidence tends to show that man had emerged from the historic Stone Age long before he tried to live in the Negeb.

Great quantities of stone circles and cairns still exist in Sinai. In our part they are not equally distributed, but are most common between El Auja and Wady Lussan, and in the hill country to the south of Beersheba. They are rare to the south of a line drawn from Wady Lussan to Jebel Harun. Of all sorts and sizes, they are built of rough unshaped boulders or blocks of limestone, interspersed with large lumps of flint, and they are nearly always placed upon rising ground, often upon the tops of the most prominent hills. We have visited a great number of these and dug out a fair number, and the conclusion at which we have arrived is that in all probability none of them go back to the prehistoric

Stone Circles

Stone Age; that a small number of them, in certain districts, are as old as the middle of the second millennium B.C.; that from that date to the present time such monuments have been erected by the nomad population of the country, and that of those now existing few are older than the Byzantine period, and the vast majority are comparatively modern. Believing these conclusions to be correct we must none the less put in a word of caution regarding them. These structures conform to a tradition, as will be shown later, singularly consistent; their workmanship is, *ex hypothesi*, primitive in character, and their material is necessarily identical at all periods. Even with careful examination it is generally difficult and often impossible to fix the approximate date of any one cairn.

We could not dig every cairn we saw, and therefore we have had to base our general views upon a limited number of cases in which internal evidence was conclusive, upon analogies with these, upon arguments of association, and upon common sense. The stone monuments of the country may be classified as follows:

1. *Ring graves.* These are stone circles ranging from two to five yards in diameter, the walls one to four courses high; the interior of the ring is filled up nearly to the height of the walls and not infrequently covered roughly over with large slabs, sometimes heaped up with stones so as to form a pyramidal mound.

2. *Rectangular graves.* Small square buildings of rough stone, generally from two to four yards across. The footings of the walls often go down some two or three courses below the ground surface, and the walls themselves rise three or four courses above the ground; the interior is filled in with stones and soil, and sometimes covered over with rough slabs.

3. *Chamber Tombs.* Rectangular buildings like the last, but standing anything up to six feet high and roofed over with very large stone slabs. The best example of these was on Ras Seram; the building measured about eight feet square externally; the chamber was about four feet square and covered with four ring roofing slabs of which two remained in position. It was filled up

to half its height with stones and soil; there was no doorway or window; from its west side a low dry stone wall about seven feet thick ran in a straight line west for nearly thirty yards. This would seem to be a crude form of Ziggurat. Round one on the hill-top facing the mouth of Wady Guderat were a number of sandal marks,[1] such as are common on the sides of Jebel Harun.

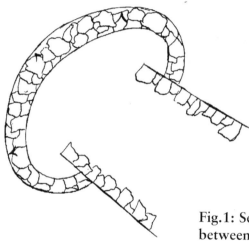

Fig.1: Semicircular shelter between Beersheba and Khalasa. 1 : 50

4. *Round shelters.* Roughly built stone rings, the wall probably never more than four courses high, and open on one side; the opening is sometimes so wide that the building is more properly described as a semicircle (Fig. 1). The floor is often sunk below the level of the surrounding soil.

5. *Rectangular shelters or houses.* Long rectangular buildings

---

[1] Made by tracing the outline of the sandals upon a great rock with many sharp blows of a pointed flint. A crude autograph.

generally divided breadthways by cross walls into three or more chambers communicating with one another or having separate entrances. The floors are sunk below the level of the surrounding soil, and the lower courses of the walls are of large blocks with smaller stones above. The walls were never more than three feet high. Sometimes there is a combination of 4 and 5, a circular room being set in the middle of a long rectangular building whose width corresponds to the diameter of the circle.

6. *Sheep pens.* Large rings with roughly built low walls of small dry rubble.

7. *Dead man's piles* or *Makatal.* These are small cairns of rough stones put up where a dead body has been found; the man is very often buried elsewhere, and the cairns merely mark the spot at which he was murdered.

8. *Memorial heaps, "Shehadat".* These are small stone piles like the last, but made close to, and in connection with, the actual grave, being built by the relatives of the dead man, either at the time of the funeral, or on anniversaries. By the grave of an important person there may be a great number of such small cairns. The long line of stone piles on the crest of Jebel Muweilleh, which made Palmer think that this must be the site of a great city, are simply such memorial heaps connected with the few large ring-graves that are dotted about on the hill-top.

9. *Ritual heaps.* Mounds of small stones with a sacred or semi-sacred connection, on to which any passer-by may throw another stone; probably he does not know his reason for doing so and could not account for the sanctity of the spot; but presumably somebody knew once, and he feels that he has acquired merit by carrying on the tradition.

10. *Roadside heaps.* Small cairns or heaps piled up by travellers along the roadside to express their feelings; generally the feeling is one of relief at having climbed a particularly steep part of the road, or at having arrived at a spot from which the travellers get a good view over the country they wish to reach. Our camel men made such piles, and so on one occasion (south

of Wady Lussan where there are hundreds of such heaps, great and small) did the cook, though he was a Christian from Mosul, sophisticated by a long sojourn in Jerusalem.

11. *Boundary heaps* or *guide heaps.* Piles set on hill-tops either to mark the boundaries between the grazing-grounds of different clans, or to accentuate some natural feature by which the Arabs may take their bearings in a wild country where tracks are all alike.

12. One may add to these the 'trig-points' of the present survey, which are often not to be distinguished by the visitor from the heaps classified as 8, 10, and 11. This is a very large class.

The dates of these various types of mound can best be discussed after we have given in full such detailed evidence as was forthcoming for the limited number of examples which we were able to examine.

THE CHRONOLOGY OF THE STONE MONUMENTS

On a small hill close to the Government station of Kossaima was a group of ring graves, all presumably of one date. On the north side of many of them were found the fragments of pottery vessels that had been placed against the face of the ring wall; the pottery was thin and very hard, of a gritty clay, hand-made, and baked in an open hearth, red on the outer faces, and black or grey in the section; all sherds were much weathered and sand-polished. Four graves were cleared out by us. The first was quite empty. The second, which measured 1 metre across internally (Plate Vl), and had walls of upright stone slabs resting on the rock surface of the hill, contained about 40 centimetres of light soil, and also produced no results; in the third, near the top of the filling, were the fragments of a flat-bottomed jar, of the usual type of ware, much rotted by the action of salt, together with fragments of a large, well-turned, hand-made vessel of a grey clay burnt on the face to a light pink, and of another pot of very gritty black clay. The fourth grave produced a few decayed bones of a young child,

Kossaima

29

and a fragment of bronze wire, apparently from an ear-ring. On the analogy of pottery found at Muweilleh and Ain el Guderat we should attribute these graves to the second millennium B.C., and perhaps rather to the first half of it.

Wady el Guderat

Near the mouth of the Wady Ain el Guderat, on a mound of the foothills, was a group of perhaps fifty graves. The stone rings were rather oblong than round, lying E. by W., and occasionally a larger stone at each end of the ring made a kind of head- and foot-stone. All around on the surface were many sherds of hand-made pottery of the Muweilleh and Kossaima types, and of wheel-made wares resembling those found upon the Tell el Guderat. Two graves were dug. The shafts were sunk in the hard sand, rather more than a metre deep, and the body was laid in a recess cut in the south side of the shaft, and closed by large flat stones leaned against the wall. The bodies were extended on their backs, the heads west, the hands by the side. The first grave produced (low down in its filling) two sherds of hand-made pottery and a scrap of bronze; the second two fragments of wheel-made vessels; the graves must be connected with the settlement on the tell, and would belong, therefore, to the middle of the second millennium BC.

Tell El Seram

In the middle of the Wady el Seram, some three miles from El Auja, there is a long, saddle-backed hill, with steep sides and straight, narrow top, running N. by S., called Tell el Seram; on it are nine cairns in a row (Plate IV, 2). At the north end are two circular cairns; then a rectangular pile some two metres square, standing three cairns high. Next comes a rectangular house cairn (Class 5) of four compartments, precisely like others we had seen in the Wady el Abiad. Beyond this the monuments are in pairs, a small rectangular structure, and a larger round cairn; further on a large square cairn (Plate IV, 2, and Plate V), with a small ring near its north side; and at the south end of the hill two pairs of large and small stone circles. At either end of the hill is a low, straight wall, running N. by S., not touching the tombs, but obviously in connection with them. From No. 3 onwards all make an absolutely straight line running ten degrees east of north. Cairns Nos. 4, 5 and 7 were dug. The walls of No. 5 went down about sixty centimetres to bed rock; the interior was filled with light lime, in which were the bones of a child in very rotten condition – their original position could not be ascertained. In the large cairn (Class 7), under a filling of small stones and sandy lime, placed within a rough cist of stone slabs, were the bones of a man, extended on the right side, the head west, the face turned to the south (Plate V). Nothing was found with the body. The bones were remarkably fresh and strong; the skull only had been smashed. This was noteworthy, as the lime in which these lay has generally a bad effect on bone, and together with the Mohammedan disposition of the body is an argument for a late date. Probably this grave is of the same type as those burials 'in stone cists within circles' described by Palmer. Accurate dating evidence, however, was obtained by digging on the house site (No.7), which undoubtedly stands in close relation to the tombs. The place was littered with potsherds of the types most common in the rubbish heaps of Khalasa, at Esbeita, and generally in the Byzantine cities. The conclusion is obvious. We have here the huts and the graves of the nomad people who, throughout and after the Byzantine period, kept their flocks of goats and their camels on the rough hill pastures. Just as the modern Beduin, living a similar life, obtains his household vessels from the kilns of Gaza, so these, his forerunners, used the same pottery as did the more civilized dwellers in the towns and valley farms – a pottery which also, in all likelihood, was the product of the Gaza kilns. Ring tombs, similarly dated by pottery to Byzantine or slightly post-Byzantine times, have been noticed by us at Bir Rakhama, Ain Kadeis, Abda, El Auja and Esbeita. North of Khalasa we dug two circular hill-top cairns, close to both of which Byzantine or Arab pottery was found; in one of these was a flattened lead bullet. Not less important is it that the modern Arab, here in the south, generally makes graves of the same form; thus, close to Kossaima we photographed (Plate VI) a modern ring-grave of precisely the same type as the cairns of the second millennium B.C. on the other side of the spring; a rag on the grave kept up the tradition of the offering placed beside the ancient grave. A better illustration of offerings at a modern grave – though the grave is not a circle, but of the normal Arab type – was photographed at Ain Kadeis (Plate XII, 2); on the headstone is the dead man's skull-cap; close to it are his shirt, his headcloth, his pipe, and his camel stick, while a black Gaza pot is leaning against the graveside.

Muweilleh

There were many ring graves for which we could not find any positive dating evidence; thus, on Jebel Muweilleh the graves produced neither pottery nor any other objects, and this very absence of pottery would seem to distinguish them from the undoubtedly early graves of Kossaima and Wady Guderat; on the other hand, the group included a house ruin of the mixed rectangular and circular type, and such a ruin at Ain Muweilleh was found in connection with an early settlement dated by pottery (Fig. 2). The weathering of the lichen-covered stones on Jebel Muweilleh showed that the tombs must be of a respectable antiquity, and perhaps it is safest to assign them to the early first, or to the second millennium B.C.

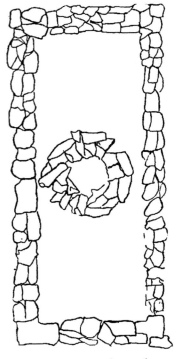

Fig. 2: Rectangle and ring on Jebel Mushrag near Muweilleh. I : 150

Very often ring graves were proved to be of modern date by their position; the Arab of these parts prefers to bury his dead in the neighbourhood of water,[1] and actual water spots being few and far between, often chooses some ancient ruin near which, presumably, water must once have existed. Thus, we found ring graves in the ruins of an isolated Byzantine farmhouse high up in the Wady el Ain, on the Tell of Ain el Guderat, on Tell Kurnub and Tell el Milah, on the town site of El Auja, etc.; these tombs were obviously post-Byzantine; many were frankly new.

Both round and rectangular shelters (Classes 4 and 5) occurred at Ain Muweilleh (*see* p. 27 – 28), where they were of the second millennium B.C. The post-Byzantine structures of the same character on Tell el Seram have already been described. Both types are still in use at the present time. A mighty circular breastwork of stones is piled up three or four feet high, and above this are heaped branches of tamarisk and broom or other desert shrubs; there is no roof. If the housebuilder is rich in the possession of a tolerably decent piece of goat's hair tenting, the shelter tends to be rectangular, the ground level is lowered inside the walls, and the tenting is stretched over the room from wall to wall, its edges kept in place by stones, and we have the second type of modern shelter, which undoubtedly corresponds, as does the first, to the houses that the desert people used three or four thousand years ago.

Dead men's piles and memorial heaps are commonly made at the present day. The modern Arabs build large things upon occasion, like the stone wall, five or six feet high and very long, seen by Russegger near the Red Sea, on the road to Sinai,[2] and they put up small piles continually; indeed, in regard to these and the remaining classes of stone cairns there is nothing to prove

---

[1] The inquisition after death by the two angels is a thirsty business, and it is more convenient to have water close by.
[2] Russegger, Reisen iii, 29 – 30.

that any one is old: and if we assume some of them to be so, it is only because we know that modern customs generally have their roots in the past, and because history quotes some ancient instances of man's inveterate love for piling stones (Gen. xxxi, 46; Josh. iv, 20).

No Stone Age In Sinai

We therefore believe that the Stone Age proper has left no monuments in the country, which in that remote period was uninhabited. The first signs of human occupation that we find are the shelters and graves of the poverty-stricken nomad folk that huddled round the scanty water of the Muweilleh springs. Their houses seemed never to have been rebuilt, and by the look of the remains they had been inhabited only for a short period. Some unknown local conditions must have persuaded people to live here for a little while.

In fact, roughly speaking, the dawn of history in the southern part at least of this district seems, so far as its remains go, to coincide with the first efforts of Egypt to conquer Syria. The tells that dot the northern fringe of the country with which our survey is concerned may well go back to a date far more remote than this; the way from Hebron by Raheiba and the spring of Muweilleh down to Egypt was a path well worn by the patriarchs long before the Pharaohs of the XVIIIth dynasty marched to the Philistine plains; but only when the relations of Egypt and Syria had already established a steady stream of traffic along the northern desert routes do there appear the least traces of permanent dwellings in the inhospitable south.

The Earliest Occupation of the Country

The poor huts of Muweilleh (which are, as has been pointed out, the poor huts of the modern Beduins) continued to be the normal type of dwelling used by the ancient desert wanderers. Only at Ain el Guderat, in the one fertile valley of the south, there sprang up a builded fortress which, in the latter half of the second millennium B.C., commanded the approach to the precious spring and guarded the fields that it watered. To a rather later date, probably to the early years of the first millennium B.C., belong two other buildings, the little hill-forts at Tell el Kasr el Raheiba, and at Bir Birein, which command the Darb el Shur (*see* p. 61). But these, like the Guderat Castle, are not really dwelling-places; they are military police stations set here for the defence of a trade route; their isolation and their *raison d'être* alike only emphasize what must have been the unchanging character of the country about them – a wilderness into which no one, save a few poor nomads, would come unless he were obliged, a stretch of ill road along which one hurried perforce to an attractive goal. These places are eloquent of the history of the country because they are so unrepresentative and so few. The same truth is pressed home by those sites to which written history would direct us, Elath and Ezion Geber, the Red Sea ports of the Phoenician league. Here there are no great harbour works, no ruins of thriving towns, but on the sandy beach and rocky islet doubtful traces at most of a little trading station where the troops of the convoy drowsed between the rare visits of the Eastern fleet.

Modern Kossaima, with its police barracks, its Government house, and its three shops, may well give us a fair picture of these guard-posts of the Jewish kings, and Akaba today is a not unworthy descendant of Solomon's seaport.

The next period of occupation in Sinai was, like the Jewish one, due to trade. The flourishing Nabatean kingdom in Petra built itself a seaport or two in Southern Syria, and made roads with guard-houses along the lines of communication. In the centre of the hill system it built the town of Eboda or Abda, probably named after a relative of Abraham, in a habitable place not far from the junction of the two roads from Khalasa and Gaza to Wady Musa. In Abda today under the debris of Byzantine monasteries, one can still find the remains of a great pillared temple which probably (*see* p. 125 – 128) dates back to the second or third century B.C. Round it and below are the ruins of what seems to have been a fair-sized settlement, with a reported 'high-place' and tombs (with Nabatean inscriptions) whose internal arrangements are those of the tombs of Petra.

The Roman town of Khalasa (*see* p. 144) may also date back

The Nabatean Period

to the second century B.C. and have been a second guardian of international trade. Its classical name was Elusa, and as Abda had its eponymous hero, so Elusa was a religious centre, with a goddess of its own so obscure and so ill-reported by Jerome, that Wellhausen[1] and Robertson Smith fall out as to her probable name and condition. She seems to have been connected with the morning star, but whether the star was male or female, and whether the goddess was that goddess called Khalasa or no, appear equally doubtful. She was certainly, however, a Semitic goddess, taken over later by the Romans. In the Byzantine period (unhappily for modern archaeologists) the city became very great and very important, and the earlier town was swallowed up in later constructions; afterwards, when Gaza was building, the masons found it easier to quarry stones from the ruins of Khalasa. The site is now a disheartening pile of tumbled blocks and stone chippings, out of which nothing can be made. Therefore we were fortunate to find the cemetery, and in it among many Greek gravestones one early thing – a dedication in Aramaic characters and the Nabatean language to a king, Aretas, who must be one of the kings of that name at Petra (*cf.* Chap. VI, p. 188).

The Byzantine Period

In the Byzantine period a deep and sudden change came over the whole aspect of Syria. The destruction of the Jewish and other little states of the East by the Romans gave Palestine for almost the first time in its history the fortune of some centuries of reasonably good government and unbroken peace. In these settled conditions Syria realized that potential wealth she always possesses. The people began to multiply, and under stress of new needs developed their land to its utmost. Reclamation schemes were set on foot, and the whole country was covered with a network of paved roads, having rest- and post-houses at intervals,

---

[1] Wellhausen, *Skizzen* iii, 44. W. R. Smith, *Religion of the Semites*, p. 57, note.

and substantial bridges over every stream. The mud huts of the peasant farmers became solid homesteads; hamlets sprang up where had been an untrodden wilderness. The villages became towns, and the old Semitic collections of squalid houses were replaced by regularly planned cities on the Roman model, with shaded porticoes and colonnades leading to marble temples, luxurious public baths, and private houses as sumptuous as palaces. About the busy streets moved a cosmopolitan crowd – Jews, Phoenicians, Persians, Armenians, Arabs – speaking to one another a common Greek, but flaunting their unconverted Oriental taste in the weight and costliness of their ornaments, and the medley of brightest colours in their effeminate robes. From the Euphrates to the Red Sea the ruins of this period transcend those of the earlier times, and bear witness to a population more numerous and more wealthy than the land has seen before or since. It would not be astonishing if the increase of population and the improvement in agriculture had led to a certain migration southwards on the part of a people who had both the capital and the technical skill to develop the unpromising soil of the south country better than their ancestors had done. At the same time such migration would naturally follow the lines of trading routes on which economic conditions offered of themselves additional resources.

Side by side with the growth in wealth of the Byzantine Empire had come about a great increase in trade with the Far East. Over Turkestan moved continually the long slow lines of camel caravans laden with Chinese silks and Bokhara carpets for the Greeks. They used to come to golden Samarkand and thence turned either through Persia, if the way was safe, or by the northern shores of the Caspian to the mart of Cherson and across the Black Sea to Constantinople. From Ceylon and the Indian ports and South Arabia came cargoes of spices and emeralds and silks to Aila and the other Red Sea ports, and passed thence by land over the desolate hills of our part of Sinai, either to Gaza for shipment to Greece or to the opulent cities of North Syria. And

International Trade

this latter route was at once cheaper and more secure than the long northern journey over the Mongolian desert. In consequence at various times (notably in Justinian's reign) we find the Byzantine Government fostering this trade, whose effects are still plainly visible along the road. Khalasa, to take but one of the towns of the southern desert, could never have employed all its teeming numbers to till the surrounding plains, carefully though they were tilled, and very great though they be. From its position at the north end of the Aila – Gaza road one can reasonably suppose its urban population supported by the carrying trade, and by the unravelling of imported ὁλοσηρικόν and the weaving up again of the mixed silk and linen fabrics that passed current in the marts of the West. Beersheba and Raheiba, lying on the same trade route, must also have had their industrial population as well as their peasant class.

Byzantine Fortresses

The Byzantine Government, devoted to bricks and mortar, was not slow to extend its protection over its south-eastern frontier. Syria, the rich and populous province of the Empire, was also a source of anxiety, thanks to the threats of its powerful and covetous neighbours on the east. The rulers of Persia and Irak, Rome's old enemies, whether encouraged by victory or irritated by defeat, were always renewing the struggle on even terms. In time other possible enemies were added to these. The Ghassanids and the country of Hira both shared in the Arab revival brought about by the return of trade to the Elamitic gulf. Persia at times threatened even this distant region, for in 570 A.D. a Sassanian took Mecca by storm and held sway in the Yemen, and in 614 A.D. another sacked Jerusalem. The Persians conquered Egypt once. It must have been the fear of these enemies, or of the more constant waspish forays of the Nomad tribes provoked by them, that turned the Emperor's attention to the defence of Sinai. The forts there are of Justinian's plan and most probably his work, but only a bureaucratic pedant could have imposed on a desert such incongruous defences, which seem intended rather to complete a theory than to meet a local need. His border system of scattered fortresses worked admirably to hold a river line or to block mountain passes, but was peculiarly inadequate against nomad raiders in a country where roads are arbitrary and innumerable. Auja, Abda, and Kurnub were walled castles with garrisons of regular troops, and there were forts at Aila and Khalasa; but for all that, the inhabitants of each town or village must needs build their houses shoulder to shoulder, and loophole the blank outer walls for rudimentary defence.

But if these great buildings were primarily due to the Emperor's inelastic scheme of imperial defence, yet in all we find their proper warlike character modified by features peculiar to this district, and suggestive of another influence.

In addition to their corn and wine and silks, the people of Syria had a second commerce in their unlimited holy places, and, indeed, in their sanctified air. In the Christian-Byzantine period these commodities were the more prized as the temporal influence of the Church increased, and bishops became professed politicians. Churchmen lived in the palace, and piety fled to the wilderness. The Sinai desert shows all these things. At Auja, castle and church dispute the hill-top: at Kurnub the church has it. The castle at Abda is an annexe of the convent, and at Khalasa the fort was a cure of the bishopric of Gaza. And if in these larger centres we see the Church wedded to the State, in the smaller we find no less clearly the religious devotee attempting to hedge himself off from the secular world. The three great monasteries of Esbeita were the nucleus of the little town that huddles round them; Tell el Sawa is nothing but a monastery with its dependencies; and the group of buildings conspicuous on the rock promontory of Mishrafa is a Byzantine 'laura' whose monks climbed up from their isolated cells on the cliff-face to the common chapel above.

Monasteries

The influx of population into the country north of Ras Seram and Abda brought about there a remarkable change. Monks, soldiers, and merchants must all eat, after their degrees, and food had to be provided despite the unwilling soil. Every flat stretch of valley or upland was put under cultivation. Across every wady,

Byzantine Agriculture

not only in the broader watercourses, but where the rain torrent had cut channels far up on the rocky hill-side, low walls were built to catch the flood-borne earth in a staircase of terraced fields, and later to fan out the rush of the torrent over a great space, that the gathered soil might not be carried away, but might retain on the steps such moisture as it received. Olive yards were planted at the foot of hills, and vines were induced to grow on the flint-strewn slopes of disintegrated limestone. So thorough was the laborious agriculture of the period that its remains are the first and the last things to catch the eye of all travellers in the desert. The great barrage of Kurnub, with its thirty-six feet of smooth masonry, is not more wonderful in its place than the tiny remains of little lonely farms, miles apart, on the bleak upper slopes of Jebel Magrath. To find stone-built houses in solitudes, broken terrace walls in every wady, and long rows of flint heaps that mark ancient vineyards, makes so deep an impression that it is easy to see things in a wrong perspective and to forget the uneconomic origin of it all. We have probably sufficiently explained away the towns. Where they are not purely military or religious foundations they owe their existence to the trade routes, and are in no way determined by the quality or extent of the plough-land about them. Were it otherwise the splendid upper reaches of the Wady el Hafir, larger than the tilth of Auja, of Khalasa, of Raheiba, of Esbeita, and not remote, would have been the site of a city greater than these. But this wady lay off the high-roads, and so its solitude was disturbed only by scattered farms.

The Ancient Rainfall

The truth is that the land was poor, desperately poor,[1] and that all this labour and capital and ingenuity were contributed by enforced habitants to redeem somewhat the horrid conditions of their existence.[2] Geographers of great experience have deduced

---

[1] Petrosus est, raro habet terram. (Antoninus of Placentia, § 38, *c.* 570 AD).
[2] Professor E. Huntington in 'Palestine and its Transformation' – a very interesting book.

from the present state of Sinai that the land has dried up: that the rainfall, was once much greater than it is today. Our impressions are directly contrary; but, of course, neither position is capable of proof.

Professor Huntington believes that in this part of the Near East there has been throughout history an alternation of irregular periods of comparative moisture and of drought; these can be argued partly from the migrations of peoples whose movements would be enforced by the drying-up of their old pastures, partly from the signs of settled cultivation during certain limited periods in what at other times we know to have been desert. The descent of the Patriarchs into Egypt would thus indicate a change from conditions when life in Southern Palestine was easy to those under which it was impossible; the growth and prosperity of the now ruined cities of the Negeb would denote a century or two of good rainy seasons in the desert. It would, perhaps, be unreasonable to ask what increase in the present rainfall is necessary to satisfy Professor Huntington, but from the tone of his book we judge that he would require a considerable prolongation of the spring rains of late February and March. It is, indeed, the failure of these spring rains that so often brings to nothing the feeble agriculture of the Beduin. Sinai today gets a heavy rainfall in winter, usually quite enough, were it only distributed over a longer period, to ensure a satisfactory crop. The fault from the farmer's point of view lies not so much in the quantity of rain that falls as in its limitation to the coldest months of the year. Our opinion is that, broadly speaking, these climatic conditions have been always the same, and that any agricultural prosperity the desert has known was due not to any change in them but to the greater adaptability of the then inhabitants. We have, we think, made it clear that at no time prior to our era was there any period of settled occupation in the desert. There is no evidence of a Stone Age. The "tells" and city ruins so common throughout Palestine and North Syria cease abruptly on the north fringe of the Negeb; except for Tell

The Early Period

el Ain el Guderat not one exists south of the Beersheba plain. In this early period, therefore, there were no towns, and the beggarly remains at Muweilleh are enough to show that life in the desert then (and presumably, therefore, the condition of the desert) was the same as it is today. In the Greek period, Khalasa and Abda guard the Nabatean trade-route, but offer no better an argument for the fertility of the surrounding country than the Government station of El Auja at the present day. It is only when we come to the Byzantine period, with its towns, its villages, and its scattered farms, that we need serious arguments to combat Professor Huntington's conclusions.

Stored Water

We believe and shall attempt to show that the prosperity of the Byzantine Age was wholly due to the conservation of the normal water supply and to improved agricultural methods. The towns and homesteads of the Byzantine Negeb relied entirely, as to some extent does modern Jerusalem, upon stored water. A few had wells, but even there the cisterns were no less important. Esbeita, where there is no well at all, has as many caves hollowed out below it as it has constructions above; each house, on the average, had two cisterns; every street was graded down to a catch-pit; every courtyard and roof, even the flat ground outside the town, fed some underground store. Along the main roads huge pillared cisterns were excavated (see Plate VIII, 1), usually at the foot of a rocky hill, along whose side ran a rough trench or low catchment-wall to lead the rainwater to the tank's mouth. Similar cisterns were cut by the scattered farms, and in the upland pastures, as at Khoraisha behind Ain Kadeis, where the tank, whose roof is supported by a single massive pillar (see Plate XXIII, 1), is filled by a tributary of the Wady Khoraisha. At the time of our visit this *haraba* had received no fresh flood for two years, but still contained many feet of water and supplied the flocks of all the Arabs for miles round; since our visit the torrent has come down again and filled the cistern to its brim. There are many such *haraba*s in the country and, when the catchments are maintained, Arab tradition seldom speaks of one running dry. There can be no question that for domestic purposes the Byzantines relied entirely upon stored water; it is also certain that the normal winter rains of today would suffice to fill their cisterns, that the spring rains would generally serve to replenish them, and that the water so stored in these huge and innumerable reservoirs was enough to supply men and cattle until the rainy season came round again.

A striking feature of the Byzantine houses is the absence of wood. Wooden doors there must have been, but even the smallest houses were floored with stone slabs and roofed by ponderous arches carrying a flagged ceiling; even the cupboards were niches in the wall with stone shelves. Obviously there was no timber in the country which could be spared to make cottages of the raftered type common in the pine and poplar districts of Syria or in the palm-tree oases of Central Arabia and the Nile Valley. Again, although Sinai is a limestone country yet we find the Byzantine builders going to great inconvenience to avoid the use of lime; they only built with it when absolutely necessary, in water-reservoirs and the like, and even then they preferred where possible to hew out of the solid rock. This sparing of lime must point to a scarcity of fuel. Had skilful agriculture been aided by an increased rainfall during the centuries of Byzantine prosperity we should certainly have expected a more abundant stock of both wood for fuel and building-timber.

Scarcity of Wood

Another argument can perhaps be based upon the present level of the water in Byzantine wells. The greater number of these have been filled up, but where they have been kept clean and are in constant use the water rises, so far as one can judge from the masonry of the wells, to the ancient level. Had the country got drier one would have expected the water-level to have sunk considerably, even if the wells themselves had not required deepening; but nowhere is this the case. At Khalasa, Bir Birein, and Bir Hafir, for instance, the water is fairly near the surface. The same argument is supported by the very

Old Wells

different conditions of the well at Raheiba.[1] Here the diggers had to go down three hundred feet into the rock before they tapped a spring – good proof that when the Byzantine town was built there was no greater supply of surface water than there is today. The great well was cleared out a few years ago and water found at its original level, but the Beduins got no profit from their work. The great depth was too much for the strength of their frail ropes, so they returned to their cisterns, and travellers are fast filling up the well again by dropping in stones to hear the boom of the waters in the bottom of the pit. The history of Raheiba was repeated at El Auja when the Turkish Government cleared out one of the town wells and found plentiful water at the old Greek level. They were so pleased with the discovery that they brought a steam-engine to pump it up, characteristically ignoring the fact that an engine requires fuel. The absence of the latter caused the experiment to fail.

Grain Stores

The water store-pits find their complement in the many underground granaries, intended doubtless to contain and conserve the surplus corn of a successful harvest. These granaries are everywhere frequent, and when lined with masonry are generally mistaken by travellers for water-cisterns. The similar pits made by Arabs in hard soil, with no stone lining, or burrowed out in the rocky sides of a wady and walled up when full, keep barley, wheat, and millet in good condition for years.

Terraces and Hedges

The elaborate terracing system of the Byzantines, which turned to account the natural filtration of the rainwater through the earth, was the main secret of their agricultural success. Hedges of tamarisk were planted along terrace walls and round fields (*see* Plate II, 1, a landscape near Khalasa) at once to bind the light soil,

---

[1] The digging of this well has been attributed to Isaac, but it is more likely to have been sunk by the Byzantines to supply the bath-house that stands by it.

to break the force of the winds, and to attract moisture. We noticed that wherever these terrace walls are preserved, and especially if their hedges yet remain, there the modern Beduin prefers to sow his corn and there the crop is in best condition. The use of tamarisk for hedgerows is perhaps one more sign of the prevailing drought of the country, for it is one of the few shrubs which, without irrigation, will withstand the heat of summer and autumn in the desert of today, and probably that same hardihood recommended it for the same climate in Byzantine times.

But while the terrace walls kept for the soil the benefit of winter rains that nowadays run to waste, the iron ploughshare of the Byzantine drove a far deeper furrow than does the twisted branch with which the poor Beduin scratches the surface; the grain was nearer to the underlying moisture, and was better sheltered from the heat that now scorches its shallow roots. We believe that today, with ordinary methods of dry farming, the Negeb could be made as fertile as it ever was in Byzantine times; only, with so many better parts of the world's surface waiting to be reclaimed, it is not worthwhile. In estimating that past fertility we must remember that, of the wide stretches of old plough-land still visible, not more than half would be sown in any one year, and that even then this half might in spite of all care fail as often as not of its yield. It was because the crop was at best so precarious that the area of cultivation was so great, in order that the surplus of favourable years might be stored in the many underground granaries against the lean years to come. We know, too, that upon occasions corn was imported out of Egypt.

To sum up the processes of the Byzantine time, one may say that the Greek government found an unreclaimed desert – for no single terrace wall is of any other period than the Neo-Greek – and that it pushed roads through it, and built forts and trading towns and castles along the roads; and that private people penetrated far into the desert not for gain but in search of solitude and uncontaminated space for hermitages. These churchmen farmed their little steads, and sometimes husbandmen and

Summary

herdsmen and the camel-men of the road huddled their tents or rough stone shelters around the monasteries, until there arose a village or hamlet about each water-cistern. This in the north only, for near Kuntilla and Themed only gazelles and snails can find a livelihood. The written records of the time, recitals of pilgrims, and chance references in the pious lives of monks, tell us of the great and holy population of the desert. If, in addition, we had had preserved to us the account books of the merchants, or the sailing lists of the Red Sea ports, we should have a complete picture of the Southern Desert under Byzantine rule.

The Arab Conquest

The end of it all came suddenly. The fears of the central government had forbidden arms to the provincials. Heraclius had drained away the garrisons of the Empire for his Persian campaigns: without hands the effete fortresses that survived a Beduin raid could not withstand the organized forces of Mohammedanism. The persecuted Jews threw themselves into the hands of the more lenient Arabs: the equally persecuted Monophysites and Jacobites looked on at the passing of official Christianity without regret. Before the Arab power the cities of the south melted away. Once we thought we saw traces of resistance and bloody destruction: elsewhere the stoppage of trade no doubt put an end less painful but equally abrupt to the life of the community. The upland tent-dwellers inherited and neglected the farm-works of the Christian husbandmen. Such of the latter as remained, though they continued to use Gaza pottery and Byzantine coins, must soon have fallen into a Semitism of speech and life. The Mohammedans only admitted the communal existence there of such Jews of Akaba as had not been turned into apes for despising the Sabbath. To these, as to the great Monastery of Sinai, Mohammed is said to have given a charter. The rest of the country was converted to Islam, and became the abandoned wilderness of today.

It has had little or no history since. In the days of the Arab sovereignty, when Egypt and Syria were at peace or war in alternate decades, North Sinai acquired its present strategic importance as the most defensible frontier any country ever possessed. The coast road then, and in the time of the Crusades, became a well-trodden highway of commerce, while the pilgrim road from Suez to Akaba represented the religious interest. The interior of the country was not visited by historians. Once Amaury of Jerusalem, in trying to cut off a threatening move through the 'Desert of the Children of Israel', marched south from Gaza till he came to a place which he recognized as Kadesh-Barnea. Unfortunately, he recorded no details of his discovery. On two occasions at least Arab Sultans also crossed by unusual routes. Once Saladin found the coast road blocked to him, and Renaud of Chatillon exercising wild activities in Kerak. He therefore marched with some thousands of men south of the pilgrims' road to Themed and Akaba, and thence slipped through to Damascus by way of Maan and the Syrian pilgrims' road.[1] Nearly a century later Baibars marched along the Shur road by Hassana to Muweilleh, and then by Nagb el Ribai (Petra) to near Shobek.[2] He had only a few men with him, and suffered from lack of water on the road. Since the time of the Crusades, Sinai has been stirred up by Turks and Egyptians, and by Napoleon, but without any very exciting incidents. Of late years it has been under Anglo-Egyptian control, and has fulfilled its rôle of buffer-wilderness in comparative peace, except for difficulty in checking the tendency of certain large boundary pillars to travel westwards.

[1] This has been noted by Clermont Ganneau in the *Revue Biblique* for July, 1906.
[2] *Cf* Quatremère in *Journal Asiatique*, 1835, tome xv, pp. 31 – 34.

CHAPTER III

THE DARB EL SHUR AND THE NORTHERN TELLS

When those long caravans that cross the plain
With dauntless feet and sound of silver bells,
Put forth no more for glory or for gain,
Take no more solace from the palm-girt wells.

(from 'The Golden Journey to Samarkand' by James Elroy Flecker)

North Sinai a thoroughfare: Holland finds a road from Egypt to Muweilleh: Between Hebron and Beersheba: Khalasa: An early fort at Raheiba: A cistern: Wells at Bir Birein: A fort there also: Ras Seram: Muweilleh. THE NORTHERN TELLS. – Abu Hareira: Abu Irgeig: Tell el Seba: Tell el Sawa: Khirbet el Watan: Khirbet Hora: Tell el Milah: Imshash el Milah.

I

The Darb el Shur.

By virtue of its position, Northern Sinai has always been the thoroughfare of Asia and Africa, or, more particularly for the historian, of Syria and Egypt. For this purpose use has been made at various times of three great roads. One of these, the most favoured commercially, is the northern coast road by Gaza and El Arish. Another, used sometimes for military purposes in the Crusades, was the southern route by Themed, Akaba, and Maan; parts of this second route seem to be hinted at in the Book of Exodus as the main route of the migrating Jews. The third great route, known to us as the Darb el Shur, and made famous by Abraham and Isaac, ran from Hebron direct to Egypt, without touching Gaza or the Mediterranean. It must have had particular attractions when the northern route was closed by unsympathetic aliens holding the sea coast of Palestine.

Roads Across the Desert

The scarcity of settlements and water-holes on the possible lines for such an inland route makes the search to recover its stages not a hopeless one. There is a strong *prima facie* probability that its course remained the same from the earliest times throughout the Greek period to the present day, and that if we can combine remains of all these periods into one great road we shall have found the Patriarchs' way into Egypt. The Rev. F. W. Holland followed up such a route, tracking his quarry by the water-holes. He showed lines from the Suez Canal quite suitable for a tolerable party, coming by various groups of water-holes as

A Limited Choice

far as Jebel Muweilleh. Baibars, the Sultan of the thirteenth century, followed this road to Muweilleh, and names water-holes among those recorded by Mr. Holland. However, this district was outside our survey; we therefore accepted Mr. Holland's evidence *en bloc* as leading to an eminently reasonable conclusion, and set ourselves to find a decent route from Hebron to Muweilleh.

The Modern Darb el Shur

Naturally, we took the existing one, which every Arab knows, though few pass along it now save on tribal business. The days of trade-caravans between the merchant princes of Syria and Egypt have passed away. We took this dead highway, however, and looked along it for road-stations or wells or engineering works to mark its use in antiquity. It begins at Hebron, a gateway of Jerusalem and Judea, and runs to Beersheba. This part lay in settled country, then as now, and does not need discussion. Beersheba is a natural watering place for one accompanied, as Abraham was, by his own nomad clan and its due property of sheep and camels. The wells lie in a wide rolling plain, not ill-watered, with forage enough at most seasons of the year, and a little to the east was Sheba, a fortified Canaanite town, held, perhaps, in Abraham's time by Abimelech, where provisions for the way could be bought by passers by.

To Khalasa

From Beersheba the road runs down to Khalasa, where it cuts the Gaza – Petra or – Akaba road. We have no proof that Khalasa existed before the Greek period, when it was a Nabatean town dependent on Petra; but the knowledge of its easy and constant water supply may well be older, and in the present special circumstances of the ruins evidence of early occupation would remain undiscovered. From Khalasa the road runs westwards, and is now marked neatly enough by the remains of tamarisk hedges of Byzantine period. It crosses a low ridge and then runs along the broad and fertile valley that leads down to Raheiba from the north. About two miles before it reaches the Byzantine ruins the track passes close to the foot of a conical hill which juts out from the limestone cliffs, where their line is broken by the mouth of a tributary wady; and on this hill we found a small fort or watch-tower, whose remains are known today as El Kasr el Raheiba. (Plate VII, 1)

The building was a little rectangle, with chambers at the south end, and an open courtyard with a double row of chambers on the north, where probably the entrance once had been. We divined so much from the very wasted and encumbered foundations of dry rubble – the walls were rough and undressed

An Early Blockhouse

Fig. 3: El Kasr el Raheiba.

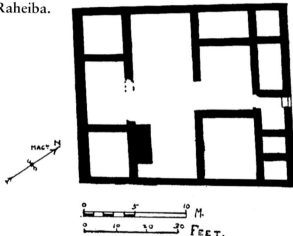

– which now alone mark the site of the building (Fig. 3). On the surface we found fragments of late pottery scattered about; but many of them fitted together, and they obviously belonged to one vessel broken on the surface after the destruction of the building. After hunting round very carefully we found on the hill-slopes some earlier sherds, in particular two distinct pieces of fine ring-burnished haematite-stained ware, of a sort ascribed by Macalister to the Second Semitic period (1800 – 400 B.C.), but certainly also in use some five hundred years later. These early sherds, interpreted in conjunction with the lack of Byzantine material, must be taken to prove that the building was a little fort or watch-house set here to guard the road, perhaps at the time of the Patriarchs, or perhaps during the Red Sea adventures of Jewish kings, Solomon or Jehoshaphat. The pottery is Syrian, an argument against Raheiba having been an Egyptian outpost.

The road, after passing the Kasr, avoids the Byzantine town on the slope, but continues on the valley bottom, not far from the great well, three hundred feet deep, which some would like to identify with the watering place made by Isaac for his flocks at Rehoboth – a name which appears today at a point near Khalasa. A stone-lined well on such a scale as this of Raheiba is, of course, very unlikely to have been the passing labour of a nomad chieftain.

A Reservoir

The road becomes clearer after passing Raheiba, for it enters on the desert proper, where it has not been ploughed up, in its course south-south-west towards Auja. Auja, however, is only a Byzantine site, and the road passes two or three miles to the east of it in the wide plain out of which the Wady el Abiad runs towards Esbeita. Here the road is today a broad well-marked ribbon of many parallel tracks. We photographed it as it rose to a slight ridge of limestone in which a large rock-reservoir had been hewn (Fig. 4). This reservoir,[1] lying to

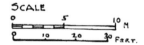

SCALE

Fig. 4: Rock reservoir near Bir Birein.

the east of the road, had been recently cleared out, and the ground about was littered with Byzantine pottery, for, like most of the rock-cut cisterns of this country, it is of Byzantine date;

---

[1] The pit was 12.30 m. x 11.60 m. (40 ft x 38 ft), and is now 40.20 m. deep. The roof, which has fallen in, had been carried on four square columns cut in the chalk; there was a stepped descent to it on the south side, whilst above the pit a ditch and bank of chalk drawn round the lower slope of the ridge caught the rain-water flowing off the hill-side and led it to the cistern.

but its presence here, to serve the needs only of travellers (there were no house ruins in the neighbourhood), is of interest, as proving that the road was still an important highway in the days of the Later Empire.

From here the road ran nearly due south, cutting across two small cultivated wadies separated from each other by a stony

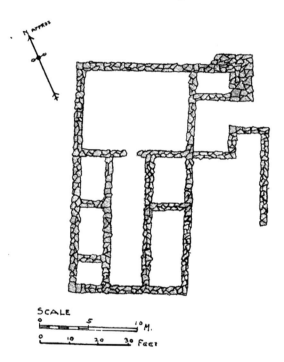

Fig. 5: Sketch plan of building on hilltop commanding Bir Birein.

SCALE

ridge, and thence by a little pass between shrub-covered slopes on to the shingle plateau dividing the upper reaches of Wady Abu Ruta from the Wady el Hafir. The descent on the Hafir side of this plateau bears unmistakable signs of artificial grading to make its slope easy. The road passes thence across the Wady el Hafir, and over broken country, past a curious stone construction of long rough walling on a hill-side – a water catchment – until over a rise it commands a view of the valley and wells at Bir Birein (Plate VII,

An Early Blockhouse

2, and Plate VIII). The date of the wells is of course impossible to determine. North of them are plentiful Byzantine remains; but to the south-west of them, on the crest of the high rocky bank that limits the valley, we found ruins of a rude building that appeared very ancient (Fig. 5). It is in quite hopeless condition, and our sketch plan is as bad. All the walls are of rubble, dry built. The square tower and *dowar*, or stone circle mentioned by Palmer, still exist, but are obviously the stone framework of brushwood huts, and the pottery about them is of the latest Byzantine or early Arab period. The larger building of our sketch plan (Fig. 6) is more interesting, and a very little pottery, found below it on the hill-slope (the probable position for early remains), was some of it hand-made, some ring-burnished haematitic ware, like the wares of the Kasr el Raheiba. The ground plan of the building above is not distinctive: it may be an early building: it may have been modified in Greek times, or then only built on the site of an early one. Excavation could do nothing in such a rubbish-heap of stone. In any case the point is not important, since the pottery is sufficient to show us an early fort on the hill-top like that at Raheiba, of the same period, and no doubt part of the same system of police patrol.

From the wells the road skirts the gravel mounds on the south-east of the wady, and cuts across the plains of the broad upper valley, past terrace walls and hedges of

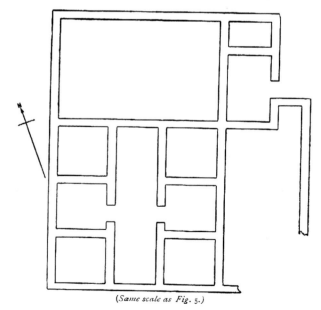

(*Same scale as Fig. 5.*)

Ras Seram   Fig 6: Sketch plan of early building on hill-top Bir Birein.

the Byzantine period. Gradually the ground gets more stony, and the path, still clearly marked, begins to ascend some low limestone hills leading up to a regular pass between two peaks crowned with stone cairns. It was curious to note how the friction of feet has polished to a creamy whiteness, as smooth as fine marble and as slippery, the larger rocks that lie flat in the path. At the top of this pass we came suddenly to a descent like a steep gully into a broad flat plain, ringed about with a beautiful amphitheatre of cliffs and steep mountain slopes, but open on the west for many miles; across the wide valley bottom the ancient road strikes direct for Ain Muweilleh (perhaps ten miles away), leaving the spring of Kossaima a couple of miles to the south. *Muweilleh* From the foot of this descent a track, and a very difficult one at that, runs straight to Ain Kadeis. By the roadside, near the water pools at Muweilleh, are the house ruins described in Chapter IV. Thus from Khalasa at easy stages on the way we were able to find stations—Raheiba, Bir Birein, Muweilleh—all of a Semitic period, which prove a considerable traffic passing then between Hebron and Egypt by this inland route. Our sphere did not extend beyond Muweilleh to the west, and so we contented ourselves with the notes of Mr. Holland for the continuation of the way; the more readily as from the top of Jebel Mushrag we could distinctly see the great road running 'down into Egypt' across the flat basin of the Wady el Arish towards Jebel Welal, and Jebel Yelleg visible on *Jebel Yelleg* the distant sky-line (Plate IX).

II

The Northern Tells

In the Southern Desert there are scarcely any sites of high antiquity. The tells, the artificial mounds that in Syria mark the ruins of ancient cities, are frequent in the Philistine Plain, but cease with its southern limits. In the open country between the

The distribution of Tells

coast and Beersheba, and to the east of Beersheba itself, there are many more or less imposing mounds, but beyond the fringe of stony and barren hills that divide these fertile lands from the desert proper the very word has lost its significance, and from here to the Red Sea the little post of Wady Guderat is the only true 'Tell' that we could find.

Since the former survey of Palestine did not include quite all of the plain of Philistia, a few of its ancient sites fell within the limits of the present survey and are shown on the new map. Not all of these were visited by us, but a mere visit can give very little information; in their origin the tells must date back at least to the Early Bronze Age, but the surface remains illustrate for the most part only the latest period of their occupation. Excavations have already proved that the material civilization of Palestine remained at a consistently low level down to Roman times; buildings are of the roughest description, sculpture is unknown, inscriptions are very rare, metal-work can boast no artistic merit, and even pottery in most periods compares ill with that of other countries. It is therefore not likely that much can be learned from the surface of the ground; we must be content to find evidence for an approximate date which is almost certainly not the earliest and quite probably not the latest in the history of the occupation of the site.

Tell Abu Hareira

Tell Abu Hareira, on the southern road from Gaza to Beersheba, is a very large mound, partly natural but artificially scarped, that rises over the Wady Ghazza; it consists of a great citadel mound and a lower town mound with an earth rampart. On the top of the citadel is a shrine of the saint, and the whole surface of the tell is covered with Arab graves. There were quantities of Arab potsherds littering the ground, most of them probably due to offerings deposited at the graves, for there were no signs of actual occupation in Arab times. On the slope of the citadel were found a few sherds of Canaanite pottery of the pre-exilic period. The mound is one of the finest in the south country.

On the northern road eastward from Gaza, some five miles

west of Beersheba where the track crosses the Wady abu Irgeig, *Abu Irgeig* are two very small tells side by side. Round them are the remains of a large Byzantine village, whose cemetery lies a little to the north of the road. Both the mounds had been capped by late buildings with roughly built rubble walls and floors of rubble and beaten earth. The pottery in and round these buildings was Hellenistic, with a few Byzantine sherds intermixed. No earlier pottery was visible, though the mounds themselves were undoubtedly of early date.

Some three miles west of Beersheba, on a promontory of fairly high ground between the Wady el Seba and a tributary that here *Tell el Seba* joins it from the north, stands a lofty tell known as Tell el Seba or Tell Imshash el Seba (Imshash=Wells). The top of the promontory seems to have been occupied by the lower town which was defended by the two torrent-beds and by the citadel which stretched from bank to bank behind it. East of the citadel the ground is much broken and covered with mounds and stone ruins; some of the former may be early; the latter are Byzantine and include a church of considerable size (the foundations only remain) with a building at its east end; the ruins are those of a large village, not of a town. About half a mile to the west, in the wady bed, is a well, covered over with a modern well-house; during much of the year water can be found in shallow pits dug in the wady. A number of native huts occupy the site of the Byzantine village, where coins and inscriptions have been found; the Arabs showed me a coin of Quietus and a tombstone of one Stephanus dated TOY ⊂̄Κ IND B̄I (probably 550 A.D.).

The pottery on the top of the great tell was nearly all Seleucid; there was nothing Roman or Byzantine, but there were a few sherds of earlier date. On the east side, some twenty feet below the top of the mound, walls of rough rubble showed upon the surface, and in the soil below these a certain amount of pottery was found, all of early date; several characteristic rims, a jar handle,[1] and a fragment of poorly burnished red ware belonged to Macalister's Third or Fourth Semitic periods, and should be dated between 1200 – 800 B.C. Further down a few fragments were found which might be of earlier period, including some hand-made pieces. The height at which unmixed Semitic pottery occurred points to a very heavy substratum of pre-Hebrew culture. On the opposite bank of the wady, now cultivated land, were found a few painted sherds of the type found at Khirbet Hora. In Joshua xix, 2, Beersheba *and* Sheba are mentioned together as being in the lot of Simeon. As we have seen, Beersheba possesses no tell or sign of ancient occupation; probably in early Semitic times the settlement or city was at Sheba only, this being the modern Tell Imshash el Seba, and the famous Beersheba, the Well of Sheba, lay three miles west of the city, out in the wide pasture grounds to which nomads such as Abraham would bring their flocks when the southern pastures failed – just as the Arabs of the Negeb today drive their flocks northward to Tell Imshash when the drought has left no greenstuffs on their barren hills. It is not unusual to find an ancient town near to but not enclosing its water supply (*e.g.*, Raheiba and Abda), but in this case Sheba could get water enough from its water-holes and wells in the wady. Perhaps the very fact that Beersheba was out in the country away from the jealous town, and open to all comers, gave it its importance for the wandering ancestors of the Jews. If, as seems certain, Beersheba took its name from the then existing town of Sheba, the modern name Bir el Seba, 'The Seven Wells,' must be a mere corruption. Since eight wells are known to exist, it has no ground in fact or in tradition.

Tell el Sawa Tell el Sawa, some eight miles east of Tell el Seba, properly

---

[1] A handle of this type occurred in Beth-Shemesh Tomb 4, at the period of the Jewish monarchy.

speaking does not deserve its name; it is a fairly high natural hill, one of the range that shuts in the rolling plain of Seba on the east. The north end of the hill rises in a steep knoll; its south end tails away into a narrow ridge, and on this lower level are the remains of buildings. Under the knoll is a large square building, clearly a monastery, with a church on its north side and cells lining the south. The church had one apse only, that of the central aisle, the side aisles being square-ended, and the floor was of plain white mosaic. North of this were other ruins of houses, and a small square tower of two rooms with very solid walls rising to a second storey; this must have been a military guard tower; but the whole place is small and unimportant. There are several cisterns on the hill-top, and on the east slope traces of buildings, caves, and terraces. The tower is of the usual Byzantine limestone, well dressed, some of the blocks having drafted edges, and the apse of the church was lined with the same material; but all the rest of the walls were of a solid flinty conglomerate (of which these hills are formed), deep rust-red in colour and enormously hard – the blocks into which it is split are often a yard square and as much as two feet thick, regularly cut and well trimmed to a face. There are no traces of earlier occupation, and no such artificial mound as would justify the name 'Tell' applied by local custom to the site.

Some four miles to the west of Tell el Sawa, near the Seba road, is a small mound overlooking a cup-like valley in whose sides are several rock-cut cisterns or water-holes; it is known as Khirbet Watan. On the surface are visible walls of limestone rubble, one faced with cement, and quantities of Roman and Byzantine potsherds, showing that there was once a large farm or small hamlet, easily accounted for by the proximity of water and the fertile character of the surrounding plain. Below the surface, however, were found a few Semitic fragments including some red-faced ware with finely drawn horizontal bands of pebble-burnishing that should belong to the Second Semitic period (c. 1800 – 1400 B.C.). This, too, was at best a very small settlement;

Khirbet Watan

but it is perhaps of interest to find at that early date isolated homesteads side by side with the great defensive city mounds, witnessing, one may suppose, to a settled and peaceful occupation of the country.

A little to the north of Khirbet el Watan, on the summit and western slope of a fair-sized hill, lie the ruins known as Khirbet Hora. On the surface this site much resembles that of Tell el Sawa, though it is on a considerably larger scale – a collection of scattered buildings all of squared blocks of red flint conglomerate, littered with Byzantine potsherds and a few fragments of early Arab glaze. The houses were rectangular, with courtyards in the regular Byzantine manner, and rock-cut cisterns were everywhere; no church ruins could be distinguished. To the north-west of the main site there was a small hillock of decomposed limestone which contained a lot of pottery, and here, mixed with Byzantine sherds, there occurred a few examples of ring-burnished ware, handles and rims, of the later Second or Third Semitic periods. A more interesting discovery was made on the site of the Byzantine town itself. At the north end of the town an attempt had been made in recent times to clear out an old cistern, and the surrounding soil had been a good deal disturbed in consequence; at another point on the south-east the rains had partly denuded the edge of the hill outside the line of buildings, and sweeping away the surface soil had exposed one or two patches of the underlying gravel. In this gravel, and in the upturned soil by the cistern, mixed up with later sherds, were found small fragments of hand-made pottery with geometrical patterns painted in red or black on a light surface – usually on a hard ivory-white slip over a somewhat coarse reddish-grey body.

[The authors ask me to add a few words about the Hora sherds, of which they have submitted some thirty, mostly minute, fragments. Out of this number, four seem to me wheel-made, and two are rims of bowls or very large jars in coarse grey ware, washed with red and painted with plain bands on the interior face and the rim: one has plain brick-red bands, the other purplish-

Khirbet Hora

black. Both rims are rolled over externally. So far as I can see, these rims should belong to vessels of the Second Semitic period, and so also may a tiny fragment of red, unwashed, wheel-made ware, ornamented with finely-combed festoon incisions, and another fragment, wheel-made, with faint purplish bands.

The rest of the sherds, all painted except one, a red unwashed and unslipped fragment, ornamented with a coarsely-combed festoon, are hand-made, and for the most part slipped, *i.e.*, washed over before fixing. The designs in red, purplish-black or ochre, seem to have been, on exterior faces, vertical bands or combinations of these with lozenges and triangles, often chequered and, on interior faces, horizontal bands. Both faces of one vessel were sometimes painted. The fragments seem to belong mostly to jugs or cups, but they include no rims, bottoms, or handles. The designs are such as are more proper to the Second Semitic, and even the Third Semitic, ware of Gezer than to the First or the Pre-Semitic ware. One fragment, finely slipped, painted and polished and showing vertical bands of purplish-brown alternately chequered and fretted, is of typical Third Semitic design; but it is hand-made. Were it not for the fabric, I should have no hesitation in referring all these fragments to the Second and Third Semitic periods; but in view of the fact that they are hand-made, and show designs not dissimilar from the early painted ware of Carchemish, which is of late Neolithic or very early Bronze Age date, I feel a little doubt. Nothing quite like them was found at Gezer, but since the pre-Semitic ware there is farther removed from them than are the later wares, and it is a far cry to Carchemish, I incline to regard the Hora sherds as a local fabric of late Second and early Third Semitic period (say not earlier than the middle of the second millennium B.C.), whose early characteristics are due rather to the remoteness of the site, which has retarded the adoption of the wheel, than to prehistoric date. Hand-made sherds found in Jerusalem, and decorated in late Third Semitic style, resemble these Hora sherds in types of pattern, but are of different clay. It looks as if South Palestine continued primitive methods of fabric to very late times. D. G. H.]

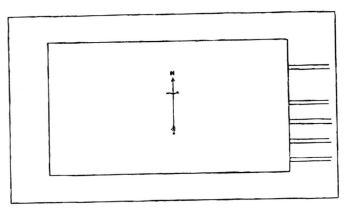

Fig. 7: Fort of Tell Milah. I : 100

Tell el Milah

Tell el Milah is a large artificial mound, not very lofty, in shape a regular oblong, lying east and west, with a somewhat lower 'annexe' at its western end; the top is flat, the sides are fairly steep. South of the mound, and separated from it by a broad shallow depression now dotted with Arab graves, is a large straggling ruin, a collection of houses built in flint conglomerate, all of Byzantine date. This may support the identification of Tell el Milah with the Malatha or Malis (Eusebius) of Byzantine writers. In the hollow to the north of the mound are three wells which give water all the year round: others are said to exist but have not been cleared, and the local Arabs, fearful of trouble with other tribes should their water supply be too invitingly copious, have no wish to clear them.

The summit of the tell is occupied by a large rectangular building with walls dry-built of blocks of flinty conglomerate and of rubble (Fig. 7); these are now level with the soil and in many places cannot be traced. The building measures 84.00 m. east by west by 56.50 m. (277 ft. by 202 ft). No external buttresses were visible. An inner wall runs parallel to the heavy outer wall, the distance between them being on the north (and south ?) some six metres (about 20 ft), on the east ten metres and a half (34 ft. 6 in.), and on the west eighteen and a half (61 ft). The two walls are joined at frequent intervals (generally of three or four metres) by cross walls which divide the intramural space into a series of chambers. The centre of the enclosure sinks to a slight hollow and shows no signs of building; it may well have been an open courtyard. Arab graves, of very recent date, cover the whole top of the hill. Over the surface, which was much disturbed by the gravediggers, were strewn Byzantine potsherds mixed with a few of earlier (Semitic) date. On the sides of the hill the earlier sherds predominated and included ring-burnished wares and fragments of broad-rimmed bowls, apparently of the Second and Third Semitic periods, perhaps 1500 – 1000 B.C. The main point of interest was to decide whether the walls of the fort went with the earlier or the later pottery – whether they were those of a Byzantine stronghold or of an older Canaanite population. Without excavation this could not be definitely ascertained. The material of which the walls were built was that used in the late buildings of Tell el Sawa and Khirbet Hora, but it is the material that would naturally be employed in this district at any period of history, for it lies most nearly to hand. Scraping a hole a couple of feet deep against the outer face of the wall we found Byzantine pottery exclusively in the upper stratum and a few fragments of earlier ware lower down. The evidence was inconclusive; perhaps the analogy with Imshash el Milah, pending proper excavation, may turn the balance in favour of the earlier dating of the Tell Milah fort.

Between four and five miles west of Tell Milah, on the north bank of the wady, was a small and low mound, not dignified in the neighbourhood by the name of 'Tell', though its artificial character and the ruins of which it is composed are sufficiently obvious. On the opposite bank are a number of water-holes, some of them stone-lined, called the Imshash el Milah, and these give to the ruins the only title they can boast.

Imshash el Milah

The little mound is covered with modern graves (a woman was being buried there at the moment of our arrival) and this makes its examination less easy. One could see, however, that the place had been a small 'Kala'at', closely resembling that of Tell Milah. There was the rectangular enclosure, longer north by south, with a fairly heavy outer wall and a row of intramural chambers against it; the outer wall was of large roughly-squared coursed blocks of flinty conglomerate, the inner walls were of smaller rubble. Some outer buildings were attached to the north face of the main fort but were too ruinous for their character to be ascertained. Scattered over the mound were a few fragments of Byzantine pottery, probably to be explained by the existence of some small ruins of the same date that lie close to the tell: it is quite possible that the Byzantines as well as the modern Arabs chose the ruins for their graveyard; but the bulk of the potsherds were early and included such fine examples of continuous ring – or spiral – burnishing as could only be attributed to the Second Semitic period (perhaps 1800 – 1200 B.C.). There could be little doubt that the building here was of the same date as the mass of the pottery about it, and that the few later sherds on the surface were of casual introduction; and that being so, it is difficult not to attribute the very similar building on Tell Milah to an equally early date.

CHAPTER IV

AIN KADEIS AND KOSSAIMA

But this is a question of words and names
And I know the strife it brings.
I will not pass upon any your claims.

(lines 5-7 from 3rd stanza 'Gallio'e Song' by Rudyard Kipling)

i. Ain Kadeis – Conformation of the district: The two 'plains': Notoriety of Ain Kadeis: Visitors: Trumbull's description: Our opinion on it: The springs, grass, fig-trees, bathing-pool. ii. Muhweilleh and Kossaima – The Kossaima plain: Ain Muweilleh: Kossaima. iii. Ain el Guderat – Wady el Ain: Wady Ain el Guderat: The aqueducts: The great reservoir: The tell: The spring. iv. The Antiquities of the District – At Ain el Guderat: The Arab remains: Byzantine things: A reservoir: A village: Roman pottery: The early period: The tell: Its plan: Pottery: Early graves: Kossaima: Muweilleh huts. v. The Kadesh-Barnea Question – Not proven.

Below the Negeb proper, and divided from it on the west by a broad depression, is a mass of steep white hills, grouped in a cluster of peaks and ridges that have different names among the different Arab tribes, and from different sides. The westernmost part of the range (on the map called Jebel um Hashim) runs down from the central height in a spur called Jebel el Ain, and afterwards in a long broken chain of less notable hills extending to Jebel Muweilleh, a flinty peak some miles within the Egyptian border. This chain of foothills is important geographically, in that it divides two water-systems. To the north of it is a running-together of wadies into a plain about Kossaima, and to the south of it is another running-together of wadies to simulate a second plain, which modern writers have called the plain of Ain Kadeis (Plate X). This second plain is held in by considerable hills: on the east is Jebel el Ain, a rugged bow of cliffs in limestone and flint, with only one possible way over it; on the north is the watershed already mentioned, a procession of pointed hills; on the west and south there are no steep places, but rows of inconspicuous ridges, slowly adding up to a modest height. Looked at from these boundaries the contours of the lower ground fall flat, whereas in

The Southern Plain, falsely called of Ain Kadeis

reality the whole surface is irregular, running up here and there into tolerable hills, and all seamed with stony torrent-beds. The soil is sandy, between stones, and there are only rare traces of ancient cultivation. The Arabs – husband-men here without hope – still plough each winter a little of the further wady beds, and in wet years reap a harvest. But Ain Kadeis is the only water of the district, and that a spring on the westward slopes of the great mountain far up the Wady Ain Kadeis.

The name Kadeis[1] was so reminiscent of Kadesh-Barnea of the Israelites, that as soon as it was recorded of a spring it naturally loomed up in western eyes with an importance inexplicable locally. The Arabs know nothing of a plain of Ain Kadeis: to them the name is that of a water-spring in a small valley called after it, and the great area of low land outside the mouth of this valley is not a plain at all, or connected with its tributary wady in any way by name. Yet one party of travellers after another set out, either from Syria or from Egypt, with this obscure water-hole as their avowed object. Ain Kadeis is too small to water the flocks of other than the few poor families who live near it, and, as we found, too remote from all roads to come to the notice of such Arab guides as live at any distance. But this native ignorance was interpreted as deep-seated policy, and so foreigners came to believe that the spring had remained, from the time of Moses, still a holy place (we do not really know whether even Moses thought it holy) – some great head of water in an oasis too beautiful and too precious to be disclosed to Christian eyes. Its Arabs took on a sinister character: they became by degrees inhospitable, sullen, fanatical, treacherous, bloody. And yet all the time, had the world but known it, the place had been seen, measured, and described by Palmer on his visit in 1870,[2] with his usual minute accuracy

---

[1] Kadeis, in Hejazi Arabic, is a scoop or bailer used in the bath for purification. The Sinai Arabs use such scoops (of wood) to lift up water from a shallow well. It does not mean 'holy', as Trumbull and other writers have assumed.
[2] *Desert of the Exodus*, ii, 350.

and vividness. The account given by Rowlands, who was the first to see the spring in 1842, while mainly recording his personal emotions, tallied well enough with Palmer's in essentials; and there the matter would have ended, but that a Mr. H. C. Trumbull, an American, spent a single hour at the spring in 1882, and wrote round his visit a very large book. with fantastic descriptions of the valley[1] and wells. The work, however, was plausible, and has unfortunately been accepted by biblical geographers[2] as the authority on the district. As for the remainder of Trumbull's book, it is full of varied argument, often irrelevant, some philology, and a large confrontation of the views of everyone, good or bad, who had mentioned Kadesh-Barnea throughout the ages. His account, which we had with us at Ain Kadeis, says (*Kadesh-Barnea* pp. 272, ff.):

'It was a marvellous sight! Out from the barren and desolate stretch of the burning desert waste we had come into an oasis of verdure and beauty... A carpet of grass covered the ground. Fig trees laden with fruit nearly ripe enough for eating were along the

---

[1] We need not give measurements of the valley. They have been published admirably by Professor George L. Robinson, McCormick Seminary, Chicago, in articles in the *Biblical World* in 1901 and 1910. He gives a plan of the valley and springs, with photographs. His whole description is so clear and accurate that it may well be regarded as final.

The account in the *Homiletic Review* of April and May, 1914, by Professor Coborn of Alleghany Coll., Meadville, Pa., is not worth discussion.

In the *Revue Biblique* for July, 1906, the French Benedictines have done work as good as Professor Robinson's in accuracy and authority.

In Z.D.P.V., vol 37, part i, Dr. Kuhtreiber describes his visit made in March, 1912. His is the fullest and best account of Ain Kadeis in print, and we regret that ours was written before we saw his article. We supplement him, however, in some details.

Dr. Musil, in his heavy book on *Edom* (ii, pp. 176 – 181) gives good photographs of the valley, and a very poor description.

Of older writers one should mention Holland, who is faithful, and in particular the second letter of Rowlands. He was astonished at Trumbull's discovery, and, though in old age, set out at once to Egypt, visited Kadeis, and wrote him a simple account of his trip, published in the *P.E.F. Quarterly* for July, 1884.

[2] e.g., Hastings' *Bible Dictionary*, art. Kadesh-Barnea.

shelter of the southern hill-sides. Shrubs and flowers showed themselves in variety and profusion. Running water gurgled under the waving grass.... A circular well, stoned up from the bottom with time-worn limestone blocks, was the first receptacle of the water... the mouth of this well was only about three feet in diameter, and the water came to within three or four feet of the top. A little distance westerly from this well and down the slope was a second well, stoned up much like the first, but of greater diameter.... A basin or pool of water larger than either of the wells, but not stoned up like them, was seemingly the principal watering place. It was a short distance south-westerly from the second well.... Another and yet larger pool, lower down the slope, was supplied with water by a stream which rippled and cascaded along its narrow bed from the upper pool; and yet beyond this, westward, the water gurgled away under the grass... and finally lost itself in the parching wady....

'There was a New England look to this oasis,[1] especially in the flowers, and grass, and weeds.... Bees were humming there, and birds were flitting from tree to tree.... As we came into the wady we had started up a rabbit, and had seen larks and quails. It was, in fact, hard to realize that we were in the desert, or even near it. The delicious repose of the spot after our journey over the arid gravel waste under the blazing mid-day sun was most refreshing.... Our Arabs seemed to feel the soothing influences of the place, and to have lost all fear of the Azazmeh. After a brief rest on the grass they all stripped and plunged into the lower and larger pool for a bath.'

A note by Dr. Trumbull should in justice to him be reprinted with this extract of the text. He said: 'In writing up this description from my hurried notes made on the spot, I find room

---

[1] On this compare our photographs.

for question at one or two points, as to the distance and bearings of the several wells and pools one from another, but I give the facts at these points as accurately as I can recall them.'

As a general comment we can only say that this account is as minutely accurate in its measurements as it is inaccurate in its descriptive matter. The valley of Ain Kadeis is unusually naked, even among the valleys of the south country. At its mouth it is a broad, flood-torn wilderness of stone, about which a torrent-bed twists from side to side, shallow and spreading in the longer stretches, but cut twelve or fifteen feet deep through limestone shingle at the bends. In the side of the valley are the last remains of rough terrace-walling, and near by, a little to the north of the wady entrance on the sand-hills, we found ancient remains. There were eight poor ring-graves, some sherds of Byzantine pottery, and a few rough stone foundations that might in courtesy be called a farmhouse. These late Christian remains seemed to us probably to mark the highest level of the population of old Kadeis.[1]

After the entrance the valley quickly draws in and becomes, if possible, more stony than before. On each side the hills are very steep and bare, and shine painfully white in the glare of the sun. There is nowhere any green place, or any smooth ground, until the actual spring is reached; instead, great polished boulders have rolled off the cliff-sides into the stream bed, and at times half block the water channel with their huge bulk. In and out of such as these, over small and slippery stones, up and down the steep torrent bank leads the rough track to the wells. In all its length the Wady Ain Kadeis is a most unmitigated desert.

The springs themselves are made up of two or three water-holes under a cliff (Plate XI). From these flow out steady trickles

---

[1] Though Mr. Pickering Clarke, in the *P.E.F. Quarterly* for October, 1883, says 'the city itself was possibly a Hittite shrine ... from a city so important the whole district round would take its name.' We will not print comments on this.

of water, very good and sweet ('like sugar' say the Arabs), constant throughout winter and summer. They unite in a tiny stream which runs under the rocks, forming occasional pools, for about a hundred yards, and then comes to a stagnant and smelly end beneath a mighty boulder. The flow of water is a plentiful one for the needs of the few nomad households that now are the miserable population of the valley. Certainly they could not water there at one time all their little flocks for lack of room (our men brought our camels two by two), but in this dry country the smallest running water is a precious thing, and so Wady Kadeis, in spite of its lack of pasture and of smooth ground for camping, has always two or three families living in its side-ravines, and the local Arabs have profited by the opportunity of constant water to establish a graveyard on a hillock near at hand (Plate XII, 2). The goats of these Arabs, and their camels, continually driven to the well, have formed round it a patch of manure heavy enough to hide the boulders underneath, and to give root-hold to a little grass. This tiny plot, existing on sufferance of the winter floods, is the verdure that in Trumbull's eyes blotted out the sterile slopes around: just as the fig trees, from which his patience presently expected ripe figs, are two or three stunted roots of the uneatable wild sort, growing under cover of some larger boulders in the torrent-bed round a corner below the springs. The biggest of these bushes has old gnarled branches growing to more than a man's height, but the others are diffcult to find[1] (Plate XII, 1).

Trumbull celebrates particularly the flowers of the valley, but they are only the common bloom of all the dry country, which flourish for the few days after rain till the sun's heat cuts them down. While they last, one who peers between the rocks throughout all Sinai will see a garden in what from a few feet off

---

[1] Professor Coburn finds food for thought in the saying of his Arab that no man had ever planted those trees.

is blasted wilderness. Ain Kadeis, with its running water, is, of course, a little richer than most places at such times. Lastly, the pool into which Trumbull's Arabs, after stripping, plunged so rashly to have a bath, is only about a foot or eighteen inches deep, and full of very large and sharp stones. Our guide also washed his feet in it.

II

Muweilleh and Kossaima

The chain of foothills, insisted upon in the beginning of this chapter as the watershed between the northern and the southern plains, is crossed by many paths. One or more ascends each saddle between the peaks, and runs out into the northern plain between the mouth of Wady el Ain and Jebel Muweilleh. These roads are very easy ones, and the largest, which leads down direct upon Kossaima, has on its southern slope the footings of a ring-booth or two, and a few ring-graves of uncertain date. There is another path, more difficult, which passes from the valley of Ain Kadeis over the spur of Jebel el Ain, and descends into Wady el Ain not far from the mouth of Wady Ain el Guderat. The hills between the roads are striking little peaks, steep and sharp for the most part, curiously eaten out and furrowed by the sand-blast and the winter rains, very white, sometimes capped with a point of harder limestone scarped like a pyramid, sometimes rounded into huge half-drums, like clustered organ-pipes eighty or a hundred feet high.

The Foothills

The northern plain is a great contrast to its neighbour on the south. About Wady Ain Kadeis stretch great wastes of dry watercourses, winding among the sand-hills, and for the whole district there is only the petty spring of Ain Kadeis remote in a difficult valley. On the north of the watershed there are certainly some sandy stretches, and stony parts where limestone ribs and

The Northern Plain

knolls crop out of the flat; but much of the country is earth capable of ploughing, and some of it quite fertile tilth. In place of the solitary Ain Kadeis are Ain Muweilleh, in a soft wady bed; Ain Kossaima, a plentiful running of water in the sand; and Ain Guderat, a great spring, not set in a dung-heap like Ain Kadeis, or sand-choked like all other Negeb springs, but bursting straight from the rock, and running down a deep green valley of lush grass in swift irrigation channels, or in a long tree-shaded succession of quiet pools many· feet deep. This plain about Kossaima (which also seems to have no one local name) runs from Muweilleh on the west to the foot of the great pass of Ras Seram on the east. In fortunate years it might be very fruitful; and in the worst seasons its crops cannot entirely fail, thanks to the irrigated valley of Ain el Guderat – the only large stretch of corn-land under running water which we saw in all the southern waste. These exceptional advantages, which make this plain the only readily-habitable spot in the desert, seem from the remains in it to have been as obvious to its old-time rulers as to the British administrators of Sinai today.

Ain Muweilleh

Ain Muweilleh[1] is a convenient starting-point in a description of the particular features of the district in detail. It and its hills are the western limits of the good land, and anciently it must have been the most thronged spring, since the old inland route from Egypt runs under the cliff-edge of Jebel Mushrag to the water, and climbs up the wady bank just beyond on its straight way to Ras Seram. On the east side a low limestone shelf borders the valley, and upon it lie a few rude ruins of an early period, to be discussed more particularly later on when we come to treat of the allied remains at Kossaima and in Wady Guderat. Below this limestone shelf and between its steep edge and the flint screes of Jebel

---

[1] The name Muweilleh means a salty place. The description is a correct one.

Mushrag is penned the wady, a broad sandy bed full of deep-rooted tamarisk trees. The drinking water is little more than a group of shallow pools, green with slime, in the sandy bottom, which is sodden and slippery with the heavy damp for many yards around. The place is peculiarly unattractive, but at the same time very wet, and near it must have been a constant camping ground. It cannot, however, have had any large or settled population, since the possible plough-land is limited to the wady bed, and is sufficient only for the needs of an inconsiderable village.

In passing from Muweilleh to Kossaima the great road to Syria is left to the north, and a smaller track, tending steadily uphill, leads in about an hour to this, the second spring of the northern plain. In Palmer's day Kossaima seems to have been a very barren spot,[1] but the Sinai Government, when establishing a police post here, dug out the spring, and cemented about it a basin with a long canal to take the overflow (a stream as big as Ain Kadeis) to a drinking trough and reservoir. Below the reservoir the soldiers have made a garden in which are palm trees and fruits. The plain for a very wide space about the water-head is covered with great beds of rushes, and white with salt. The government post consists of two or three stone-built houses on little limestone hummocks above the spring. Beyond them on the north are some early graves, discussed in Chapter II with the other graves we found.

Kossaima

---

[1] Photographs of Kossaima, before Bramley, are to be found in Musil's *Edom*, vol. ii, pp. 183, 185.

III
Ain el Guderat

Wady el Ain

From Kossaima the path to Ain el Guderat leads at first over a plain of flat soil dotted with small bushes as far as the mouth of Wady el Ain, and then up this great wady for about a mile to the sharp turn on the left which leads into the tributary valley of Wady Ain el Guderat, called also locally Wady el Ain for saving of breath. The flat soil of the Kossaima plain is sand in summer, and very treacherous mud after rain. The Arabs plough some part of it each autumn, and when the rain is plentiful their crops are splendid, but if there is no rain they lose their labour for that year. The extent of clear soil hereabout makes this one of the most important plough-lands of the neighbourhood. It is now not fully cultivated, since the needs of its present scanty population are satisfied with a little part; but there is room enough for the work of many men. Wady el Ain the greater is rather stony, but with here and there patches of clear ground, reputed better than the plain outside for the amount of moisture always present in the soil. Nearly every winter this wady runs down in a little flood, and very often in its upper course one can find water in the water-holes (*themail*).

Wady Ain el Guderat

The smaller valley, Wady Ain el Guderat, opens unpromisingly from Wady el Ain on the east. The usual road cuts across low banks of limestone dust and chippings, like giant rubbish heaps, which extend from the north side of the tributary valley to beyond its middle. After them comes the rough mouth of the water-course, and beyond again, going southward, hummocky ground of crumbled limestone. This debris of floods in the entrance explains how travellers looking for Ain el Guderat have gone up and down the main Wady el Ain without seeing any traces of it. It is quite a narrow valley, edged by hill slopes so precipitous and lofty that it may well be called a gorge. On the south the wall of these limestone steeps is for a great way unbroken, falling at times in a sheer drop of a hundred feet to the soft grass of the meadows beneath. On the north it is a little more open, in that there are two or three places where side valleys run in, and offer difficult ways to the Arabs when they want to pass out directly northward to Ras Seram and Syria. On the west, across the main Wady el Ain, the view is cut off abruptly by the knife edge of Jebel el Ain, with a stone heap on the crest of it. To the east is the heart of the hills (Plate XIV). These cliff-boundaries shelter the valley from the sun of the morning and evening, and enclose it in an air of remoteness and quiet somewhat spoiled by the resonant echoes they throw back.

When first seen from the foothills of the mouth the lower part of the valley appears green or yellow with the crop according to the season, and has goodly acacia trees standing at intervals along its edge. The soil is many feet deep, and of very clean earth, a little light perhaps, but wonderfully good for Sinai. From the fading out of the cultivated land at the mouth to the source of the water may be two miles or so, and the width of the bottom varies from one hundred to four hundred yards. The watercourse in the middle is not, as in all other valleys of the hills, a sprawling moraine of loose boulders, but is a clear channel, cut five to fifteen feet into the ground, steep banked, and generally from three to ten yards in width. It thus wastes only an inconsiderable part of the valley space, and its depth gives it content enough to carry off all ordinary floods without damage to the fields on each side. An occasional great flood may sweep the whole place, levelling trees and washing out the soil, as happened two years ago; but normally the lower reaches of the torrent-bed are dry except when it is raining, or when the cultivators, having finished the watering of their land, turn the stream of their little canals back into the proper bed.

The Valley

Each side of the valley is marked off sharply from the hill slopes by a line of large broom bushes, as great as trees, which push their roots into the abandoned ditches of two old irrigation channels. That on the south side is only a dug ditch, winding along the contour of the hills, till it comes to an end in a great Byzantine reservoir situated in the very mouth of the valley, at the

The Aqueducts

junction of its south side with the east side of Wady el Ain. The reservoir is a great work, four-square, and about twenty yards each way, built in the usual style of the precise Greek masonry, laid in line, and it still preserves in one corner the opening of the sluice, which let out its water as required to gardens on the flat land round the elbow of the hills. The reservoir is, however, now long abandoned, half filled with earth and stones, and its conduit is only useful to the *rethem* trees.[1] The northern aqueduct is carried up higher, and is built of masonry and very poor mortar; it is nearly all destroyed, and, therefore, very difficult to trace. It may also have gone to Wady el Ain, but more probably it was made only to bring water to a little Byzantine village whose remains yet exist in a bay of the northern slope, near the beginning of the outer foothills. The present waterways are only ephemeral, a deeper furrow among the crops, as such canals must always be, made each spring and destroyed each winter in the Arab yearly interchange of plough and fallow.

The plough-land is broadest on the north side of the stream-bed, and on this side also are the threshing floor and corn pits of the Guderat tribe, in front of the ruins of the Byzantine village

The Tell

mentioned above. Behind them, up a valley, the main road goes out to Ras Seram; east of them the valley draws in suddenly; and in the very throat of it lies a small tell, or mound of ruins, blocking up the road (Plate XIII). Against one side of this mound grows a spreading acacia tree; under the other runs the torrent, and round about are heaps of small building stones and pottery and ashes. Round the bend the valley opens out into a splendid field, with some large trees along the stream, and beyond this again are more fields, up to the dam across the water, in which the irrigation ditches have their start. The Arabs do not care to

---

[1] It is perhaps worth noting that Trumbull (*Kadesh-Barnea* p. 280) suggests that Moses may have mistaken this Christian reservoir for Hazar-Addar of Numbers xxxiv, 4.

cultivate above this point, and so the winding valley floor is filled by a dense thicket of reeds, in the midst of which the stream, now in long pools eight feet deep, edged with flags and bulrushes, moves more slowly. The spring proper[1] is yet half a mile higher, where a buttress of limestone runs into the valley (Plate XV). From the foot of it the water gushes out strongly in three little spouts thick as a man's arm, from deep, narrow fissures in the rock. The noise of the falling water, the Arabs say, is so great that a man cannot hear himself speak; perhaps, for the water's sake, they use a gentler utterance than their wont. The plain of reeds goes far above the spring, and the land is still moist. Indeed, five minutes' walk higher up is a built aqueduct of stone and lime leading out of the hill-side and running across the valley. It probably points to another, but now forgotten, spring which watered these upper fields.

The Spring

IV

The Antiquities of the Kossaima District

In the valley of Ain el Guderat are remains of many periods of occupation. The latest are the Arab graves of the Guderat tribe on the top of the little tell, and the excavated Arab corn-pits at the foot of the Ras Seram road. There are other Mohammedan graves – old ones – below the great Byzantine reservoir in the valley-mouth, which are set in a medley of walls running about the platform below the reservoir. There may have been buildings here, but more probably they are only conduits and retaining

Arab Remains at Ain el Guderat

---

[1] Ain el Guderat means the spring of the earthenware kettles, or small spouted pots. Whether it refers to the rush of water, in contrast to the slow welling up of Ain Kadeis, or to actual pottery, we know not. The French fathers (*Revue Biblique*, July, 1906) call it Ain el Mufjer. The spring is sometimes called el Mufjer locally, to distinguish its force: but this is not a proper name.

walls of terraces in an irrigation scheme; it would be a very good site for water-gardens, and probably on the abandonment of these the Arab conquerors took the ground as a suitable graveyard. The tombs are only rings and ovals of stones very roughly arranged; on some stones were varieties of tribe-marks, and there was one little stone of the flat disk type, common in Byzantine cemeteries, with a rude cross scratched on it. Facing this cemetery, across the valley, is a large underground corn-store of the ordinary bell shape, but lined with rubble masonry all the way up.

Byzantine Remains in Ain el Guderat

Of Byzantine remains the reservoir already described is by far the largest and most important; it and the conduits on each side of the valley prove that in the Byzantine time not only was the whole of the valley-bed proper in cultivation, but work was extended beyond, over what is now the waste land of Wady el Ain. The Greek population must therefore have been more numerous than the present owners of the valley, or have been assured of a larger market for their produce. One can well imagine that in years of drought Ain el Guderat fed all the saints of Central Sinai.

The Byzantine village on the north side of the valley, at the spot where the road to Ras Seram runs into it, is a collection of very simple huts. The remains now visible are those of from fifteen to twenty poor small houses, built in unshaped rubble. The plans of them are not very apparent, for the Guderat tribesmen have dug out their corn-pits among them, and, as their threshing floor is just below, they usually, for a few weeks in each year, move their camp to the old village site, and pile up its stones in a fresh arrangement every time along the back and side curtains of their tents. None the less, the foundations are certainly Byzantine, for the ground all about is red with the hard ribbed pottery of Gaza make, peculiar to Christian ruins everywhere in this part of Sinai. There is no permanent settlement of Arabs in the valley, through their fear of the climate. It is believed that anyone who lies there in summer (whether man or beast) will be attacked by an intermittent fever of peculiar strength; indeed, even the cooked meat of animals which have fed in the valley is declared dangerous by the local authorities in hygiene. As a matter of fact, the large deep pools of the upper river must be admirable breeding-places for mosquitoes. Starting above this Byzantine village, and running eastward along the hill-top, there is one of the long and puzzling walls which, like those elsewhere in the Negeb, appear to start and go on and end so aimlessly. It is a wall of dry stone, perhaps three-quarters of a mile long in all, and still perfectly preserved. It has been piled up very carelessly, from two to three feet thick, and from three to five feet high. It runs reasonably directly along the hill, never at the crest, but always a little way down the valley slope; it crosses gullies on the hill-side, without varying its height or taking any regard of them; in one place it is broken by plain openings, flanked internally by a square enclosure, a few feet each way, like a pound, or a temporary shelter. Its purpose is mysterious. Being on the downward slope of the hill it would not keep anyone out, and, besides, it runs only from one side-wady to another, and so would not really protect anything. It cannot be meant to keep human beings enclosed, for any child that could crawl would overpass it; nor would it pen any sheep or goat. The only Arab animal that would find such an erection impassable would be a camel, and, perhaps, the wall is the monument of some tribe's exasperation in herding camels. The beasts have a perverse habit of wandering up a steep hill-side and becoming incurably lost, and this wall, if supported by fences across the valley at its two ends, would prevent their escape entirely. The present Guderat tribe disclaim all responsibility for the work; but they are comparatively new-comers in the district.

When walking across the valley of Ain el Guderat between the Byzantine reservoir and the village site, we picked up near the torrent bed some pieces of *terra sigillata*, the haematite-stained polished pottery of Roman period. The only fragment of recognizable shape seemed to be that of a cup of a very late type. There was also, however, a piece of one of the shallow round-

Roman Remains at Ain el Guderat

bottomed cups or little bowls of haematitic ware, with classical ornament moulded in relief on the outside, which occur plentifully in North Syria in deposits of the 2nd and 1st centuries B.C. These pottery fragments had almost certainly been brought by water to their present position, and we could find no traces of the site of the Hellenistic settlement from which they probably came.

However, all the rest of Northern Sinai can show ruins and remains as good as these. The great interest of Guderat is in its tell,[1] which seems to contain a ruin of a period not represented elsewhere in the Negeb, save in the hut ruins of Muweilleh, the graves at Kossaima, and, perhaps, in the little guard-houses at Bir Birein and Raheiba on the great road between Hebron and Egypt. Tell Ain el Guderat is by far the most important of these, since its walls stand ten feet high, its ground plan is intelligible, and its pottery bears witness to greater wealth and refinement than we suspected in the other places.

Tell el Ain el Guderat

The tell is a little mound about 200 feet long and 120 feet broad, fairly regular in shape, and stands now in a heap from twelve to fifteen feet high above the corn-fields. The sides are very steep, and at first the whole thing looks only like a pile of round water-worn pebbles and ashes, without system. This, however, is seen not to be so as soon as one digs anywhere. The water-worn stones then appear as the filling of walls faced, not certainly with ashlar, but with limestone blocks selected off the hill-sides with regard to their squareness of shape and convenience of size for loading on a camel and for laying (Fig. 8). The design of the building was a long rectangle, with square towers of slight sally at the four corners, and a small tower in the middle of each face. The walls were built hugely thick to a height of ten feet above the

---

[1] First recorded by Dr. Kuhtreiber, in *Z.D.P.V.*, vol. 37, part i.

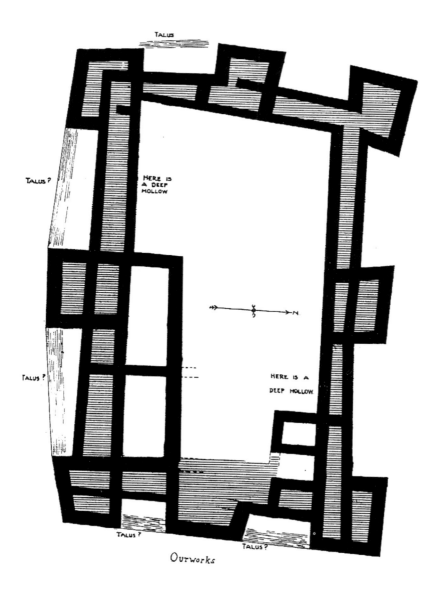

Fig. 8: Fortress at Ain el Guderat

ground, when their solidity seems to have ceased, and they became mere shells of built stone, with a series of rooms or corridors in their thicknesses. The walls are faced with well-laid blocks, some as much as three feet long, but all thin and light; the filling is of river pebbles, large rough stones, and mud. Between the towers the wall seems to have been sloped out in a talus, which near its base lines up with the outer faces of the towers; from that point it was carried down vertically for perhaps two or three courses to the ground. In our view the plan of the building is superior to its execution.

We dug into one of the rooms on the top of the wall and found that its sides were standing a yard or more high, and from this, and from a good deal of surface-scratching while following walls, we have ventured to reconstruct tentatively the whole building as described. It demands, of course, far more thorough investigation than we gave it, with our two or three men, in the three days we were able to spare. Captain A. W. Jennings-Bramley, Governor of Sinai, was good enough to grant us an emergency permission for the *sondages* which we undertook.

So far as the western half of the fort is concerned, a single row of chambers in the wall top, and the tower rooms, seem to have been the only accommodation provided. The ground level within the high walls of this half was very low, full of soft dust and quite clear of any indication of walls. The depth of it is, perhaps, only six or seven feet. The eastern half is, however, a sort of platform, level with the present top of the enceinte, and with obvious signs of party walls that crossed and recrossed it, making a complex of chambers. We had no time to ascertain to what depth these inner walls descended; probably the whole end of the fort is banked up, since otherwise they would be from twelve to fifteen feet high. Outside the main wall of the fort on this eastern side was a low tongue of land bearing traces of less important buildings. We could see no signs of a gateway leading into the fort, though such presumably exists.

As seen on paper, the plan might recall that of the great fort at

Abda; actually its style of construction distinguishes the building altogether from any Byzantine-Christian or Arab work that we have seen elsewhere. The plan again is not unlike that of some Egyptian forts of the XIIth and XVIIIth Dynasties; the material is different, for the mud-brick of the Nile valley was an impossibility in the Sinaitic desert, but the parallel is perhaps not insignificant. A better indication of date is given by the pottery. There was not much of this upon the surface; light ashes, rubble and building-stones from the fallen walls and lumps of clay, that may have formed the roof, had buried everything; but in the little room which we cleared and in the debris of the sides of the mound we found any quantity of broken sherds. There were both wheel-made and hand-made wares, but the Egyptian types for which we first hoped failed us altogether: the pottery was purely Syrian. Many large vessels were of a greenish grey clay, turned on the wheel, not unlike the 'gulla' wares of the Nile, but not to be identified as such. One piece of a cup or tumbler in strongly ribbed reddish clay, which might by Egyptian analogy be late, has parallels in Syria that date back to the tenth or twelfth centuries B.C. There were fairly numerous sherds of the line-burnished haematitic ware (hand-made) which occurred also in the guard-houses of the Darb el Shur and have been, in South Palestine, assigned by Macalister to the Second Semitic period (perhaps rather they belong to the whole period 1800 – 900 B.C.).

Some fragments of fine painted pottery, at first sight closely resembling some Cypriote fabrics, might belong (also on the analogy of South Palestinian sites) to the end of the second millennium B.C. Together with these, there were fragments of rough hand-made wares, thin-walled, of gritty clay burnt very hard in an open hearth, which are identical with those found in the graves at the mouth of Wady el Ain el Guderat, in the ring-graves of Kossaima, and in the hut dwellings by the Muweilleh springs.

The evidence furnished by our brief scratching of the soil is not enough to fix the date of the building with any accuracy. It enables us, however, to say that we have here in the neck of the wady, commanding the finest water-supply in all the desert, a building which from the thickness of its walls may well have been a fort, of Syrian or Semitic, not of Egyptian origin. It is connected in culture and probably in date with the early hut-settlements and graves that cluster round the other water-sources of the district. It was occupied for a comparatively brief period, in the latter part of the second or the beginning of the first millennium before our era. Various tempting theories lie obvious to hand, but only thorough excavation can profitably solve the character of what is beyond question an interesting and important site.

Flints at Ain el Guderat

In the valley of Ain el Guderat we found a worked flint. It may of course have been a prehistoric one, and, if so, the place would be distinguished as the only Stone Age site we noted in our part of Sinai: but more probably it is of Arab manufacture and comparatively modern. The tribesman is a great maker of flints, and Ain el Guderat, with its flocks and herds, is a place where they must use many flints each year. Another unpromising object is a cave in the south wall of the valley: it is a very simple hole, hewn in the cliff-face about three hundred yards above the tell. Its mouth lies about a hundred feet above the ground, and is reached by an easy path. The cliff is of very soft stone, and so the roof has scaled in large masses which bury the floor deep in chalk and dust. The opening of the cave is very nearly its greatest width: it seems once to have had side chambers like a Byzantine tomb, but there is no evidence at all of early date. The Arabs say that it was dug to extract salt from the rock.

Guderat Graves

The early graves of the Guderat valley are treated by themselves in Chapter II, p. 30. Historically the point of importance in connection with them is that their pottery is that of the tell (except for the lack of painted ware) and that of the Kossaima graves combined. They thus provide a useful link between the various remains of the Kossaima district. The graves at Kossaima also are described in full in the chapter dealing with burials (Chapter II, p. 29 – 30), and from them one may presume

Kossaima Graves

a small rude settlement in Kossaima also at the Guderat period. We were not successful in finding any house ruins there: they may have been destroyed, or we may have missed them; but the point is unimportant as we found plenty of dwelling-houses and a few graves of exactly the same type at Muweilleh. The ruins there, close to the water-pools and the small cave described by Palmer, appear to be those of a little village containing perhaps thirty 'houses' of a temporary character. The houses are very small, some rectangular, some circular or semicircular. They are now represented by very low heaps of large pebbles, so few in number that they must nearly all have been like the hut of our guide from Ras Seram. His house, which he had furnished with a coffee-pot (for making shrub-coffee) and a water-skin, was a crescent of piled-up stones, three or four courses high, caulked with tamarisk leaves, and topped with tamarisk boughs to keep off the wind. He had rested a few branches horizontally across the wall, anchoring them with stones, to provide himself with the luxury of a roof: if he was cold he lit a fire between the horns of the crescent. The only huts at Muweillah not like this were two or three more magnificent rectangular ones, belonging to those fortunate owners who had a tent-cloth to roof them in. The pottery about the settlement was almost entirely the roughest hand-made type of the district. There were only two or three sherds of the finer wheel-made wares.

Muweilleh Ruins

The castle of Ain el Guderat is so enormously better than the remains about it that one is inclined to ascribe its erection to some outside agency. It is as much above the huts of Muweilleh as the police station of Kossaima is above the hut of our old guide from Ras Seram. On the other hand, of course, there is no land and no water at Muweilleh that would justify a large village, The Rev. Caleb Hauser, in the *P.E.F. Quarterly* of April, 1908, does not agree with us here. He identifies this Muweilleh with the biblical Makkelath, and the Latin Mohaila, the military station in the *Notitia*. In Christian times, he says, it must have been the seat of an archbishopric, since Palmer found there traces of Christian occupation. His first point is etymology, in which we are incompetent; in regard to his second there are no material classical remains to make probable a Roman post. As for the Christian remains, Palmer, whom he quotes, in describing them, is carefully exact upon the two insignificant and widely separated holes in the chalk which still exist, each with a little cross in red painted on the wall.[1] All Sinai, Palestine, and Syria are littered with similar remains. And there is no reason why these particular caves should have ever contained an archbishop. There was probably another Muweilleh below Aila on the road to Sinai. It is, unfortunately, a very common Arab place-name.

V

Kadesh-Barnea

It would perhaps be improper to close this chapter without any reference to the vexed question of Kadesh-Barnea. The unfortunate vagueness of the Pentateuch geographically, and its lack of synthesis historically, cause the end of all such controversies to be a deeper confusion than the beginning: therefore, so far as possible, we have kept out of our pages any reference to the barren literature of today which wrangles over indeterminable Bible sites. In most cases the strife is about a Hebrew name, and its possible reappearance in a modern Arab form. That glib catchword 'The Unchanging East' has blinded writers to the continual ebb and flow of the inhabitants of the desert. It is hopeless to look for an Arab tribe which has held its

---

[1] Père Jaussen, in the *Revue Biblique* for July, 1906, has drawn plans of these caves.

present *dira* for more than a very few generations: and to expect continuity of name, as in settled districts in Syria, is vanity. A second factor to be remembered is that the Jews were an unscientific people, anxious only to get through the inhospitable desert as soon as might be. Research into local nomenclature is today very difficult among the tribesmen; and it is not likely that Moses was more patient and painstaking than a modern surveyor. Probably, as often as not, the Israelites named for themselves their own camps, or unconsciously confounded a native name in their carelessness.

At the same time, by good or ill fortune, the problem of Kadesh-Barnea is a little narrower and a little more documented than most. We are told that the Jews left Ezion-Geber, and went to the Wilderness of Zin, which is Kadesh; and that the latter touched on the boundaries of Edom. We know where Ezion-Geber was, more or less, and where Edom was; though there is not the faintest light upon her boundaries. Somewhere between these points the children of Israel seem to have spent nearly forty years. We have no safe clue as to the numbers of the tribes, nor do we know their social condition; and this capital ignorance qualifies all discussion as to how they were disposed. There must, however, have been at least some thousands of them. They may have been genuine nomads, scattering to all the corners of the desert in groups of two or three tents, in which case Moses was an even better organizer than we knew, to gather his people again and launch them against Palestine as a disciplined army; or they may have been a tribal group keeping to one district and moving a mile or two in this direction or in that as they devoured the pasture. If this second view be accepted, then it is definitely our opinion that only in the Kossaima district are to be found enough water and green stuffs to maintain so large a tribe for so long, and that therefore the Wilderness of Zin and Kadesh-Barnea must be the country of Ain el Guderat, Kossaima, Muweilleh, and Ain Kadeis. The similarity between the names Kadeis and Kadesh need not be a mere coincidence, for the former is just as likely to be of ancient as of recent origin. The extension by the Israelites of what is now the name of a small isolated valley to a whole district can be explained by the fact that travellers coming from Akaba would happen first on the low country at that valley's mouth, a country less detestable than the wastes they had just left, and might easily, as strangers, call the whole plain after their first watering-place. On the other hand, the assumption, necessary to our minds, that the place-name was extended to a district embracing other and better water-sources, undermines the identification of Ain Kadeis valley as the scene of events related as happening at Kadesh. These may have taken place anywhere in the Kossaima neighbourhood. We are told that at one well in Kadesh the Israelites found the water insufficient – and if there were more than twenty families of them, and the spring were the present Ain Kadeis, then their complaints must be considered moderate. Thereupon Moses produced the water of Meribah, so called to distinguish it from the first well. Certainly it is useless to look for this copious fount in the barren gorge of Ain Kadeis, unless we suppose that it dried up as miraculously as it appeared. At a later date Moses, writing to the King of Edom, described Kadesh as 'a city in the uttermost of thy border' (Numbers xx, 16). The word 'city' is a vague one, and probably only means a settlement, perhaps a district, like the modern Arabic *beled* which is used to mean town, village, district, or country. In the former sense it might be used of such hut-settlements as those of Muweilleh and Kossaima; but would most temptingly apply to the fortress of Ain Guderat, should we assume – we cannot prove it – that the fort was already built when Moses came.

Strategically the Kossaima district agrees well with what we know of Kadesh-Barnea. The Darb el Shur, the road of their forefathers, stretching westwards before the eyes of the mutinous Israelites, suggested an easy return to Egypt (Numbers xiv, 4); the same road runs northwards to Hebron, whither the spies went up to view the Land of Promise (Numbers xiii, 21). From the south runs up the main road from Elath, one of the stations on the

Exodus route. Westwards there is a choice of roads; one can go either through Bir Hafir and the Abda district by what is now called the Darb el Sultan, the King's Highway, into the Araba, or by way of Wady Lussan, a little to the south, to Bir Mayein,[1] and thence by the Jerafi wady system to sundry roads leading into the Araba directly in front of Jebel Harun, the traditional Mount Hor. To choose today out of the innumerable hills of the country one particular peak to be the scene of Aaron's burial shows, perhaps, an uncatholic mind; but as long as the tradition of Jebel Harun passes muster, so long the existence of recognized roadways between the mountain and the Kossaima plain must influence our judgment. These roads running out to north, south, east and west – all directions in which journeys were planned or made from Kadesh-Barnea – together with its abundance of water and wide stretch of tolerable soil, distinguish the Kossaima plain from any other district in the Southern Desert, and may well mark it out as the headquarters of the Israelites during their forty years of discipline.

---

[1] Very carefully examined by Père Jaussen in the *Revue Biblique*, July, 1906, with a sketch map, and a good description of the way.

CHAPTER V

THE BYZANTINE TOWNS

They have their day and cease to be.

(line 18 of 'In Memorium A.H.H. Obit MDCCCXXXIII'
by Alfred Lord Tennyson)

Esbeita: Zephath and Hormah: Mishrafa: Abda:
Beersheba: Khalasa: Saadi: Raheiba: El Auja: Kurnub:
Akaba: Geziret Faraun.

Esbeita lies on the east side of the great Wady Migrih, just opposite the mouth of the Wady el Abiad. Its eastern bank is a long slope of flint-covered limestone, half-way up which are the ruins of the town; south of the ruins it is broken by the little Wady es Zeyatin. The only road visible in the neighbourhood passes under Mishrafa and runs south, keeping close to the west bank of the Wady Migrih; Esbeita therefore lies well off its track (Plate XVI, 2).

Wady Migrih is the last place in which one would expect to find a town. It is not on the line of the desert trade routes, and it is peculiarly barren. On the east great stony slopes, and on the west limestone cliffs, shut in a wide valley where stretches of drift-sand divide rolling banks of flint-strewn rock. The ravines high up the hill-sides have been terraced into tiny soil-plots, but even Byzantine industry could do little with the main valley. Under Mishrafa there are a few patches of old tilth, but for the most part the grey-green scrub alone refuses to admit the impossibility of life amongst the stones, while the flint-heaps on the foothills show where vines gave up the struggle long ago. Wady Zeyatin, as its name shows, may once have been an olive-yard, and three or four stunted olives still survive there; but it is a narrow little valley without much room for trees. The only arable land from which Esbeita could have drawn its food supply lies two miles and more away from the town in the Wady el Abiad. Here, in spite of the sandy character of the soil, through which the *seyl* waters have cut deep channels with precipitous crumbling banks, much of the broad valley bottom could be made moderately fertile in good seasons. It shows everywhere traces of old cultivation (Plate XXII, 2); the lower foothills are marked out with rows of vine-heaps, the flat land is still in furrows, and in the middle of the wady is a small ruined hamlet with vine-towers and walled gardens. It seems strange that the town should not have been placed here rather than on its sterile hill-side so far away. One can only suppose that the monks, who presumably first settled there, chose with intent a spot whose barrenness, equal to that of the Thebaid, might exercise them in good works, and that the lay folk, later comers, chose to build their houses under the protection of the monasteries, though forced to go to a distance for their food.

There were no living wells at Esbeita. Water could be fetched from some *haraba*s, rock-cut cisterns, about a mile and a half away to the north-west, in Wady Migrih, or from Wady Themail, further to the south; but the people generally depended for their supply upon the great reservoirs in the middle of the town and upon the countless cisterns with which the rock is honeycombed (Plate XVII, 1, 2). There was one cistern at least in every town, and the streets and open places served as so many more; everywhere were runnels and long banks of earth and stone to catch the rainwater and to carry it to the tanks; even outside the town one such banked conduit followed the wall-line and led to cisterns and to the few poor garden plots that lie on the lower western slope.

These Byzantine cities of the south have so strong a family resemblance one to another that it would be tedious to describe them all in detail with vain repetitions; and since Esbeita is the best preserved of them it may well serve as a model for the rest (Fig. 9). Esbeita is small, measuring some 450 metres by 350 metres, and of irregular shape, an aggregation of haphazard buildings rather than a town laid out on a plan. Properly speaking it is not walled, but the walls of private houses and of their gardens along its outskirts are continuous, and form a complete girdle, broken only by small arched gateways at the ends of some of the streets. So flimsy a bulwark was useless, as events proved,

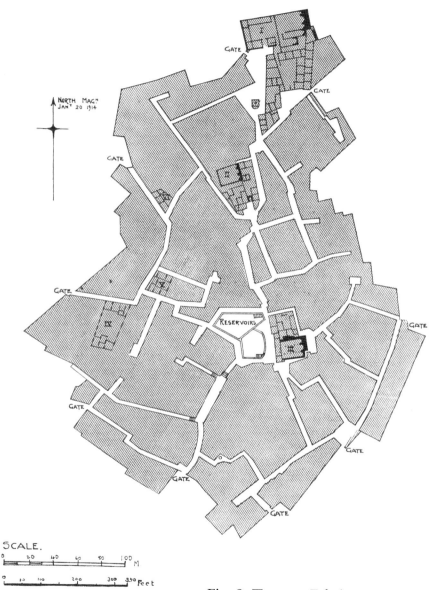

Fig. 9: Town at Esbeita.

99

against a properly sustained attack; but a blank dry-stone wall can stop a Beduin raid, and was considered sufficient not only for a monastery town like Esbeita but even for the fortresses of Abda and Kurnub.[1]

In the centre of the southern part of the town is a great double reservoir of irregular shape open to the air, with sides of masonry and of rubble concrete; each of the two basins has steps leading down into it. The northern streets drained into the reservoir. From the reservoir the main roads of the town run out in all directions. They are of varying widths (though four metres is about the average) and full of turns and angles, following the outline of houses built at hazard. To the north the ground slopes gently upwards, but it falls away sharply to the south-east; the south-west road from the reservoir ran down an old wady bed and was broken by steps, and the narrower lanes also that joined it from the west ended in flights of steps upon the main street. Such is the state of the ruins that it was not always easy to determine even the principal roads; from them short blind alleys branch off frequently to give approach to the centre of the larger *insulae*, but these alleys were more often than not so encumbered with debris that they could not be distinguished from the courtyards or even from the rooms of the houses about them.

There are three churches in the town, one at the extreme north end, one a little way to the south, and another fronting on the reservoirs; all are of the stereotyped Byzantine plan of which we shall see many examples in other towns. Attached to each of them is a large building, presumably of a monastic character, and the three together comprise a not inconsiderable part of the builded area within the town. The churches will be described in detail later.

---

[1] Palmer, in *P.E.F* Quarterly for 1871, p.33, published a good sketch plan which we only saw after our own was complete. The new plan adds but little to the old, and is published here merely to illustrate the text.

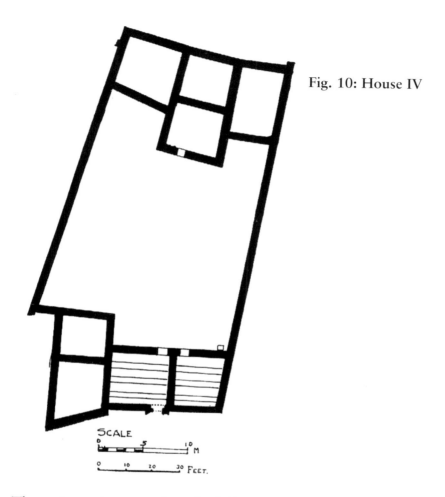

Fig. 10: House IV

SCALE

The private houses, though differing a good deal amongst themselves (Plate XX, 1), are all modifications of the 'courtyard' type prevalent in the country throughout this period, and faithfully reproduced by the modern dwellings, *e.g.*, of Beersheba. The main feature is an open courtyard, generally entered through a vaulted chamber, but sometimes giving directly on the street, on which front the living-rooms; these sometimes run round three sides of the square, more often they lie at its two ends. In the normal house the main block is composed of three chambers in a row, of which the central one, a vaulted *liwan*, opens with its full width on the courtyard and gives access to the rooms on either side. Naturally the plan varies with the shape of the building plot and with the size of the house; thus the building marked IV on the plan (Fig. 10) – so large and solidly constructed that it may well be government offices rather than a´private house – is a good example of the norm. By a door with well-moulded jambs the entrance is through a vaulted room, flanked by two other chambers, into a very large courtyard, at the far end of which are the open *liwan* and the living quarters. In the building V the rooms run round three sides of the courtyard, the entrance being through one of the southern chambers (Fig. 11). In VI, a small irregular house (Fig. 12), the doorway leads straight from the street to the courtyard; the *liwan* and the two side chambers lie on the left, and the far corner of the court is taken up by another small room. Many of the houses were quite large, with wide courtyards and even gardens that took up much of the available area of the town and made it far less populous in reality than its dimensions would seem to show. Immediately south-east of the

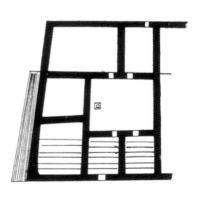

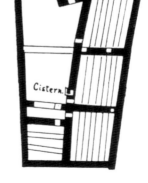

Fig. 11: House V   Fig. 12: House VI

reservoir the houses were small and crowded, many being but booths open to the street, and of one storey only, but the better class houses were seldom cramped. These latter were generally of two storeys; the high walls that lined the streets were blank, since windows faced inwards on the courts, and there was no attempt at external decoration. The sky-line, broken by the lofty naves and campaniles of the churches, may have been picturesque, but the narrow streets must have been, save for the bazaars, as dull and unsavoury as those in the native quarters of any modern Syrian town.

A peculiar feature of these Byzantine buildings is clearly brought out in the photograph on Plate XX, 2. The lower storey is built of blocks of hard yellowish limestone roughly split in the quarry; the upper storeys are of smoothly-trimmed chalk that turns honey-coloured with exposure. There is a constructional reason for this. The hard stone is preferable when it is merely a question of bearing top weight; the chalk is soft for such a purpose and was therefore never used in the lower parts of walls except on an interior face when, as in the apse of a church, the form of the building demanded that the stonework should be truly laid. The masons were unable to cut the hard limestone to a good surface, and therefore for an arch or vault requiring shaped *voussoirs* they had to content themselves with chalk; and since the ease with which this could be cut would make it cheaper, and it is a lighter stone, it was invariably employed for upper storeys.

The scarcity of wood and the cost of importing it practically forbade its use in house-building. Everywhere stone was employed in its stead. Wall-cupboards were made with cut chalk slabs; windows and narrow doors were flat-roofed with long blocks of hard limestone, and broader apertures were arched. The floors of upper storeys were also of stone (Plate XXII, 1). Broad rather flat arches spanned the rooms at intervals of about a metre, their springers resting on large blocks of limestone that stood out from the wall-face as corbels or were carried down to form pilasters. The spandrils of these arches were levelled up with rubble walling, and across, from one to the other, were laid limestone slabs, above which a packing of small stones and mud or lime formed the floor proper. The photographs of a room in house V on Plate XXI show this method of construction; some of the cover slabs had fallen, but others can be seen resting upon the rafter-arches. Doubtless many of the roofs were flat and constructed in the same way, but there may also have been vaults of small rubble and lime built over a centring, as in the bath-house at Raheiba and, probably, in the naves of the churches.

The groins or arches that supported the ceilings of adjacent rooms were set in line with one another to counterbalance their outward thrust, and the outer walls, if not supported by cross-walls beyond, were often buttressed with a stone talus. The danger of the collapse of what was practically dry-stone walling under the pressure of an arch was quite realized by the builders; the talus-buttress was very commonly employed, and sometimes added to a wall already built and perhaps showing signs of weakness. The great apses of the churches, in spite of their height, required less support because of their better masonry; the sides were sometimes buttressed, but only up to the clerestory. The backward thrust of the apse is, however, counteracted by a heavy talus, which was either solid, or else a hollow complex of chalk arches and retaining-walls set at various angles and sheathed in a skin of sloping limestone masonry.

Most of the building is with mud mortar; lime is also used, but it is generally of a very poor quality, little more than powdered chalk and water. In the reservoir the rubble walls are grouted with an excellent hard lime; the same is occasionally seen as the pointing of wall-faces whose interior is but mud-grouted, and a very thin but good lime is employed in the chalk masonry of the church apses. But for the most part the lime was unburnt, and like the mud from which it can hardly be distinguished, it has been washed out from between the stones, with the result that the walls now appear to be dry-built.

The bonding of blocks in a wall-face was carefully observed, but walls are poorly bonded together and more often merely butted on, even when of the same period and plan; occasionally at the corners of buildings, however, L-shaped stones were employed to give greater strength and coherence to the angle. Walls were generally formed of two skins of facing-blocks with a filling of mud and rubble: virtually there was never any attempt at through-bonding, and so two dangers were incurred – the falling away of either face and the bulging of the wall through the weight of its filling. Probably to this defect is due the builder's fondness for double walls. A skin of fresh masonry was often applied to an existing wall when this had not to meet any outward thrust; its own faulty construction demanded this makeshift.

On the hardest limestone, which is semi-crystalline and full of fossils, only the roughest hammer-dressing was employed, the blocks remaining for the most part only approximately square as they were split in the quarry. On an intermediate quality of stone, which is fairly hard but more uniform in grain, most of the dressing is done with the hammer, but occasionally on the outer face of the block there was used a toothed drawing tool which leaves long, close striations. The chalk stones are shaped with a fine-toothed drawing-tool and with the flat adze: the *voussoirs* are cut remarkably true and the jointing is excellent.

Such decorative work, as there was, was executed always in soft stone, but at Esbeita the buildings were even more simple than was the rule in other towns. Capitals of pilasters were generally plain voussoir-shaped or at most had a band of simple indented pattern shallowly engraved; arches were occasionally picked out with a similar pattern or a band. The shafts of columns were not infrequently treated with plain belts in relief. The door of the central monastery, of which a drawing was published by Palmer, had collapsed when we saw it, and its key-stone had disappeared. The south door of the northern monastery, which was almost entirely masked by a later talus-wall (*see* Plan, Fig. 14) had moulded jambs with grotesquely decorated capitals (Fig. 13); the doorway of the large building IV also had moulded jambs.

There were found in the churches two or three examples of simple ornament (illustrated later, see pp. 111 – 112, 114 – 115), but apart from these there could be seen no remains of decoration or inscription. Even the cemetery produced no inscribed stelae.

South of the town, just across the wady-bed, on a low flint-strewn bank of limestone, lay a small cemetery. The graves were shallow, sometimes stone-lined, rectangular in shape and covered with heaps or squares of stones; amongst these were some ashlar blocks and even fragments of columns, pointing to an occasional super-structure of a more ambitious type (*cf.* Khalasa, p. 148). There were no signs of carved or inscribed stonework.

Fig. 13: Esbeita: north church, capital of side door. 1 : 8

In the hillside close by were two large chamber-tombs, lying open and used for goat-shelters; probably there are others to be found both here and in the low limestone cliff-face that borders the wady a little distance below the town walls.

The agriculture of the district must have been carried on entirely by the inhabitants of Esbeita itself, for with the exception of the few cottages in Wady Abiad there was here nothing to correspond with the hamlets and isolated farms that abound in the neighbourhood of Khalasa. The only buildings outside the town itself are two or three presses or vine-towers in Wady Zeyatin, and, about a hundred metres south-east of the town, a single house of the usual courtyard type and a small building whose character we could not determine, though it may have been a bath. This building consists of a courtyard with two fair-sized rooms opening out of it. Along one side are a number of small compartments giving on to the courtyard, and similar compartments surround the smaller room on three sides. The walls of these compartments are of hard cement and rubble, and their floors also are of cement. Two similar buildings were found at Abda, one of them outside the town, and in the latter was a heavy stratum of ashes. The Esbeita example showed no signs of a furnace, but it was so ruinous that this fact is not conclusive. The place may be a bath-house with courtyard, dressing-room, and hot and cold baths in separate chambers. There was a large a water-cistern just outside its main entrance.

The Churches

The usual plan for the Byzantine churches in the south shows three aisles separated by arcades, and ending in round apses at the east end, the central aisle being considerably the largest of the three. The main body of the church is separated by a screen-wall pierced with three doorways in the ends of the three aisles from a courtyard often surrounded by chambers or cloisters, and containing a cistern; in one corner of this courtyard there is generally a square campanile. In two of the Esbeita churches this courtyard is reduced to a minimum, owing to the cramped area on which the churches are built; when the ground is more open, as in the case of the northern church, or of the churches at Raheiba and El Auja, it may be larger than the actual naves. Subsidiary chapels are sometimes added to the south side of the main building. The entrance to the church is always through the outer courtyard.

The apses are always built of chalk ashlar, and the apse itself is always laid out on a single centre, set back somewhat so as to make it a little more than a semicircle in plan.

The Northern Church

The Northern Church   The northern church is almost entirely surrounded by a heavy talus which did not form part of the original plan, but seems to have been added when the first chapel was built against the south side of the main nave (Fig. 14). The rough stonework of the talus hid almost completely the ornamental jambs of the main entrance, which was in the middle of the south wall of the forecourt. One jamb of this doorway had disappeared, the other is shown in Fig. 13. Entering here one passed through a vaulted chamber into the great court. The chambers which once ran round three sides of it had been almost completely destroyed, only that in the north-west corner retaining its roof ribs intact; even the walls of the others could only with difficulty be distinguished in the mass of debris that was piled high within the court, and on the north side the outer wall itself had been breached, and the inner wall of the chambers is little more than conjectural. It could be seen, however, that there had been two tiers or storeys of vaulted rooms, each provided with a niche or cupboard in the wall, and all looking out upon the courtyard. Since the court was considerably wider than the original church proper, there was no symmetry between the two. The door in the screen-wall leading to the north aisle had to be approached through a small chamber, instead of opening as usual upon the court. A corresponding chamber in the south-west of the courtyard, having an arched doorway with indented ornament on its capitals, led through a second door into a small room which, from the great heaps of fallen masonry about it, seems to have been the ground floor of the campanile; it seemed probable also that a doorway in the south side of this tower-chamber afforded a private entrance to the adjoining monastery (Plate XVIII, 2). The screen-wall was of ashlar chalk masonry; it was pierced by three small arched doorways leading to the three main aisles. Unfortunately all traces of the arcades had disappeared: no fragments even of columns could be found inside the church, so we could not tell whether the arches rested, as is usually the case, on round column shafts, or upon masonry pillars. The apses were standing tolerably intact

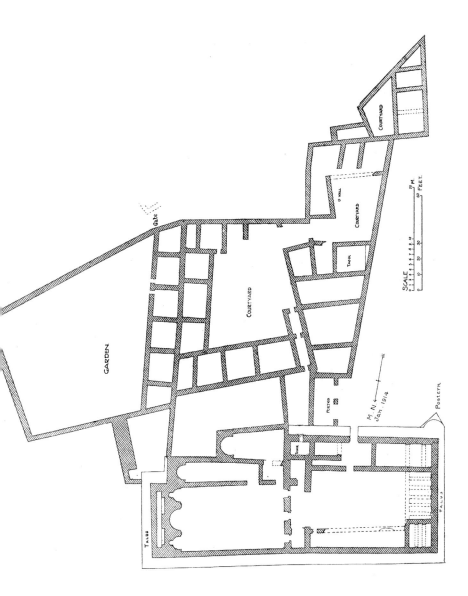

Fig. 14: Esbeita: North Church

(Plate XVIII, 1); that in the centre had a height of eight metres; the side apses stood about three and a half metres high, and there were signs of chambers above them also vaulted, whose vaults would have been level with the top of the main apse. These upper chambers, of course, served constructionally as buttresses of the central apse, but they seem also to have been actual chambers, and perhaps formed the east ends of the triforium. Since the north wall is standing (at the east end) as much as four and a half metres high, with no window apertures, and the south wall was entirely blinded by the chapel alongside of it, the lighting of the church must have been by windows set very high up, in a clerestory: and perhaps in this church there was a triforium or gallery also, to include the upper chambers over the apses of the side aisles.

Each apse had a simple string-course distinguishing the opening of the dome from the vertical wall, and the central apse had a plain projecting string round the edge of its arch. The two side apses had each a small apsidal recess at the back. The masonry of the apses was pierced regularly above the string-course with long, narrow slits about a metre apart horizontally, and half a metre apart vertically, and below the string-course by horizontal rows, 1.40m. from each other, of small square slots at intervals of twenty centimetres. At the centre of the east end the holes came closer together. In the centre of each side apse a large block had been cut away through the roof above the string course, and a smaller block on either side of it. These larger holes may possibly have held the beam ends of a canopy; the smaller slots were probably meant to take the pins of a marble facing. Fragments of polished marble (including one with slightly concave surface and the marks of a bronze pin) were found on the floor, together with a piece of a small carved marble capital, and a glass *tessera* which showed that part of the building had once been decorated with mosaic.

The construction of the roof could not be determined by us. It had certainly not been vaulted in cut stone (like the baths at Abda); it may have been of wood; the vast quantity of small chalk chippings and lime dust that covered the floor to a depth of a metre and a half rather suggested a light rubble-and-lime vault such as still stands in the bath building at Raheiba.

The south chapel was a later addition to the church. Its apse is built against the wall of the south aisle, merely abutting on it, whereas chalk ashlar is usually well bonded. The talus, which we have seen to be also later than the church, was put up to counteract a bulge in the original apse wall, whose stones were actually splitting and pushing outwards, and as it runs on to the back of the south chapel apse, it must be either contemporary with or later than that building also. At a still later period the new apse was found to be weak, and was therefore buttressed by a skin wall, 0.40 m. thick, which has now, in its turn, developed a pronounced bulge.

The nave of the chapel was cut short at the west end to form a small chamber communicating by an arched door with the south aisle of the main church, and giving access by a low door crowned with a flat arch of wide, thin slabs to a second chapel. The apse of this is of the same masonry, and boasts the same string-course as is found in the original church, but the chapel is undoubtedly of considerably later date. The south wall, of the roughest rubble masonry, abuts on the late talus of the campanile, and runs at a very different angle from the other walls. In it there are three windows, three metres above ground, and seventy centimetres wide. The walls must have been mud-washed. On the apse are traces of paintings, and two holes cut in its dome above the string-course may have been for the supports of a canopy. To the south of the church,

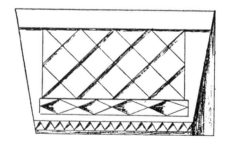

Fig. 15: Esbeita: capital in Loggia S. of N. church (monastery) 1 : 8

Fig. 16: Esbeita:
head of post
N. church
(monastery) 1 : 9

and in connection with it, there extended a large building forming a complete *insula*. Probably it was a monastery. Unfortunately it was dreadfully ruined, and presented, therefore, few features of interest; little more than the ground plan could be made out, and some details even of the plan were too conjectural to be drawn. The building was divided into two main parts and an annexe. The eastern part consisted of a large court or garden, with a straight range of six cells opening on to it. The western part had a large, irregular courtyard surrounded on three sides by vaulted chambers. The door was in the south wall. A narrow vaulted passage in the north-west corner of the court leads through into a chamber from which, it would seem, a door under the campanile gave access to the church. An open space, lying behind this chamber, separated the monastery buildings from the wall of the south chapel. On the other side of the chamber, in the recess between the main or public door of the church and the north-west corner of the monastery, was an open *diwan* or loggia, having two arches that gave upon the church square. The arches rested on capitals, decorated with trellis pattern (Fig. 15), and two post heads (Fig. 16) found here may have formed part of a balustrade separating the loggia from the street. One of the rooms on the west side was occupied by a large, open, stone-lined tank; in the adjoining small courtyard there was a cistern. The southern annexe consisted of five rooms opening into a small court, the whole laid out on a different angle to the main block, and on a plan adapted to the lines of existing streets; it was ill-built and is particularly ruinous.

The central was the most ruined of the three Esbeita churches

(Fig. 17). The narthex, which, thanks to the narrowness of the ground-area, was contracted to the width of a mere passage, was heaped so high with debris that but little of the screen wall was visible, and the position of the three doorways could only be approximately planned. Inside the church there was no great depth of rubbish over the floor; its whole area was strewn with column-drums (having a diameter of 0.52 m.); but none of these was in place, and the intercolumniation was therefore uncertain. Of the three apses only that of the south aisle remains intact; the

The Central Church

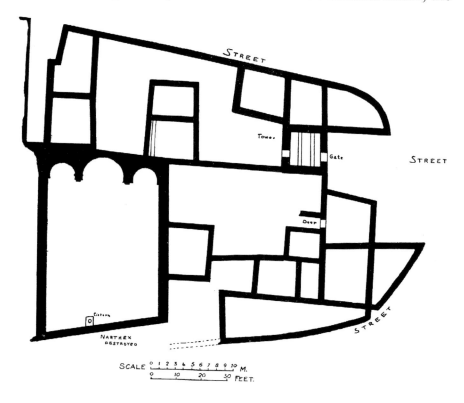

Fig. 17: Esbeita: central church.

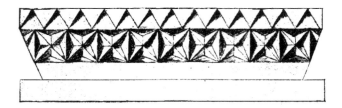

Fig. 18: three-sided pilaster-head,
central church. (1 : 8)

top of the central apse and the whole of that of the north aisle
have collapsed. The apses are as usual of chalk ashlar: probably
they were once painted (Plate XIX, 1).

The south wall is standing to a height of five metres and has
no windows: the lighting of the church must therefore have been
by a clerestory. There does not seem to have been a triforium.
Over the south apse there are no traces left of an upper chamber.
The south wall, which stands high above the top of this apse, is
of flimsy construction, not strong enough to take the outward
thrust of an upper vault, and shows no signs even of pilasters to
support the springers of the arch-ribs of the aisle roof proper. On
the other hand there are scattered about in the church several
pilaster-heads (Figs. 18, 19), roughly decorated with geometrical
carvings and one large bracket (Fig. 20) which has no projection
for in-bonding. Presumably, therefore, there were pilasters butted

Fig. 19: Esbeita: pilaster-head,
central church. (1 : 8)

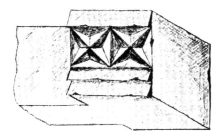

Fig. 20: Esbeita: bracket,
central church. (1 : 8)

against the wall, but not bonded in to it, which supported the cross-ribs of the vault; but such jerry-building would not allow of a second storey. The side aisles must have been quite low, and the height of the south wall is due to its being the back wall of the monastic building beyond.

How the church was roofed it is impossible to say. There was not sufficient debris to account for a rubble and cement vault supported on ashlar ribs, and the stone voussoirs lying about were not enough for the arches that certainly existed, much less for any ashlar vaulting. No traces of burnt wood were visible on

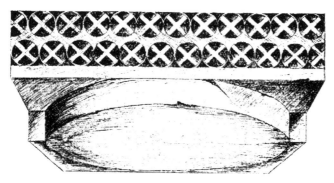

Fig. 21: Esbeita: engaged column-drum, central church. (1 : 8)

the surface; but on the whole we inclined rather to the theory of a roof of timber overlaid with earth lying across the rib arches.

The cistern-mouth, usually found in the middle of the outer court, was in this case inside the church, at the west end of the central aisle. Close by this was a drum of an engaged column having a narrow square cap with rosettes carved along its edge (Fig 17).

Attached to the church was a monastic building (see Plan, Fig. 17) which occupied the greater part of the *insula*. The main entrance was at the south end, under a tower flanked by two irregularly projecting wings and fronting on a small open space. This is the gateway figured by Palmer (*Desert of Exodus* ii, 375), the most elaborately decorated piece of architecture in the town; but since Palmer's day it has been largely destroyed – the carved jambs have fallen down and the lintel with its curious heraldic ornament has apparently been removed and sold. The tower, which is solidly built, still stands two storeys high and seems to have had a third storey. Passing through its lower chamber one enters a small irregular courtyard with a cistern in its centre, a room on either side and two facing the gateway; past these a narrow passage leads to a small courtyard with two rooms fronting on it. In the middle of the west wall of the first court there seems to have been a doorway, but it is almost completely obliterated by piles of debris. It gave access to a third courtyard surrounded on all sides by chambers; these buildings were all two storeys high. In the middle of the south side was a passage leading to the two rooms of the projecting south-west wing. From the north-west corner, doors through two adjoining rooms led to the narrow space between the screen-wall of the church and the enceinte wall, which in this church took the place of the ordinary forecourt.

The whole building was, with the exception of its front door, devoid of ornament; it was also in so ruinous a state that its plan was difficult to determine and in some smaller respects is incomplete.

The South Church

The south church was of the regular plan (Fig. 22). Its forecourt or narthex, separated from the body of the church by the usual screen-wall of chalk ashlar pierced by three arched doors, was small and sufficiently narrow to be vaulted over; a door at its south end led to the ground-floor chamber of the campanile, now much destroyed but recognizable by its complex of constructional walls and vaulting. This tower was probably never very high, as its walls are not particularly thick; at present it consists of two low storeys, each lit by a window in its south wall. These windows were shielded from profane view by a high, thin wall, which, running in an irregular curve, enclosed a sort of light-well and shut off this face of the tower from the public street.

The east end of the church was standing fairly complete (Plate XIX, 2). There were three apses forming the ends of the three aisles: the two smaller of these had arched apsidal recesses, with chamfered edges whereon was indented moulding, let into their back walls; the larger central apse had round its arch a simple, herring-bone incised pattern; but otherwise the apses were quite, plain without even a string-course to emphasize the springers of the dome. The side apses had each three square holes cut in the roof as if for a baldachino.

The aisles were separated by arcades of six columns decorated with bands, incised or in relief: the drums showed a diameter of 0.55 m. and there was a space of 2.05 m. between the columns. The voussoirs were plain. No capitals were visible on the surface of the ruins. Part of a capital carved in chalk with a simple tooth moulding was found, but

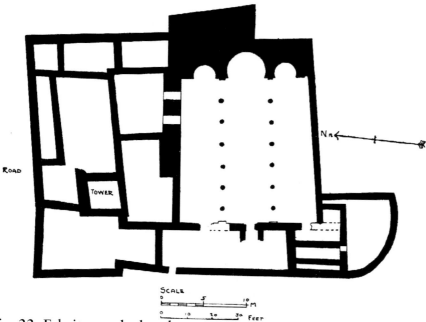

Fig. 22: Esbeita south church

it was on a small scale and probably came from a door.

Over each side apse was a vaulted chamber with walls of chalk ashlar, but these seem to have been walled-off on the west side and it is difficult to see how access to them was obtained. The north wall of the church stands fairly high with no sign of windows, and had monastery buildings against it. The south wall (ruined down to ground level) was too thin to have supported more than a single storey; the church must therefore have been lighted by a clerestory, but there was no ambulatory connected with the chambers over the side apses. These chambers do not seem to be merely constructional, so were probably approached by stairs from the side aisles.

The church was singularly barren of stone-carving; on the other hand it showed more traces than remained elsewhere of the *tempera* painting which must have been the commonest form of church decoration.

On the central apse no more than a few faint traces of colour survived. In the southern apse alone could any coherent design be distinguished, and here the colours had faded under exposure to the light, most of the surface had been scraped away by iconoclasts, and rain-water had brought down lime from the upper ruins and left a thick white deposit over the whole wall-face. Only by wetting the stone were we able to make out and roughly to sketch the original painting. The subject was the Transfiguration. In the centre is Christ, full-face, with hands raised and brought together over the breast. The *chiton* was seemingly of light pink edged with gold, the *himation* of dark blue; the halo was a plain yellow ring with white centre; the vesica of light pink. The figure was too much damaged to be copied. Below the feet is a semi-prostrate figure, probably of S. Peter, and beyond, on the spectator's left, a kneeling figure identified by a fragmentary inscription ...ANNIC, in red paint, as S. John; turning half-round to the front he raises his left hand, as if pointing to Christ. A few lines on the right of the vesica are all that is left of S. James. On either side of the apse, a little distance from the central group, a blurred mass of red colour seems to represent figures standing on a slightly higher level than the Apostles: these are presumably Moses and Elijah. Below the feet of the figures is a broad red band. The tooth-pattern round the arch of the small recess was picked out in red and blue, and its vault was roughly painted in red with a coarse network pattern, each mesh having a cross as filling-ornament. The recess in the northern apse was similarly decorated, but the design on this apse itself was indistinguishable.

It is clear that Esbeita came to a violent end. All the gates of the town have been blocked with roughly-built barriers of stone, and stone barricades have been piled across many of the streets; everything points to a desperate attempt to hold the place against an enemy who ultimately took it. Moreover the whole evidence of the ruins is to the effect that the town's occupation ceased suddenly and uniformly. There are many cases of alteration or reconstruction of buildings, such as must occur in the life of any town, but there are no signs of gradual decadence or of practical desertion. Here and there the stones of fallen walls have been used to make new water-runnels, leading to such cisterns as were not blocked by debris, but this is clearly the work of nomads who visited a site already in ruins. The water-courses block streets or run through house-sites: many are of comparatively recent date, several are still used by the Arabs. It all looks as if the people of Esbeita had left the town one day in a body, and had never returned to it, and their houses had fallen to decay simply for want of anyone to repair them.

The beginnings of the town are almost as clearly defined. The alterations and rebuildings show no development, just as they show no decadence; considering the poor construction of the houses, they are indeed remarkably few. There are no remains that point to a time before the building of the town on its present lines, nothing that goes back to a pre-Byzantine date. The earliest pottery found upon the site is not earlier than the third and may well be as late as the fifth century AD; the rubbish heaps of the town are small – very different from those of Khalasa – and argue a short period of occupation, Though the site is fairly deep in debris, yet, as it stands upon a shelf of rock, it is not difficult to see that there is nothing earlier underlying the present buildings. What Palmer took to be the remains of a broad, early wall running round outside the present limits of the town is really only the earth and stone water-channel of which mention has been made above. Esbeita is a Byzantine town pure and simple, founded not very early in the Christian era and destroyed, not long afterwards, by the Arab conquest.

Zephath and Hormah

Palmer (*Desert of the Exodus*, ii, p. 379), following Rowlands, identifies Esbeita and Mishrafa with Zephath and Hormah, scene of the discomfiture of the mutinous Israelites when, after the return of the spies, they attempted a direct advance into Palestine. This identification has been followed by other writers. Palmer supposes that Mishrafa was originally Zephath of the Amorites, and that the name was later transferred to the more important lower town (Esbeita), when the Israelites gave the name of Hormah to the hill fort on the occasion of its destruction at their hands.

All archaeological evidence absolutely contradicts any such theory. Neither Mishrafa nor Esbeita had anything to do with Israelites or Amorites, or existed before the Christian era.

The identification was a purely fanciful one, based on the similarity between the names Zephath and Esbeita. Should it be argued that the archaeological evidence is at best negative, and that Esbeita may have inherited the name Zephath though on a new site, and that the ruins of the older town may have escaped our notice in the neighbourhood, we cannot, of course, deny this possibility. But it must be pointed out that in the biblical account of the raid on the land of deferred promise (Numbers xiv, 45) mention is not made of Zephath, but only of Hormah. Even if in this context Hormah is a proper name rather than meaning 'destruction', it is a name that could be applied to any scene of defeat; thus in Numbers xxi, 3, it is given to Canaanite cities in the neighbourhood of Arad destroyed by the Israelites. This Hormah, therefore, is not the same as that of Numbers xiv, 45. Only in Judges i, 17, are Zephath and Hormah coupled together. In fact, there is nothing in the Bible record to connect Zephath with the abortive invasion of Palestine by the mutineers against Moses. The only Bible reference to Zephath (Judges i, 17) would seem to place it farther north, in the neighbourhood of Arad, Gaza, and Askelon; there is nothing except a resemblance of names to connect Zephath with Esbeita. Zephath, Palmer says, means a watch-tower, which description is not applicable to Esbeita (and his theory of the transference of names is hardly a tenable one); and the actual evidence afforded by the sites definitely excludes their antiquity.

Five thousand yards from Esbeita, on the opposite side of the valley, are the ruins known as Mishrafa. Here, between two wadies which run into the great Wady Migrih, there juts out a long spur of high ground with steeply sloping sides ending in a limestone outcrop which stands sheer two hundred feet over the flint-strewn slopes of the valley's edge. Behind, the spur widens and divides, Y-shape, the two arms like cols leading back to the high table-land of the Negeb and separated by the cup-like depression of a deep wady head.

Mishrafa

Approached from Wady Migrih, especially if one be coming from the north, the appearance of the place is very striking (Plate XVI, 1). Buildings can be seen crowning the hill-top; square towers of ashlar masonry rise from its edge; and at intervals other towers, their feet planted twenty or thirty feet down the scree slopes, lean like great bastions against the scarped face of the rock.

On a nearer view the place is less impressive. Behind, across the neck of the spur, runs a flimsy dry-stone wall, never of more than a man's height, with a narrow arched gateway not even defended by a tower.[1] Of the enclosed area, a goodly proportion was taken up by

[1] Plans of Mishrafa (both bad) are given by Palmer, *P.E.F. Quarterly* 1871, and Musil, *Edom.*

three shallow basins or catch-pits lined with stones and mud, communicating by means of narrow openings with one another and with a debris-filled cistern.[1] They are, of course, intended for the conservation of rain-water, and they afforded the only supply available for the inhabitants of Mishrafa; but then these were hermits. There are only two buildings on the hill-top proper. One was a small house of three

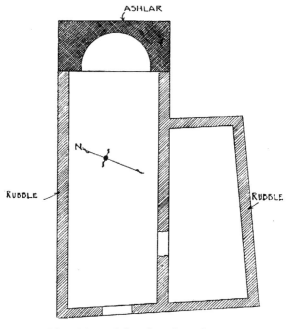

Fig. 23: Mishrafa, church. 1 : 260.

vaulted rooms opening into a courtyard; the other was a small church with one aisle, a single apse, and a small square-ended side chapel (Fig. 23). The apse was of chalk ashlar, the walls were poorly built of small rubble; there were no signs of decoration.

Besides these, there are some seventeen buildings along and against the cliff. Every one of these apparently consisted of a small two-roomed house of chalk ashlar, built low down against the rock face (the bastions of our first distant view), and of a smaller square tower on the edge of the hill-top, seemingly

---

[1] These are the stone circles mistaken by Palmer for the remains of a prehistoric fort.

independent, but really connected with the lower building by a shaft hollowed out through the rock. There can be no doubt that this is a monastic community, a 'laura' wherein each recluse (or pair of recluses) had two lower cells and an upper tower, while the church served their common need, and the house on the hill-top was perhaps the guest-house or the lodging of the brother superior.

There is no trace of early work in stone, and no early pottery visible upon the surface; and as the rocky surface is quite bare of soil, it can be safely affirmed that there is nothing below ground older than the existing building. Mishrafa, on its exposed hill-top, looking over a barren land, was not likely to gather about it the houses of lay settlers, as did probably the monasteries of Esbeita; it ended as it began, a hermitage. Though monastic buildings are common enough in this southern country, as at Tell Sawa, Abda, and El Auja, yet this is interesting as the only example that we found of a hermitage retaining the system of isolated cells gathered about a common centre.

The town of Abda is built upon the top and down the steeply shelving face of an isolated rocky spur, some three hundred feet high, which should connect with the eastern hills, but runs out into the broad valley wherein join the torrent-beds of Wady Ramliya and Wady Murra. As one climbs over the low ridges (that to the south-west shuts off the upper waters of the Wady Ramliya), and first comes in sight of Abda, the view is an impressive one (Plate XXIV, 1). The town is seen in profile. Upon the summit of the hill, which seems higher than it really is, rise the long walls of the well-preserved fort; the well-nigh precipitous face of the rock is blotched with black cavern mouths, half masked by the honey-coloured masonry of their ruined house fronts. At first, indeed, these caves are the only evidence of man's occupation visible; but as one comes closer the whole slope from sky-line to hill's foot is found to be a mass of tumbled ruin. The rock face has been cut into terraces – four irregular steps upon which stood houses whose front rooms were of ashlar masonry

Abda

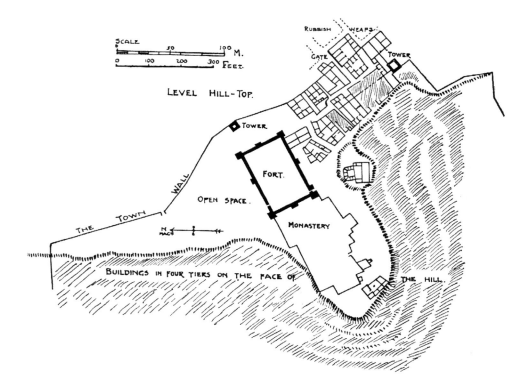

Fig. 24: Abda: sketch plan of upper town.

backed against the rock face, while their rear rooms were caverns hewn in the rock itself. When the tiers approached too closely, the floors of upper caverns have collapsed into those below. Not the buildings only, but often the rock walls themselves have fallen forwards and crushed the houses of the lower terraces; the paths that joined them have fallen away or been buried deep in debris.

These ruins occupy the two sides of a small tongue projecting westwards from the main block of the hill (Fig. 24). The flat summit of the spur is entirely taken up by one great complex of buildings. At the eastern or inland end of this is a fortress (Plate

XXIV, 2), a long rectangle whose heavy ashlar walls with square projecting towers enclose a wide area unoccupied by buildings (Plate XXIII, 2); at the west end, overlooking the town, is a monastic building amongst whose numerous chambers and courts can be distinguished the remains of two churches. To the south of the fort lay a small quarter composed for the most part of fairly large and well-built houses, probably those of officers of the garrison. The outer walls of them, fronting on the flat ground of the hill-top, were continuous and formed a defence-wall which was prolonged northward so as to enclose the fortress and a stretch of unoccupied land beyond it; it was a poor low wall of dry-stone rubble masonry, but was strengthened by two small ashlar towers two storeys high, one at its south end, one towards the north over against the east end of the fortress (Plate XXIV, 3). At either end the wall turned sharply down hill, and seems to have been carried round the whole area of the Lower Town; but it was too ruinous and fragmentary for its course to be followed with any certainty.[1]

Abda has been visited by several travellers, including Palmer, who made a rough plan of the fort; the site was carefully examined and planned in 1904, by the PP. Jaussen, Savignac, and Vincent, whose excellent publication in the Revue Biblique (Nouvelle série 1, 1904, pp. 403 – 424), had I but known of it, would have spared me the trouble of much repetition and would also have enabled me to re-examine and check certain points which, single-handed as I was, I missed altogether. Thus, engrossed in the town buildings, I failed to see either the 'Roman' camp on the northern point of the hill-top or the 'High Place' to the south of the Upper Town; for these I can only refer to the authority of the Jerusalem Mission. To compensate in some

---

[1] As marked on the plan in the *Revue Biblique* 1904, p. 404, it is not really the outer wall of the town at all. Nearly half the buildings lie outside its line as there suggested.

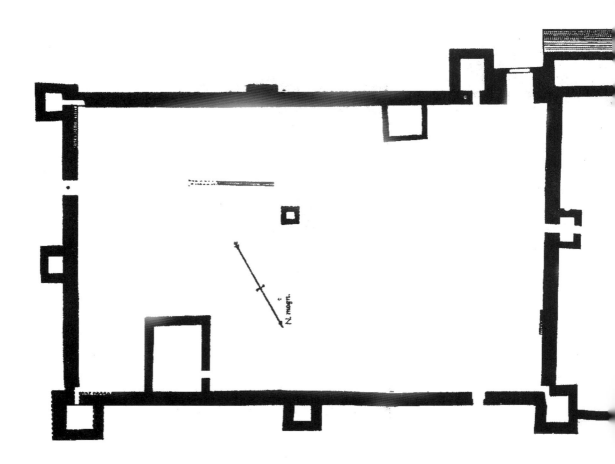

Fig. 25: Abda: fortress and monastery.

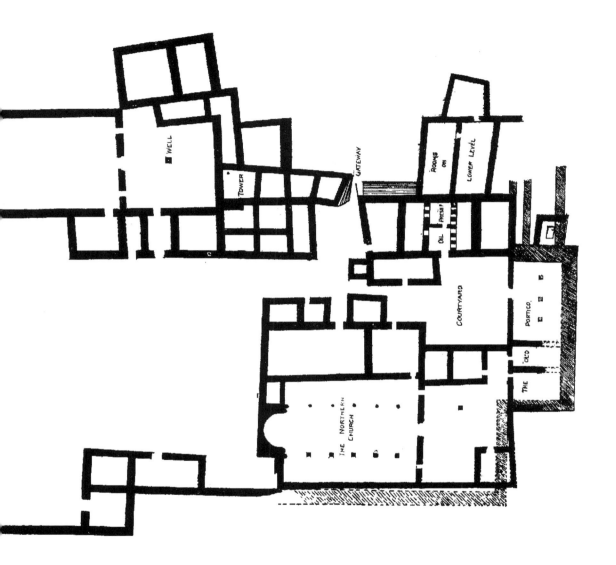

measure for this lapse, I discovered under the ruins of the monastery the remains of a great Nabatean temple, dedicated perhaps to the hero Obodas, whose tomb was at Eboda.

Between the east end of the fortress and the enceinte wall also beyond this, running under the rubbish heaps of the Byzantine town, there could be traced the walls of stone buildings which clearly were of earlier date than the houses now standing and had been intentionally destroyed, and their sites carefully levelled, at the time when the latter were built. From the debris that had been thrown into their ruined chambers to form the new plateau I picked out fragments of Greek pottery of the third or early second century B.C. It is obvious, therefore, that we have here not the immediate predecessor of Byzantine Eboda, but a settlement separated from it by the lapse of several centuries, the Nabatean town where Obodas was worshipped.

The buildings that form the western front of the monastic building are very remarkable (Fig. 25). The point of the tongue of rock has been levelled and left open; from this there rises a massive retaining-wall six metres high, forming a podium to the building above. The floor, supported by a series of cross walls joined by rough arches or horizontal tie-slabs, was flush with the general floor-level of the buildings behind; for this podium only masked a natural rise of the rock from the western tongue to the main plateau on which lay the monastery and fort. Solid as the structure was, much of it had collapsed in a cascade of great wall-blocks and column drums, but on what remained the bases and even the lower parts of the shafts of several columns were still to be seen standing in their original positions. The buildings above were at first sight so confused a complex of irrelevant walls that former visitors had abandoned the site as of little interest. On a closer view, however, evidence of two distinct periods was obvious. The columns still in position had been joined together by curtain-walls which had concealed their existence, and in these walls were re-used building-blocks and fragments of cornice and ceiling. The columns were not originally part of the existing monastic building. Moreover, the retaining wall of the podium and one or two other walls in its neighbourhood are quite distinct in character from those of the monastery, the fort, and the houses of the town. The stones are larger and better cut. They seem to come from a different quarry, for instead of being honey-coloured they are more nearly white, hard, and very rich in fossils (fossils are rare in the yellow limestone). Generally, too, these stones are rectangular, whereas the Byzantine masons, influenced by Roman tradition, preferred to cut their stones wedge-shaped behind so as to bind in better with the rubble filling of the walls Even with these criteria it was not always easy to distinguish relative dates, for the later builders not only incorporated whole existing walls in their own scheme of things, but also built new walls out of old material; such reconstructions could only be distinguished by the misplacing of stones (*e.g.* the dressed face might be laid downwards) or by an admixture of yellow stones. However, by eliminating what is obviously late, *e.g.* the walls that block the colonnade, the stair-tower at its south end, and the small chambers in the north-west angle, we are left with what can only be the western facade of a great classical temple. The lofty podium twenty-three metres long and crowned by a double row of columns, projected nine metres in advance of the main front which, if the building was symmetrical, had a total width of fifty metres. On the south the angle formed by the projection of the podium was filled by two long parallel walls which seem to have contained a staircase or ramp giving access to the temple from the lower ground of the hill's point. The columns of the outer row were six in number, of which five could be traced; they were regularly spaced; the bases were square, or stood on square blocks raised slightly above pavement level – the drums measure 0. 55 m. in diameter; the capitals were simple, a square cap over a simple roll moulding. The inner row consisted of eight columns arranged in two groups of four each with a wider spacing between the groups; the drums of the columns had a diameter of 0.60 m., the bases are round (Fig. 26). The southernmost column of this inner row lies almost as it fell; the capital is missing, but the remaining drums give a total height of 3. 60 m. for the shaft, a very probable measurement. On looking more closely at the ruins of the northern church we notice, first, that the two colonnades dividing the aisles differ in character, the north colonnade having square bases (the shafts are missing) while that on the south has round columns on round bases; secondly, that both the measurements of these, and their moulding, agree with those of the temple façade; and thirdly, that both rows of columns are continued westwards beyond the needs of the church, the western columns being embedded in and hidden by the screen wall. Further, one base appears in position in the atrium of the church. Clearly this is only the northern colonnade of the original peristyle temple, re-used without further change by the church builders. Probably excavation on the south side of the temple site would bring to light traces of the corresponding colonnade under the heap of debris that there cumbers the ground. The north wall of the temple has disappeared, as has the wall of the church, but the two seem to have coincided. Unfortunately the cella has been completely destroyed, or, if traces of it remain, they are buried under the chambers and courts of the monastery. This great temple, grandiose in plan but extremely simple in detail, is certainly not of Roman origin;[1] it must, together with the houses that lay along the hill-top behind it, which were dated by pottery fragments to the second or third century B.C., belong to the Nabatean Kingdom of Petra. It is not surprising to find an important Nabatean outpost here. Its existence indeed was known from the remark about the cult of Obodas practised here, quoted from Ouranios by Stephen of Byzantium; its *raison d'etre* is explained by its position between Petra and the Mediterranean

---

[1] Not only is its style different from what analogy would lead us to expect in a Romano-Syrian temple of imperial date, but the methods of construction are quite un-Roman. An imperial temple of this size and in this position would not have had mere dry-stone foundations, with the material for concrete abounding everywhere.

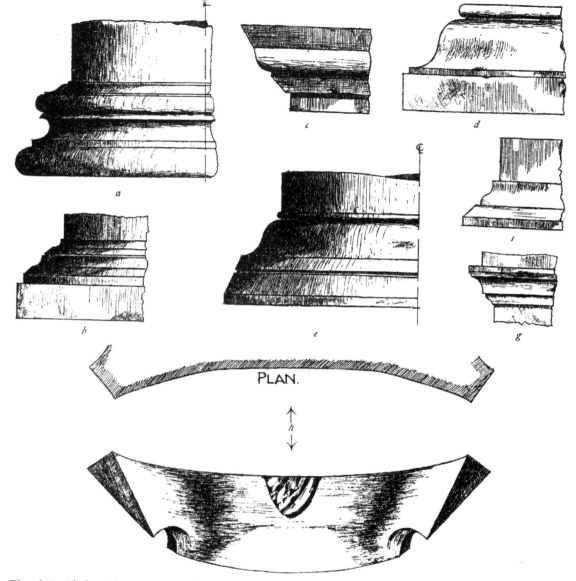

Fig. 26: Abda: Limestone architectual members from site of North Church. 1 : 8

a. Column base in north church.
b. Column on square pedestal in chamber to west.
c. Cornice near east end.
d. Cornice (or base ?) outside east end.

e. Column base at east end
f. Cornice, est end
g. String course in south-east chamber.
h. Sketch of plain capitals.

ports. It is true that the Tabula Peutingeriana puts Eboda on the road between Elusa (Khalasa) and Aila, and does not show any cross-connection between Eboda and Petra; but by the time that map was compiled the trade of Petra had ceased to exist. Moreover, it is true that, while there is a road from Khalasa to Abda, this road, in the neighbourhood of Abda itself, is extremely bad. From Abda a reasonably good road runs south to Sahala, and this is perhaps the road of the Peutinger Table. From Abda to Petra two roads are possible, but both are bad and one is not really practicable for a laden caravan. The best Petra road runs direct from Khalasa[1] to Nagb el Gharib, leaving Abda to the south-west, then crosses the Wady Murra, runs past Ain Gattar and W. Merzaba (being here called the Darb Sultaneh, the King's Highway) and joining the Kurnub road at Ain Weiba makes across the Araba to Petra. Eboda therefore does not lie on the main road from Petra to the Mediterranean, but it is between two roads, and to guard a desert track from the raids of nomad tribes there is required not so much a stationary fort as a base for patrols. Abda may well have served such a purpose; the position of the hill, rising out of a large and fairly fertile plain, and perhaps also some religious considerations, may have determined the actual situation of the town. When Petra was destroyed by the Romans, Eboda was no longer necessary and seems to have been deserted, falling gradually into decay. Only when the Khalasa – Aila route was revived, as the Peutinger Table shows that it was, did the old site again become important, and the ruins of the Nabatean town were razed or re-used for the construction of the Byzantine fort and monastery.

I have not mentioned here the Roman camp lying to the north of the town.[2] Judging by its plan, it is of quite late imperial date.

---

[1] *See* on p. 189 a Nabatean inscription found by us at Khalasa, illustrating the through connection between the two towns. Khalasa itself may even have been a Nabatean foundation.
[2] *See Revue Biblique*, 1904, p. 414.

Though I did not see it, I venture to doubt the theory put forward by its discoverers that it was dismantled and that the fortress and wall-tower were built out of its material. The stone dressing of these buildings is precisely in keeping with their period, identical with that of Esbeita and El Auja; with all due caution I should suggest that the camp was a rather rough and temporary affair not much earlier in date than the fort itself, possibly even used while the fort was building.

Perhaps the caves were all originally Nabatean tombs re-used as dwelling places by the Byzantine settlers. If so, they were so radically re-cut by these latter as to lose all their original character. It is equally possible that many of them were used in the earlier as in the later period for houses, and that the Nabatean town extended down the rock face as well as over part of the upper plateau. However that may be, the great tomb south of the town (Fig. 27) is the only one that preserves its funerary niches, and in it alone were found remains of Nabatean tomb-ornament. Unfortunately the stelae that were built into the wall of its little vaulted fore-chapel had borne only painted inscriptions of which now no trace remains; only the lintel and door jambs (Figs. 28, 29) were carved, and one stela adorned with two small busts long since defaced (Fig. 30).

The portico of the Nabatean Temple was, as we have seen,

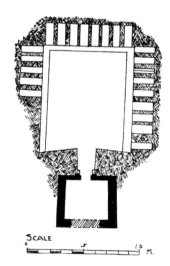

SCALE

Fig. 27: Abda: great rock tomb.

Fig. 28: Abda: carved lintel. 1 : 9

divided up by curtain walls into small cells. The old ramp or staircase had been destroyed, and to replace it a small stair tower was built with steps radiating from a central pillar. Behind the portico was a small irregular courtyard surrounded by vaulted cells; one of these on the south seems to have been used as an oil-press. A cell at the north end of the portico communicated by a small doorway with carved capitals (Fig. 31) with the narthex or ante-chapel of the north church. Here, as in the portico, the

The Monastery

flagstones of the old temple peristyle were preserved, as also its columns; two of the latter, however, had been shifted to flank the doorway in the screen-wall giving on the central aisle. There was only one apse, supported on either side by two columns; the side aisles were square ended, though that on the south seems to have had a small vaulted

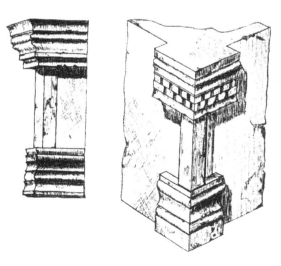

Fig. 29: Abda: carved Jambs. 1 : 7

room at its east end. A large capital with rude carvings of a bird and a man (Plate XXIV, 4), a decorated *voussoir* and a moulded string-course (Fig. 32) seem to belong to the apse. The church was dreadfully ruined and presented few points of interest.

From the small courtyard a narrow passage led between irregularly built chambers, past a gateway in the south

Fig. 30: Abda: stela with 1 : 8

wall, into the Great Court, a large open space stretching from the east end of the north church to the fort and past the main north wall to the south church; chambers lined a part of its north and south sides. On the south a door gave access through a vaulted passage to the atrium of the south church; this as usual was surrounded by cells. To the west stood the campanile; in the centre was a large reservoir. The screen door giving on the central

Fig. 31: Abda: carved capital in soft limestone of door-jamb in room west of north church. 1 : 7

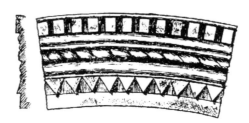

Fig. 32: Abda: moulded string-course. 1 : 8

aisle was elaborately decorated with pilasters and crosses with simple capitals and a plain moulded lintel (Fig. 33). The east end was a high piled mass of débris, but the three apses seem to have been unusually deep, their sides being continued by a vaulted passage prolonging the colonnades. Only one column was in place, so that the intercolumniation remains uncertain. At the east end, on the line of the north colonnáde, there was found in the rubbish covering the floor a marble slab measuring 1.50 m. by 0. 50 m. bearing the funerary inscription of Zacharias, son of Erasinus (Fig. 34 and p. 234) Probably this stone gives the date

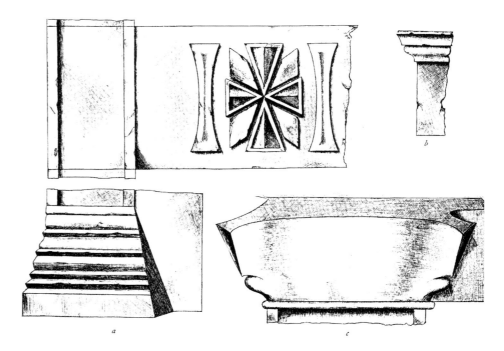

Fig. 33: Abda: south church. Details of main door in screen. 1 : 16

a. Jambs (same on North side)
b. Lintel.
c. Capital.

of the consecration of the church, 581 A.D. A curious point was that the wall of the corner tower of the fort was prolonged over the roof of the apse – an obvious gain from the defensive point of view; and this may well be an argument for the monastery and fort being contemporary.

The fort is simply a rectangle, with square angle and side bastions; the walls are from 1.20 m. to 2.00 m. thick. In the corners are stairways to give access to the wall tops and towers (Plate XXV, 1). There are no window apertures. The towers consisted of two storeys, their chambers roofed in the usual way with stone arches and cross-slabs. The main doorway was in the south-west corner, defended by two flanking towers. The doorways leading to the towers had flat lintels with relieving arches above: the small north gateway had a double arch – a wider and higher arch on the inner wall-face, and a smaller arch on the outside. Above the door, on the outer wall-face, was a cross and the monogram IMΓ. In the door-jambs AW were the deep slots for the locking-beams. In the east wall was a small undefended gateway leading to the intramural area behind the wall tower. The interior of the fort was empty except for some low foundations in the north-east corner, apparently those of a platform rather than of a room, and of a similar low structure

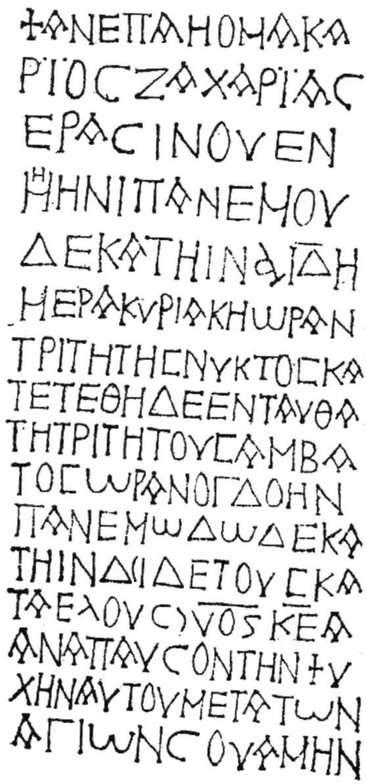

The Fort

Fig. 34: Abda: south church. Inscription (*see* pp. 186 – 187) reproduced from a blackened squeeze. 1 : 14

against the south wall. There was a large cistern in the middle of the open area, with the ruins of a cistern-house above it, and remains of an open drain leading to it from the east gate. Towards the north-west of the enclosure a curious rock, artificially cut, seems to have been a sort of rostrum. The western gate is covered by debris, and its existence was not satisfactorily verified.

The building is poor. The stones of the outer face are small, but well cut; the inner face is, in parts, of good ashlar in parts of coursed rubble. The wall faces are lightly pointed with lime, the interior grouting is all with mud. The work looks both hasty and late. In all parts of the site the same remark holds good, and, moreover, one finds many traces of work actually left unfinished – capitals half-carved, rock-hewn chambers left incomplete – a state of things quite consistent with a wholesale remodelling or complete building of the town as late as 581 A.D., the date of the south church inscription (Fig. 34), and with its equally complete destruction in the middle of the seventh century by the Arab invaders. The small size of the rubbish heaps on the hill-top agrees with the theory of a brief life for the town. Such a theory must, of course, be reconciled with the appearance of Eboda on the Peutinger Table. If it be urged that that road map was compiled during the period when we suppose Eboda to have been virtually non-existent, it can at least be said on the other hand (a) that

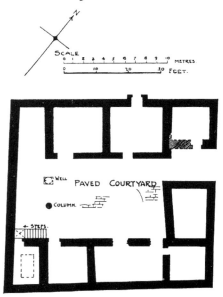

Fig. 35: Abda: isolated building on hill-top.

whatever the date of the map as a whole, we do not know to what recensions and additions it was subject, (b) that our theory does not exclude the existence of a small settlement at Eboda no less unimportant than other stations in the Sinaitic desert which actually appear on the Peutinger maps. Judging from surface indications, Abda would seem to have been built about Justinian's time, on a Nabatean site which for many years had been either deserted or sparsely settled.

The houses of the Upper Town, lining both sides of a street running nearly north by south, are all modifications of the usual courtyard type. The most elaborate is an isolated building (Fig. 35) lying outside the walls to the south (the 'fortin'of the map in the *Revue Biblique*); its front door had carved capitals (Fig. 36), and an outside staircase gave access to the second storey. Close to the south wall of the fort, on a slightly lower ledge of

Fig. 36: Abda: Limestone capital from door of isolated building. 1 : 8

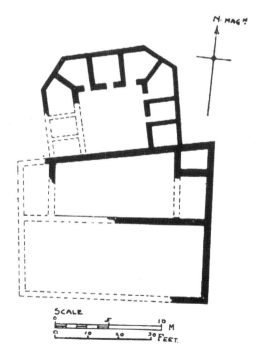

Fig. 37: Abda: building on hilltop south of fort

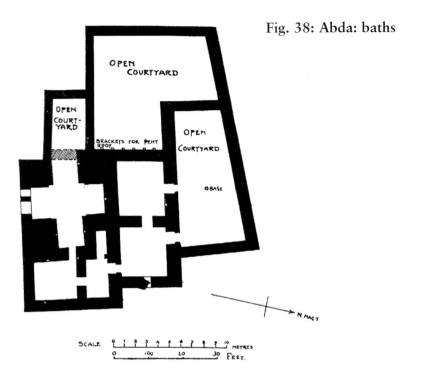

Fig. 38: Abda: baths

the rock, were the fragmentary ruins of a small building precisely like that outside the walls of Esbeita. Another similar building, also much ruined, lay on the flat ground south of the hill, a little way from the town. A hole had recently been dug in the middle of this, and showed a heavy deposit of ashes; the small cells at the north end were stone-flagged, and the walls contained lime (Fig. 37).

On the plain west of the town stands a small, well-preserved bath-house (Fig. 38). Two or three rooms have been almost wholly demolished, and the stones removed for terracing neighbouring fields; but of other rooms even the vaulted roofs of finely cut and fitted ashlar are almost intact (Plates XXI, XXII, 1). The little dome, supported on four arches, has collapsed (Plate XXV, 2). The hot air flues in the walls are noticeable, and seem to communicate with a furnace in the apparently solid mass of masonry which stands in an angle of the domed chamber; this would have been approached from outside, where there was a pent roof between two small courtyards; but the mass of fallen stones prevented the verification of this theory. On a jamb of the main doorway was a fragmentary Greek graffito 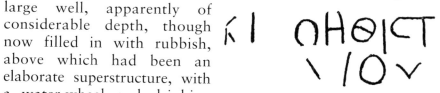 (Fig. 39). By the baths was a large well, apparently of considerable depth, though now filled in with rubbish, above which had been an elaborate superstructure, with a water-wheel and drinking troughs for cattle (Fig. 40).

Fig. 39. Abda: Greek graffito.

Not many cisterns were visible amongst the town ruins, probably because of the ruined condition of the site rather than through any real lack of water-storage; one house standing on the end of the promontory below the temple façade had a courtyard cistern of unusual size. Probably here, as at Raheiba, the inhabitants relied mainly upon stored water, and in case of need availed themselves of the big well just outside the town.

Fig. 40: Abda: well-house south-west of the monastery (for scale see Fig.37).

O WELL

In the caves of the Lower Town there was little of interest; crosses and rude decorative designs in red paint were not uncommon on the walls, gazelles and human figures appeared rarely; two graffiti only were seen, one 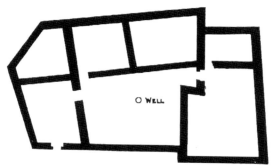 and another in Greek

ΔΟΜΝΑ
ΝΘΡ
ΟΘ
Λ

Fig. 41: Abda: Greek graffito.

faintly incised on the door-jamb of a rock-cut chamber (Fig. 41).

One point of interest about the town is its system of rubbish heaps. Here there could be seen very clearly what at other sites, *e.g.*, Raheiba and Esbeita, was present, but less noticeable, namely, that certain plots of ground were definitely put aside and marked out for the depositing of rubbish. Just outside the Upper Town, to the west, were rectangular areas surrounded by low walls, within which refuse might be shot: paths are left between the mounds, and a clear space separates them from the town wall – a sort of *pomoerium*! The rubbish heaps were quite low, very different from those of Khalasa, and did not point to any long period of occupation.

The whole plain around the town, with most of the hill-top not occupied by buildings, has been cultivated. The country is one of limestone chips, with but little flint, and there were not to be seen here the flint heaps or ridges that elsewhere marked the sites of ancient vineyards; but the ruins of one or two wine presses show that grapes were grown here also. About two miles out on the Rakhama road are two small square towers of good ashlar masonry, standing close to the roadside. Perhaps these are block-houses of the road patrols, not unlike those which the Turkish Government used to maintain along the Jaffa – Gaza post-road, or that which seems to have stood at Ain Ghadian in the south, and at Nagb el Safa and Wady Figra near the Araba on the Kurnub road to Petra.

Beersheba   The Byzantine town of Birosabon has been so thoroughly destroyed that it calls for little comment. Not only have all the old buildings been razed to the ground, but even the cemeteries

Fig. 42: Beersheba: Balustrade and post-head. 1 : 8

have been plundered in the search for stones to be re-used in the building of the modern town that overlies the ancient site. Many inscriptions have been found here, of which the bulk have already been published, and many have been sold and carried away; others are built into modern houses; a few are stored in the Government Serai. All that we found we copied and publish here; but it is quite possible that some of them are already known. The ancient town was certainly a large one: its ruins can be traced over a wide area, and the cemeteries to the north-west are very extensive. The ruins of two churches could be seen, also a fragment of mosaic pavement, and heavy foundations in concrete; broken columns and fragments of moulded cornices or carvings are common in the houses of the modern town (Figs. 42, 43); but there was nothing to be planned, nor, apart from the inscriptions, anything of interest to be noted (Plates XXVI, XXVII).

So far as surface indications go, there was no really ancient settlement upon the site. Beersheba is in the 'tell' country, but here there is no tell, no fragments of pre-Roman pottery could be found. It would seem certain that in ancient times this town was

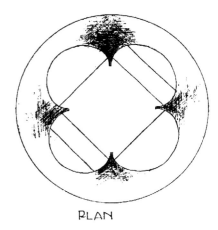

PLAN

Khalasa

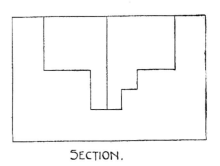

SECTION.

Fig. 43: Beersheba: font in
white limestone near the serai.
1 : 10

at Sheba (Tell el Seba), and
that Beersheba, the Wells of
Sheba, lay out in the open
tilth and pasture land where
nomads such as Abraham and
his sons would encamp at a
distance from the walled city.
This distinction between the
town and the watering-place
seems to be clearly drawn in
Joshua xix, 2 (cf. pp. 109-
110).

South of the barren
limestone hills which fringe
the Beersheba plain the
country opens out into wide
rolling sand-dunes, marked
out even more clearly as one
advances southwards by the
ruins of hedges that struggle
upwards through their
drifting yellow shroud to
mark square fields or
bordered roadways. Then a
sudden drop in the ground-
level brings one to the more
fertile soil of the Wady
Khalasa valley, a wide plain once all cultivated and still capable of
cultivation at the present day if only the water-supplies were
properly conserved as of old and the ground ploughed better than
with the crooked stick of the feckless Beduin. The hand of the
spoiler has been almost as busy at Khalasa as at Beersheba; stones
from its ruined walls have been and are still carried off to Gaza in
such quantities that 'Khalasa' has become there a synonym for
good quality limestone building-blocks. We could make out the

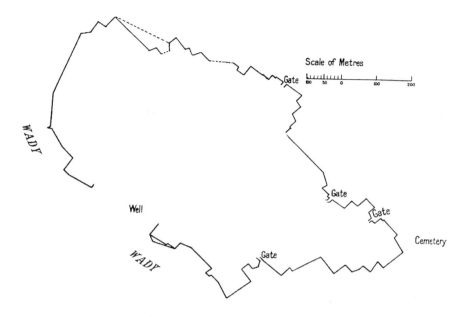

Fig. 44: Plan of Khalasa.

outline of the town but it was impossible to plan any of its buildings (Fig. 44).

Khalasa, the ancient Elusa, was perhaps a Nabatean foundation upon the trade route between Petra and the port of Gaza. There is no tell, nor did we find any very early potteries, but a Nabatean inscription (p. 188) takes us back into the pre-Christian period, and the size of the vast rubbish-heaps that surround the town point to its long life. It is mentioned as a seat of pagan worship by Jerome (Vita S. Hilarii; Comm. ad Jes. 15); and it figures prominently upon the Madeba map and upon the Peutinger Table. It is certainly distinguished in this way from the majority of the Byzantine cities in the south, which are of far later foundation. Most of the extant ruins known seem to be late in date; the inscriptions found here, with the exception of the Nabatean example previously quoted, all belong to the late Byzantine period, and it is quite possible that a good deal of the town was rebuilt when the other cities of the south were being founded. Amongst the coins found here were several of Constantine and Arcadius; Byzantine large brasses with M and DOMINIUS I PAULUS, etc., and some early Arab copper coins.

If Khalasa is the Elusath of Theodosius (*De situ Terrae Sanctae* xxvii),[1] then it was a recognized station upon the Jerusalem – Sinai road about 530 A.D. The last official mention of a bishop of Elusa is in 536 A.D., after which date the Saracens are described

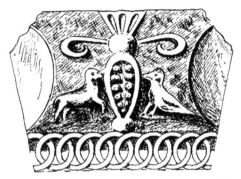

Fig. 45: Khalasa: Limestone capital from town (flat cut in two planes). 1 : 9

as giving trouble in the district; but Antoninus of Placentisa,[2] about the year 570 A.D., speaks of 'Elua (or Eluahal) in capite Eremi' upon the Sinai road and mentions a story of a bishop there, but contents himself with calling it a 'civitas'. This seems to be the last mention of it.

Probably Elusa shared the fate of the other southern cities and fell before the earlier Mohammedan invaders, perhaps a few years later than the rest because it lay further to the north. Beersheba we know to have been inhabited in Arab times.

---

[1] Corp. Script. Eccl. Lat., vol. 38, p.148
[2] Corp. Script. Eccl. Lat., vol. 38, p.211

The town lay some two hundred yards back from the east bank of the wady; but from the west bank a large building with very heavy walls projects forward over the bed of the torrent; this is probably the fort of the bishopric of Gaza. For the rest the town was only defended by the continuous though irregular line of its houses and garden-walls. In a clear space south of the fort, not enclosed by the walls, is the well that still serves the needs of travellers and of the few Beduin households encamped close by on the wady bank. The water is plentiful, but brackish and unpleasant. There are traces of other wells now filled in with debris. On the south side of the town, near the south-west corner, is a small gateway between two ruined towers; from this the outline of the town runs on in a series of

Fig. 46: Khalasa: marble capital from town. 1 : 9

rectangular returns, enclosing many small open courts or gardens, and at the south-east corner a building whose simple column bases give it some title to distinction. On the east side are two gates. The road leading from the southern of these, bordered by graveyards, runs to Kurnub; the northern gateway is more elaborately planned with its entrance set at an acute angle. Outside the walls lie great rubbish-heaps, their mound only broken by the lines of the roads, and in the north-east the mound reaches such a height as quite to dominate the town. The north part of the site is much ruined; here was the gateway through which the road ran north to Beersheba, and, by a fork just beyond the gates, north-west to Gaza: the broad tracks, bordered by hedges, can be traced for a considerable distance across the plain. A small fort, nearly isolated, and connected with the town only by a long double wall rose from the wady bank at the north-west corner of the site, separated by large gardens or pasture grounds from the bishop's fort to the south of it There were few buildings across the wady, but over the high land there the roads to Saadi and Raheiba were clearly defined by their overgrown hedges and piled sand-drifts. Along the south of the Saadi road lies a large cemetery from which we secured several inscriptions (see p. 182); here too were the ruins of what appeared to be a small funerary chapel decorated with four columns having carved capitals.

About 1 ¼ miles south-west of the town were the ruins of a fair-sized village of late Byzantine date, and a stopped-up well, lying on the east bank of the wady; remains of smaller hamlets or isolated farms cap most of the hillocks bordering the plain. It is clear that most of the once extensive agriculture of the neighbourhood must have been in the hands of this rural population, and the bulk of the townsfolk of Khalasa must have been engaged therefore in some form of trade – a trade of considerable importance, seeing that the area of Khalasa is ample for a population of twenty thousand souls. It is perhaps worth suggesting that as the town lies at the branch of the great Akaba trade-route along which, in the Byzantine period, caravans bringing silk from the Ceylon depots passed to the Mediterranean harbours and through Central Palestine to the wealthy cities of North Syria, the trade of Khalasa may have been the unravelling of Chinese and Indian fabrics, after which process the silk threads were re-woven with linen to form the ἡμισηρικόν of European commerce.

Saadi

From Khalasa a road nearly fifty feet wide, bordered by hedges, ran westward across the high plateau, climbed a sandy ridge, and then dropping to another wide plain dotted with low hills and ridges, wound between these to Saadi. Nowadays the hedges have spread untended, until the road has degenerated to a series of camel-tracks threading lengthways a broad belt of thorny scrub. Beyond the sand dunes, on the other hand, such modern cultivation as there is has destroyed hedges and tracks alike, and only here and there are vestiges of the old roadway. Then, three or four miles out from Khalasa, the road becomes clear again, passing beneath the ruined garden walls of some country villas lying at the foot of a long, low ridge of limestone to the right of the highway. Further along still the road is bordered, not by garden walls, but by a single line of small stone booths – doubtless such shops as line the main street of modern Bir el Seba – and so one reaches the ruins of the little town. Saadi was unwalled, its houses scattered over two or three low limestone knolls, all variants of the standard courtyard type (again like the modern houses of Bir el Seba), many standing in fair-sized gardens; a pleasant suburb of the more crowded business town of Khalasa.

The most prominent ruin was that of an oblong building set on a small knoll in the thickest part of the village, and in part

(1 : 9.)

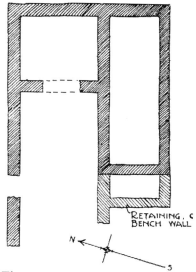

Fig. 47: Saadi: building at south end of town, and capital found in it. 1 : 200

supported by terrace walls; it boasted stone columns, but the plan, so far as it could be distinguished, was not that of a church. Immediately behind it was a well, recently cleared out, having stored water at a depth of 6.5 metres: on the well-head were hammered tribe marks ᑭ. Two large cisterns, one cleared out and containing water, which came to it from a catchment round the hillside, lay further to the south. In a building close by the cistern was found the well carved capital of a door impost (Fig. 47), and in another ruin beyond this was a stone having a simple piece of leaf ornament and a rough capital with chip-carved decoration

(Fig. 48). No other stone carvings or inscriptions were seen, nor were there any traces of pre-Byzantine settlement. So far as could be seen, the little village did not possess any church, or any building more important than the house of some landed 'effendi'. It seems to be simply the most favourable example of those agricultural hamlets which are found in the neighbourhood of Khalasa, and must have supplied the foodstuffs of the city workers; its position here is explained by the wide plain of tolerable soil that surrounds it.

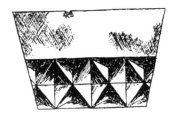

Fig. 48: Saadi: capital. 1 : 8

Not far away, across country, is another hamlet called Saadi el Raheiba: it lies on a hill-top looking over the Raheiba valley where this is joined by a tributary wady from the south-east. Most of its houses were miserable rubble-built affairs now fallen into hopeless ruin; but two small square ashlar towers still stand some twelve feet high, too full of debris for their character to be fixed. They may be watch-towers, under whose shelter poor people built their huts, and their position commanding the great valley road, immediately over against the far earlier watch-tower of Kasr el Raheiba, lends colour to this view, but there is no internal evidence forthcoming to support it.

Raheiba

The road from Khalasa runs for a short distance parallel with the Saadi road, a little to the north of it. Then winding round a hillock, where is the ruin of what might be a blockhouse, it descends a small pleasant wady between bare flint-strewn hills,[1] to work out between sand-hills into the broad Raheiba valley. This is a wide, shallow depression, between steeply shelving banks of

---

[1] From one of these, umm Athri, a number of speciments were collected to illustrate the peculiar natural fractures of these flints.

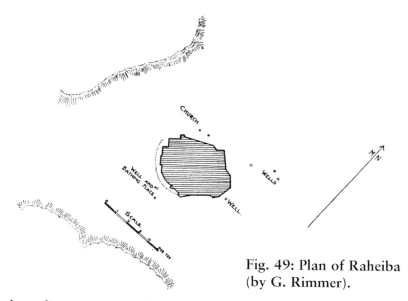

Fig. 49: Plan of Raheiba
(by G. Rimmer).

bare limestone, weathered into terraces and footed by heaps of
scree; the soil is good, and even now nearly the whole area is
cultivated by the Beduins. The great inland road to Egypt runs
down the valley; on the far side, on a spur jutting out from the
wall of hills called Tell el Kasr el Raheiba, are the barely
distinguishable ruins of a little fort that in the second millenium
B.C. guarded the trade route (see p. 52 – 53). Further up the valley
a side wady coming in from the west leads to Raheiba. One passes
first the ruins of a small village Iying in the wady amongst its
terraced fields; then the path climbs up the plateau, where we
found a crowd of Beduins watering their goats and camels at a
series of ancient cisterns which have recently been cleared out and
now store throughout the year a tolerable supply of water. On the
high land beyond these could be seen the ruins of Raheiba proper.
The town was a large one,[1] irregular in shape, and defended, as is

[1] Mr. Huntington's note in *Palestine and its Transformations*, p. 121, under-
estimates the size of these ruins, so much so that we are inclined to suppose that
he saw only those of the lower village.

usually the case, only by its continuous house and garden walls: its extreme length was 600 yards by 400 yards (Fig. 49). The ruins are still, as when Palmer saw them, a very abomination of desolation, the whole slope of the hill covered with tumbled stones and crumbling walls, through which it is difficult to pick a precarious way. Rubbish chokes the innumerable cisterns; the

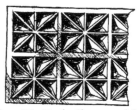

Fig. 50: Raheiba: architectual carvings. 1 : 8

courtyards are a tangle of briars; here and there the trunk of a tower, or the cracked curve of an apse, stand out above the rest, but the rain has washed out the poor mortar from their masonry, and an incautious movement will send what was yet a wall down in an avalanche of loose stones upon the formless heap below. Our photograph on Plate XXVIII, 1, serves to give some idea of this, the most lamentable ruin of all these ruined towns. It was impossible to plan the place. In the middle of the town could be seen the remains of a large church with an apsidal end, solidly-built walls, and numerous columns and column bases: two fragments of stone carvings (Fig. 50) belonged to this. Round it were buildings that might well have been those of a monastery. Next to the church was *a khan* of quite modern type, its great open courtyard with a well in one corner surrounded by a two-storeyed range of vaulted rooms. The town itself seems to have been well laid out with narrow streets at right angles to one another, and occasionally a little public square; the houses are small, and usually crowded very closely together. On the south side, where the hill falls sharply away to the main wady, the line of house walls, supported at their base by a revetment of cut stone, made an accidental, but effective, line of defence for the town; a great gateway breaks this line in its centre, and the road through it led downhill to the well and the bath-house. Close to the gate is a great reservoir, cut in the rock and lined in part with rubble masonry set in good cement, resembling the reservoirs of Esbeita; it is of irregular shape, measuring some 22.50 metres by 18.50, and is 4 $\frac{1}{2}$ metres deep; in one corner a stone staircase leads down into it (Plate XXVIII, 2). Half-way down the hill-side is a line of stones – a wall only one course high – which seems to have marked out the area beyond which rubbish had to be thrown (*cf.* Abda, p 142); the further slope is covered with town refuse. By the path that runs down from the south gate are some rock-cut tombs of ordinary type with recesses full of loose bones; two similar tombs are now used as goat shelters.

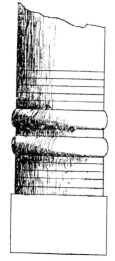

Fig. 51a: Raheiba: one of three columns. 1 : 16

On the plain to the west of the town is a large isolated church, much ruined, but apparently of the usual plan, with three aisles ending in apses at the east end. It was too much encumbered with debris to be planned. The screen-wall could be distinguished, however, and the forecourt seems to have had a range of chambers along its north side, while two chambers perhaps towers flanked the great western doorway. No inscriptions or carved work could be seen.

A large cemetery lay beyond this church to the north-west, and another on the north side of the town. In the latter we found some funerary inscriptions badly cut and much weathered (p. 186 28 – 33) which presented few features of interest, and the ruins of a small funerary chapel like that of Khalasa, whence come the columns and capitals shown in Figs. 51a-b. In the main wady to the south of the town was a large and well-preserved bath-house

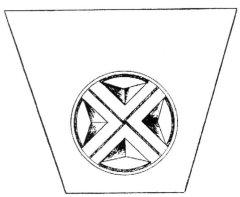

Fig. 51b: Raheiba: one of four capitals. (No scale provided.)

much like that of Abda (*q.v.* p.140 – 141). The walls were of well-cut stone, the barrel roofs and the central dome of a sort of concrete made of small stones and lime of rather poor quality; the hot-air channels up the walls showed at once the nature of the building.[1] Just by the baths was a well, the most remarkable in the Negeb, in that the water occurs at a depth of over 300 feet. The debris that filled it was cleared out only three years ago by native labour, and now that it is open the Beduins have no ropes long enough to make it useful. The well is stone-lined and seems to widen out bell-like at the bottom, where it is rock-cut: the stones at the top are deeply scored by ropes.

A short distance away is another large isolated building the character of which we could not determine: the west wall stands on a revetted podium, and the buildings seem to have been connected with the well by a wall supporting a cemented stone trough, while another (filled-up) well or cistern some 50 metres away seems also to have been connected with it.

Apart from the well, for whose date there is no evidence at all, though its upper stones do not look very early, all the remains visible above ground are definitely Byzantine. From the nature of the ground it is improbable that the existing ruins cover any early settlement, and certainly there was here no early fixed settlement

---

[1] Plans, section, elevations and photographs in Musil, *Edom*, 75 – 82.

of any importance. The identification, therefore, of Raheiba with the Rehoboth where Isaac dug a well is a theory not yet supported by archaeological evidence.

El Auja, when visited by Palmer, was still a comparatively imposing ruin, and even in 1909 Mr. Huntington[1] saw two parallel streets, 600 feet long or more, with the masonry bases of their colonnades still visible. But now the ruins are only less melancholy than those of Khalasa. An attempt has been made to establish there the seat of a Kaimmakamlik, and the ancient site has been ruthlessly plundered to provide material for the new buildings which an altered government has failed to complete. At the base of the old acropolis stand three stone houses, tile-roofed and untidily pretentious, whose upper storeys are government offices and their ground floors starveling shops; a corrugated iron roof covers the low walls of a monastery-church that was destined to be a guest-house; on the hill-top the gaunt walls of the serai, standing window-high, rise from a wilderness of stone heaps and broken tiles, more desolate than the ruins out of which they are built.

Curiously enough the same considerations that prompted this abortive scheme of Abdul Hamid were responsible for the building of the original Byzantine town. The Sultan saw here the strategic position for a government and military post that should guarantee his great forward movement against the Beduins of the desert. The Byzantine emperor fixed upon the spot for one fort in the chain that was to safeguard his territory against the roving enemies in the south who were so soon to swarm over his borders. El Auja lies indeed off the main trade-route, but trade was no longer the chief consideration; the fort is well placed to block the great Wady Hafir, which leads up from the central plateau of the

---

[1] *Palestine and its Transformations*, pp. 121 *seq*

Tih, and its garrison would command not inadequately the old Shur road that runs past Bir Birein. The wide valley would supply the soldiers with food, and water was to be found at no great depth. Actually fortresses are of little avail against a mobile enemy in a desert country where roads run everywhither; and the event proved their worthlessness here; but on paper El Auja, Abda and Kurnub may well have looked an admirable chain of defence, and if to us they seem to have rounded off a theory rather than to have met a local need, we can only suppose that that theory of imperial defence was drawn up at Constantinople and not on the marches.

The town (Fig. 52), though covering a fair area, does not seem to have been very large, for the houses were scattered and open spaces frequent. It lay on both sides of a wady, clustering under the precipitously-scarped sides of its rocky citadel (Plate XXIX, 1) The summit of this hill was occupied by a strong fortress whose heavy walls of ashlar masonry rose directly from the steep slopes or from the sheer face of the rock. The fort seems to have been composed of two parts, a lower oblong enclosure with an arched gateway at its south end defended by flanking towers, and a separate master-tower on the higher level at the north end of the hill, to which access was obtained both from the lower enclosure and directly from the town by a great flight of rock-hewn steps which zigzagged up the hill-side. The lower area is now occupied by the ruins of the unfinished serai. Only parts of its walls and of the gate tower remain, but we may suppose, on analogy with Abda, that it was an open space, the bailey of the fort; while the northern part, which is separated from it by a revetted slope and is full of cross-walls and substructures, would have answered to the keep. At the very point of the rock the walls are thrown forward to enclose a small platform in which is cut a great square well, 12 feet each way and still over 70 feet deep, lined with good ashlar masonry.

The fine church which Palmer illustrated (Fig. 53) stands on the same hill-top, farther to the south-west, joined by a curtain-

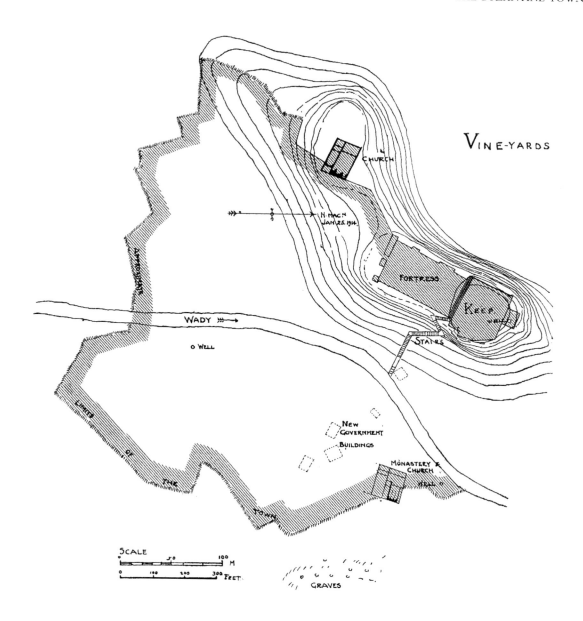

VINE-YARDS

CHURCH

N. MAGN
JAN 25.1914.

FORTRESS

KEEP.
WALL

STAIRS

WADY

O WELL

NEW
GOVERNMENT
BUILDINGS

MONASTERY &
CHURCH
WELL O

SCALE

GRAVES

Fig. 52: Plan of ancient town of El Auja.

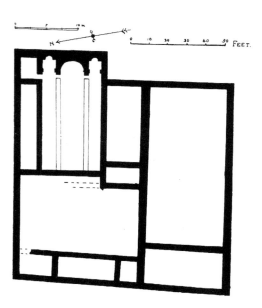

Fig. 53: El Auja: monastery church.

wall to the south-west angle of the fort. It has been sadly ruined by the Turkish builders; the facing-blocks have been pulled away and only the rubble cores of the walls are left; only the east end is standing, and even here the main apse has been utterly destroyed. The plan, whose measurements could be but approximately taken, shows a large church of the usual type, having three aisles, a side chapel on the south, and a small tower (apparently) over the chamber in the south-west corner. The architecture is the same as that of Esbeita; but here the flinty limestone blocks of the lower courses were more neatly squared, and in the church proper the inner face of the walls had been of smoothly-cut ashlar instead of plastered rubble. The 'atrium' was large, having the main door on its north side, and a bench along part of its west wall; from this wall also, towards the north end, projected a small wall whose purpose was not clear. On the north apse were traces of fresco painting. There were column-drums lying about, but the intercolumniation could not be determined; there were a few

Fig. 54: El Auja: capital. 1 : 10

pieces of mouldings, but these too fragmentary to be of interest.

There had been a doorway, leading to the town, in the continuation of the west wall that ran out from the church corner to join the curtain-wall. The outer walls of the church, as of the fort, were set in good lime mortar (Plate XXIX, 2).

Below the acropolis, on the east bank of the wady, lay a small church with monastic buildings attached. The church itself had been partly cleared, and the first steps had been taken to turn it into a rest-house: its walls stood some 6 or 7 feet high. The monastery had not been excavated, and only a few of its walls could be traced. The columns were ringed with flat bands in relief (*cf.* the south church of Esbeita); a fairly good piece of leaf-carving in marble was built into one of the modern walls, and a limestone capital (Fig. 54), in the courtyard of the mudir's quarters, probably came from here. This is the church in which Mr. Huntington[1] saw a mosaic pavement with an inscription bearing the date 435 AD (496 of the Gazan ? era).

From the town itself we could get nothing of interest; so plundered is it that many of its walls can only be followed by the long trenches made by searchers after stone. There are four deep wells still visible, of which one has been cleared and gives good water.

Only one inscription was found here, but others have been reported by other travellers, *e.g.*, Huntington *(loc. cit.)*, and give dates ranging between 436 and 519 of the local era (375 – 458

---

[1] *op. cit.*, p. 123

A.D.). South-east of the town lies a cemetery, freely plundered, and beyond this are walled and irrigated fields. On the slopes north and west of the town were vineyards: eastwards the great plain, now sparsely scattered with thornbushes, shows signs of ancient cultivation, and southwards the whole Wady Hafir is crossed and recrossed by terraces and hedges. By Tell el Seram, where a side wady narrows down to a hollow bed of good soil about a hundred yards across, bordered by gravel banks along which run dry-stone walls, the valley is crossed every fifty yards by double lines of low walling, some seven feet apart, wherein were set hedges whose shade would conserve the moisture in the narrow earth-plots, while these screens would shelter from the wind some more than usually delicate crop. The wide extent of the cultivated area, contrasting with the presumably none too large population of the town, is explained by the precariousness of the harvest in these ill-watered deserts, where a good crop must needs be stored against the inevitable lean years. At the present time the rainfall here is far less than at Bir el Seba, less even than at Khalasa, and if modern conditions held good in the Byzantine period, a proportionately wider cultivation would have been necessary to support El Auja than was required at those places. We have recorded elsewhere that in the southern reaches of the Wady Hafir, where the arable soil is almost equally extensive, there is no sign of permanent settlement at all, and the cultivation must have been then, as now, in the hands of nomads who reaped what harvest they could in a good year, and, when bad seasons followed each other too often, could return to the better-watered plains of the north.

Tell Kurnub   The ruins of Tell Kurnub have been identified by various writers with Thamara, a station marked on the Tabula Peutingeriana at a distance of fifty-three Roman miles from Jerusalem upon the Petra road. Eusebius and Jerome describe it as on the road from Hebron to Aila, at a day's journey south from Malatha (Malis in Eusebius), which again has been by some identified with Tell Milah. The *Notitiae Dignitatum*[1] describes Thamara as the garrison of Cohors IV Palaestinorum; Eusebius and Jerome call it a fortified city with a Roman garrison. The identification is not at all improbable.

A large and fairly level plain stretches east by west, bounded along the north by low hills, through which runs the road to Beersheba. To the east the view is open, and beyond the gently declining foreground one looks across the hidden gorge of the Araba to the mountains of Kerak, blue in the far distance.

Westward, low hills again shut off the valley from the open rolling uplands of Um Deifi. Only along the south are the hills really lofty – a long, flat-topped ridge, not precipitous indeed, but too steep for any but a footman to cross, and for him not too easy a clamber. The Wady Kurnub or Wady el Sidd, a broad, sandy torrent-bed, sweeps round under the foot of the ridge, which rises like a gigantic earth rampart from its bank (Plate XXX, 1) Almost in the middle of its line there is a break in the hills, and the wady, dropping rapidly, turns sharply to the south, and breaks through a winding gorge, whose rocky sides, rising sheer and inaccessible, form one of the finest pieces of cliff scenery in the south country. But from the plain this gorge is hardly suspected, for right in the middle of the rift there rises from the plain a small isolated knoll that from the north completely masks it. The wady, plunging downwards over rocky ledges, cuts it off from the south-western hills; a second and smaller tributary stream, with like precipitous banks, divides it from the south-eastern range; the hill, which sloped up fairly gently from the level plain, breaks down in great cliffs that overhang the confluence of the two torrent-beds and commands completely the passage down their gorge. On this knoll stands the fortress of Kurnub.

---

[1] Ed. Böcking, pp. 358 – 359

The Beersheba road (from which a branch track runs west to Khalasa) skirts the western foot of the castle hill, then, passing down rock-cut stairs between a smaller hill to the west and the river gorge, reaches the great dam, and running over this, climbs the rocks on the opposite bank, and creeps precariously along the face of the precipice above the ravine. The road is a bad one – worse, perhaps, now than when it was kept in repair – and another easier road from Kurnub runs half a mile eastward, and rounding the end of the long hill-wall, strikes south to meet the ravine road. So by Nagb el Safa (Plate XXXII), and across Wady Figra, one comes to Ain Weiba (where the Darb el Sultan from Khalasa via Nagb el Gharib and Wady Mura joins the Kurnub route) and thence across the Araba to Petra. But bad as it is, and was, the road was a direct one, and must have been of no small importance, especially if the Byzantine post passed this way to go down the Araba to Aila and the Red Sea. In view of this fact the military significance of Kurnub is unmistakable; the fortress was built to command the road, and of such road-forts it is the most elaborate example that we have.

The town (Fig. 55), which occupied the top and the gentle northern slope of the hill, was surrounded by a rubble wall some 3 metres high, strengthened at its angles by small towers 3 or 4 metres square, and of only one storey. Two gates open on to the low ground to the north, and on to the western slope. The wall itself, as also at Abda and other towns, is a poor affair, an obstacle rather than a real wall of defence, intended rather to resist mounted raiders than an ordered assault. The buildings occupy only part of the enclosure; conspicuous are two churches and two other large and well built structures which probably were in the nature of Government offices, and a tower, still standing to a considerable height which from the middle of the slope dominates the road to the ravine. These larger buildings occupy nearly a quarter of the inhabited town area; for the rest the houses are small and poorly built, nearly all of one storey only, not a few seeming to have had foundations only of stone and a superstructure in some flimsier

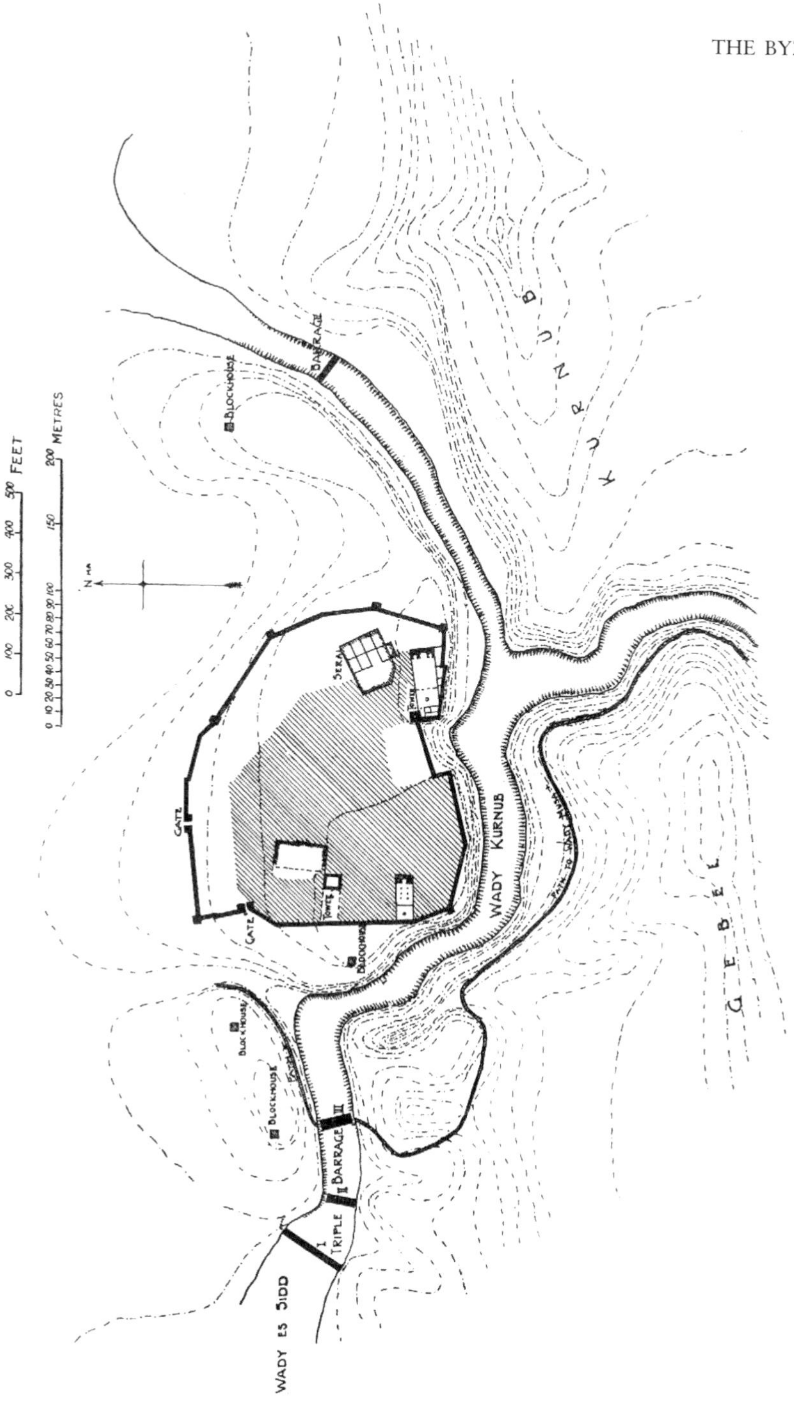

Fig. 55: Town and district of Kurnub.

material. Probably these are the quarters of the common soldiers of the garrison (Plate XXXI, 1).

The strategic importance of Kurnub is emphasized by the system of blockhouses that secure its command over the ravine road. On the eastern spur of the town hill is one of these, a small ashlar tower, built close to the ruins of an older structure, perhaps of the same type, overlooking the eastern wady. On the western edge of the hill is another tower perched immediately above the angle of the main wady. Two more towers, and the ruins of an older but similar building stand on the smaller hill to the west, above the great dam, commanding the road as it skirts the hill to cross the torrent bed. A larger building, also a small fort, judging from the thickness of its walls and their pronounced batter, stands on a small rise out in the plain by the road, just where this dips down to pass between the town and the western hillock; and further out in the plain, still close to the road line, is a sixth of these small square buildings which, though not in itself distinctive, must, by analogy with the rest, be regarded as a military blockhouse. These six towers, dependent upon the main fort, occupying the posts of vantage that best command the south road and the gorge, give to the place a character quite different from that of any other of these southern cities.

Another remarkable feature of the place is the great work by which the flood waters of the wady were kept in check. One is used to the more or less elaborate terrace walls that cross nearly every valley and torrent bed; generally these are low, roughly piled rubble walls, or more rarely, as in Wady Ramliya, well-built walls of a man's height, with faces of coursed rubble or rudely dressed square stones. Here is something different. It has been remarked that the stream-bed drops sharply down from its level in the open plain to the rocky bottom of the ravine between the hills, so steeply indeed that, unhindered, a few floods in succession might well carry away all the arable soil of the valley. To prevent this, between the western hillock crowned by the two blockhouses and the rocky side of the southern hill, in a space of a hundred metres, three great dams have been thrown across the wady. The two upper dams, serving their purpose, are buried in the soil that they have retained; the floods have deposited their water-borne soil in three shallow steps level with the wall-tops, and then, plunging over the lowest barrier, have scoured the gorge itself down to the naked rock; from this rock bottom the face of the great dam rises exposed and intact (Plate XXX, 2). This lowest dam is 24 metres long, and 11 metres high; its front is strongly battered, but even so, the width at the top is 7.80 metres. The face is of finely-cut ashlar stone, set in hard lime, packed behind with lime and boulders; the top, over which crossed the road, was paved with layer upon layer of flints set in lime, a concrete as hard as the rock itself. A few stones have been dislodged from its edge, and the masonry of the front is deeply channelled by the falling water, but the dam is still almost as solid as when it was built. Fifty-one metres up stream is the second dam, 20 metres long, and, at the top, 5 metres across, buried in the silt; it is similarly built with a sloped face of fine ashlar, and filling of boulders and cement. The third dam is 35 metres up stream; it is 53 metres long and 3.40 metres wide at the top; the front seems to have been vertical, not battered, and the height was probably not very great.

In the eastern wady, below the blockhouse, is another, but smaller dam, built of cement and stone on a natural ledge, the first breakdown of the torrent bed. It is 3 metres high, and some 20 metres long, but

Fig. 56: Kurnub: east church. 1 : 400

has not the solid strength of the great dam to the west – naturally not, since there would be here no such volume of water as in the main wady.

In the bed of the ravine there are numerous *themail*, or water-holes, which keep their supply all the year round, and there is a spring high up behind the spur of the hills on the south-west of the ravine. Tales are told of a walled-up spring or cistern with wooden barriers and a wooden trough, but no living Arabs claim to have seen it.

No inscriptions were found at Kurnub. The eastern church was large (Fig. 56), very simple in style, of the usual type with forecourt or atrium containing a large cistern, some chambers, probably for the resident clergy, and a campanile at the north-west corner. By it was a large open square. The western church was small (Fig. 57), but comparatively rich in decoration, its stone carving being better in quality than existed, perhaps, upon any other site (Fig 58 and Plate XXXI, 2). There was only one apse, the side aisles being straight-ended; three columns and a pilaster on either side of the central aisle formed the colonnade. These columns had moulded bases and richly carved capitals, and the arch of the apse was also delicately worked (Plate XXXI, 2). Round the church are buildings apparently attached to it, and perhaps monastic in character, but now too ruinous to be distinctive.

There are traces on the site of two periods of occupation. Foundations of earlier blockhouses can be seen on the hills; in the town a number of walls have been razed level with the ground at a time when the place was still inhabited, and the eastern part of the great block of buildings dubbed 'the Serai' is built of larger stones than

Fig. 57: Kurnub: west church. 1 : 400

VOUSSOIR FROM CHANCEL ARCH OF W CHURCH.

PLAN OF TOP OF CAPITAL FROM W. CHURCH.

N.β ALL ENGAGED CAPITALS.

DOOR FRAME (?) IN W. CHURCH

BASE (?) IN SAME CHURCH

BASE IN SAME CHURCH

Fig. 58 : Kurnub : Wet Church, architectural Members. 1 : 15

usual, and these of a hard white limestone, unlike the soft yellow material generally employed. Unfortunately, no potsherds or other remains could be found that would serve as criteria for comparative dating. We can only say that whereas the present town is probably of Justinian's time, there was an earlier settlement upon the site, though nothing is known about its period or its importance.

Akaba   Modern Akaba is a village of about a thousand people, and is built mostly of mud brick, or of pebbles from the beach set in mud. The only dressed stone is in the old fort, which is a rectangle with gate towers and round towers at the corners, built in stripes of pink and white, apparently late fifteenth or sixteenth century. It is now partially ruined, but still acts as military headquarters, and has troops living in it. In front of the houses of the village and the fort is a narrow strip of land, hedged and banked round, and full of palm trees; the outermost trees stand on the very beach, here, fortunately, almost without tide. The site of the present village has no signs of previous occupation; there are no old stones, and no pottery is to be found. Quite possibly the ancient towns around the bay were also made of mud brick. If modern Akaba were destroyed it would leave no trace after fifty years, thanks to the soluble nature of its materials. If ancient Aila had been all stone built, some of its blocks would have been re-used.

At the same time it is quite probable that the present site of the town has never been occupied before. It lies at the foot of the slopes of the Arabian hills, and wady after wady descends from them, each pointing direct upon the town; a flood from any one of these would sweep away every building in the place if it were not for a huge bank, which is (after the fort) the most striking thing in Akaba today. It is a great wall of earth and gravel, running along parallel with the sea behind the town, the fort, and the palm gardens, and usually from 100 to 200 yards inland. To the sea the earthwork presents a face from 10 to 30 feet high, and very steep; to the hills its top is not more than from 3 to 10 feet above the level of the ground. It is thus apparent that the effect of this earthwork has been to bank up the soil behind it (with the aid of the floods) to a very great height, and it is also sufficiently strong to deflect the water coming down from the hills either to south or to north in any case, away from the town. The materials of the bank are very clean; what little pottery appears in its strata is Arab; and local tradition has it that it is an earthwork for cannon of the time of Ibrahim Pasha of Egypt. If this tradition (not unreasonable) is true, then the earthwork, by shielding the site of the present town, has made it habitable and free from the devastation of floods. But the wall is just as likely to be much older, and to have been put up simply as a defence against these floods, before cannon were thought of.

In the houses of the present village there are two antiquities on view. One is the capital of an engaged column of the usual Byzantine shape, bearing on it a running ornament of an uncertain leaf. The cutting is rude, but the drawing not contemptible. The other is a similar capital, having on each of the two worked sides a half-length figure of a saint. The cutting and drawing of these are utterly conventional; the saints are alike, even in the mutilations that their faces have since suffered, so that it is fortunate that each bears his name in Greek cut into the edge of the capital above him; one is St. George and the other St. Isidore. At their bravest they were only very poor things. It is certainly the capital of a doorway or of a chancel-arch, and as certainly must have come from one of the Byzantine churches of Aila. Both stones were found, with the remains of the walls of a small building, in some palm gardens at the north-east corner of the beach. Just to the west of this spot is the ruin-mound pointed out today by all the people of Akaba as the site of ancient Aila. The shore, before it trends east and west, and the ruins (now merely a sandbank) run along the beach for a distance of about 250 yards, and extend as far inland. Thus Aila was a very small place at the best of times. The ruin-mound is about 10 feet deep, and appears to be clean sand without any signs of stone walls; the Arabs say, however, that these are to be found a little under the surface. The ground is covered with fragments of

Arab glass of all colours – green, yellow, and claret-coloured were the most ordinary sorts, but the abundance was very strange. There was also a great deal of glazed pottery, some of it a metallic glaze, but much of it the kind of ware manufactured generally on the upper course of the Euphrates near Aleppo in the later Middle Ages. The distinctive black, yellow, and decomposed blue of Rakka ware predominated. With these distinct sorts there was much common pottery, including several fragments of a fine red ware, very smooth faced, decorated on the outside with incised bands containing little foliations and flourishes. This all pointed to an Arab settlement of some luxury in the early Middle Ages, and its gradual decay and abandonment not later than the seventeenth century. There was also some Byzantine pottery mixed in with the later stuff, and a very little of the red-ribbed Gaza ware. The probabilities are that the classical Aila and the early Elath are both on the same spot below each other; otherwise it would be hard to explain the absence of any other ruined site at the head of the bay. There are remains a little farther inland, and these represent probably a small village outside the gates of the larger place.

There are several ancient cities mentioned as having been situated at the head of this beach of the Red Sea. There is said to be the site of one in a valley some distance to the south of the present Akaba on the east coast of the sea, and on the west side perhaps there was a settlement at Taba. The state of the country when we were there in February, 1914, was, however, unfavourable to exploration. At the point commonly called El Deir or Umrashash, where the Nagb road drops to the beach, there seemed to be no ruins whatever, unless the platforms of the Turkish guard-houses cover ancient remains. If there has been anything it has been very small.

The other point of capital interest at the head of the Gulf, after Akaba itself, is certainly the small island off the western (Egyptian) coast near Taba, called by a variety of names, but at Akaba *Geziret Faraun* commonly Geziret Faraun (Plate III, 2). The Crusaders called it Graye consistently. It is, as seen from the shore, a small double island formed of two sharp points of rock, about 50 feet high each united by a strip of sandbank raised only a few feet above the level of the sea. Between it and the mainland is a deep channel, perhaps 400 yards across. The island has been strongly fortified at several periods. All round the shore at sea level are to be seen the remains of a built wall of rough masonry about 4 feet thick, entirely destroyed down to the level of the beach. The Akaba water seems to have a curious effect of petrifaction (perhaps due to the coral there), which cements the shores into a single slab of conglomerate; this wall therefore looks as natural a tipped stratum as need be, save for the tool-marks still showing on the inner edges of some stones. The date of this first wall it is   impossible to determine. Within it there is a narrow beach of sand round the northern peak, the larger of the two rock masses of which the island is made up; facing shorewards is a square tower of split porphyritic granite, the material of the island, and of all the buildings upon it. This tower has a window or door in its face about 8 feet above the water, which is shallow; the real entrance to the fort was, however, probably from the sand beach on the seaward side. There is here a narrow path running up the cliff face, elsewhere nearly precipitous. The actual door into the fort is very narrow, and the fort itself is small, though no smaller than the top of the rock, every inch of which it covers with its buildings. In the central block or keep there are about a dozen tolerable rooms, and in the extension to the north along the backbone of the ridge there are a few more. Attached to the keep, but half-way down the slope towards the sandy waist of the island, is a little mosque with plain plastered *mibrab* full of inscriptions cut by officers and men of *H.M.S. Diana* in 1896. The southern peak of the island is nearly as high as the northern, but much smaller, and the buildings on it are more ruined. It has a tower or two still standing, and some well-made rooms and passages with barrel vaults to their roofs. On the sandbank which unites the two peaks lie half buried some rough stone huts and circles, and there is also on it a little pool of salt water, perhaps 50 yards long. It is now filled with sand and debris, but has been deeper, and probably had an entrance from the sea. Set round the pond, as though for ornament, are some drums of columns in soft white limestone. There were two similar drums in a room in the keep of the northern building, and (from their stone-dressing) they seem of different period from the rest of the place. Of course they may well have been shipped across from some ruin at Akaba.

The actual mason-work of the castle is of the worst description. It is built of small split pieces of the red granite of the island and the mainland, and there has been little attempt to square any of the stones. Around the openings of windows, and in doors, and sometimes even at corners of the buildings, are worked blocks of soft yellow limestone, very roughly finished and without mouldings. Door and window heads are usually made of palm-logs, many of which remain in a rotten condition, and in the northern half of the buildings the roofs and the *chemin-de-ronds* of the curtain walls were also of this wood, with leaf and rib overlay. The walls are nearly mortarless, but inside were plugged with a hard smooth yellow lime plaster, that the great rooms might appear reasonably habitable. The remains of this pargetting are only to be seen in some inner window openings, which are rectangular and small. These had proved too numerous for later inhabitants of the fort, and two out of three of them have been walled up. The walls are usually about a yard thick (in places, more or less), and their tops are parapeted in very simple style. The outer windows of the fort are nearly all of the loophole type, very narrow outside, and broad within. The southern half of the fort is so much more ruinous than the north that it would suggest an earlier abandonment; also its construction is so much better on the whole, with free use of lime cut stone and vaulting, that one would suspect it of being a twelfth century construction. The pottery found in it was, however, not very early; practically all of it was metallic-glazed. The pottery of the north end of the fort was nearly modern, and its abandonment may have been as recent as a century or so ago. The only stone which showed any attempt at ornament was built incongruously sideways into the head of a half-destroyed window opening to the east on the northern rock. It was a roll moulding and some angle-ribs, and looked very much like a springer of a twelfth-century French roof; but it was such a tiny fragment that no reliance whatever can be placed on it. It has certainly, however, been re-used in its present position

It is very hard to give dates to a building so characterless. There are some vaulted store-pits or cisterns that should be twelfth or thirteenth century Arab work, and the southern ruins may be of the same period, with later repairs. The whole of the north half of the fort is more like fifteenth or sixteenth century work, repaired in the eighteenth century. The loopholes and windows are some of them intended for cannon fire, and some seem more suitable for archery, so that a date in a transitional period is the most probable one. At the same time Akaba is a very out of the way place, and the roughness of the building may be due more to an emergency which forbade choice of materials than to a decadent period. The island has been planned, rather feebly, by Leon de Laborde, and his plan was republished, with very good photographs and notes, by P. Savignac, in the *Revue Biblique* for October, 1913. The fathers suggest for the building a date much earlier than I accept; the reference by Abulfeda[1] to the abandoned condition of the island in the fourteenth century does not in any way preclude a subsequent re-occupation during some crisis in the Red Sea and a partial rebuilding. Questions of dating apart, however, the account of the disposition of the rooms and defences in the *Revue Biblique* is admirably clear, and does far more than justice to the fort. The extreme poverty of the remains there struck the French observers very strongly, and they are in agreement that to try to date closely such ruins is unnecessary.

---

[1] Quoted from Rey, *Colonies Franques*, p. 399.

CHAPTER VI.

Inscriptions from Southern Palestine.

Greek : Nabatean : Arabic.

I. GREEK.

By M. N. Tod.

The following inscriptions, copied by Mr. Woolley at Bir el Seba, Khalasa, Raheiba and Abda during the course of his survey of Southern Palestine, have been entrusted to me for publication. To carry out this task adequately would call for greater leisure and knowledge than I can command, but I have at least tried to draw the attention of scholars to the difficulties which have baffled me in order that they may point out the true solutions. To the Reverend Dr. G. B. Gray I would express my warm thanks for the aid he has kindly given me in connexion with several of the Semitic names contained in the inscriptions.

I have used the following abbreviations :—

A.J.A. = American Journal of Archæology.
C.I.G.=Corpus Inscriptionum Graecarum.
C.R.A.I. = Comptes Rendus de l'Académie des Inscriptions et Belles-Lettres.
P.A.E.S. = Publications of the Princeton University Archæological Expeditions to Syria. Division III, Greek and Latin Inscriptions.
P.E.F.Q.S. = Palestine Exploration Fund : Quarterly Statement.
R.B. = Revue Biblique Internationale.
Rec. = C. Clermont-Ganneau, *Recueil d'archéologie orientale.*
Wadd. = W. H. Waddington, *Voyage Archéologique : Inscriptions grecques et latines.* III. 6.
Z.D.P.V. = Zeitschrift des Deutschen Palästina-Vereins.

Twelve of the inscriptions copied by Mr. Woolley had been previously published.

(*A*) *R.B.* 1893, 204 ; C. Clermont-Ganneau, *Archæological Researches in Palestine*, ii. 407 No. 8 ; E. Schürer, *Sitzungsberichte der Akademie zu Berlin*, 1896, 1081 No. 5.   Found by Clermont-Ganneau in the house of Saliba 'Awad at Gaza : now in the gardens of the British Consular Agency there.

(*B*) *A.J.A.* 1910, 66 ff., 426 f.   Cf. *R.B.* 1910, 633 f. ; *P.E.F.Q.S.*, 1910, 235 f. ; *Revue des Études Grecques*, 1912, 66 ; *Z.D.P.V.* 1913, 236 ff.   A photographic reproduction of the stone is given in *A.J.A., loc. cit.*   Now in the Government Serai at Bir el Seba.

(*C*) *R.B.* 1903, 428 f. No. 8, with a photographic reproduction of a squeeze.   Cf. *Rec.* v. 370 f.   Now in the Government Serai at Bir el Seba.   A rough limestone block, badly cut, worn, and defaced by a plaster wash.

(*D*) *R.B.* 1903, 279, 426 f. No. 3 (with photograph of squeeze).   Cf. *Rec.* v. 370, viii. 77; *Revue des Études Grecques*, 1909, 321 ; *Bull. Corr. Hell.* 1907, 332 f., 420 ; *R.B.* 1908, 150.   Now in the Government Serai at Bir el Seba.

(*E*) A fragment of the famous Byzantine Edict of Beersheba.   *R.B.* 1903, 279 (with photograph of squeeze), 429 No. 9 ; 1906, 86 ff. (= *Rec.* vii. 185 ff.).   Now in the Government Serai at Bir el Seba.

For other portions of this important document and general discussions of its contents see also : *R.B.* 1903, 275 ff. ; 1904, 85 ff. (=*Rec.* vi. 210 ff.) ; 1906, 412 ff. ; 1909, 89 ff. ; *P.E.F.Q.S.* 1902, 234, 236, 269 ff., 385 ff. ; *A.J.A.* 1908, 344 ff. ; *C.R.A.I.* 1905, 541 f. ; *Rec.* v. 130 ff., vii. 257 ff.

(*F*) *R.B.* 1905, 252 No. 9 and Plate X.   In the floor of a house near the cemetery, Bir el Seba.   Limestone slab, deeply and clearly cut.   The previous editors were unable to see the right-hand portion of the stone.   Mr. Woolley's copy (Plate XXXIV. F.) thus serves to correct in several points their restoration of the text.   We must read

['Εντα]ῦθα ὁ μακάρ(ιος) - - ρο διάκονος κατε[τέθη] ἐν τῇ ιε' τοῦ μη[νὸς 'Α]πελλέου ἰνδ(ικτιῶνος) ὀγδόης +

Apellaeus 15th in the Arabian calendar corresponds to December 1st.

(*G*) *R.B.* 1905, 255 No. 19*b* and Plate X. Khalasa. Limestone slab, with inscription incised and painted red.

(*H*) *R.B.* 1905, 255 No. 17 and Plate X (*C.R.A.I.* 1904, 303 f.). Khalasa. Limestone, very roughly cut.

(*I*) *R.B.* 1905, 255 No. 16. Khalasa. The variant readings of Mr. Woolley's copy are as follows :—l. 1 ΥΠϹ *i.e.* υπέ instead of υπζ'; l. 2 there is no letter after Π; l. 5 has Χ as fourth letter with Μ or Ν beneath it in the following line, instead of Μ surmounted by a small χ; l. 7 has ΑιΕ, l. 8 ΠΡ (in ligature) ΟϹΠ, l. 9 ΚϹϹΚ.

(*J*) *R.B.* 1905, 255 No. 15 and Plate IX (*C.R.A.I.* 1904, 303). Khalasa. Limestone.

(*K*) *C.R.A.I.* 1904, 299 f.; *R.B.* 1905, 249 f. No. 3 and Plate IX. Of this inscription Mr. Woolley saw only a photograph.

No. 5 (below). See footnote *ad loc.*

The remaining inscriptions have not, so far as I know, been previously published. The sign $\frac{1}{10}$ (or $\frac{1}{5}$), which follows references to the Plates on which the copies are reproduced, denotes that those reproductions are one-tenth (or one-fifth) of the size of the original stones.

Bɪʀ ᴇʟ Sᴇʙᴀ (Bᴇᴇʀsʜᴇʙᴀ).

1. In the Government Serai. On a *tabula ansata* of coarse limestone, roughly cut : 0·33 × 0·25 m. Plate XXXIV.

Εὐτυχῶς ᾠκεδομήθη ὑπὸ Ἀλεξάνδρου καὶ Βοήθου καὶ Ἀλκιβιάδ(ου) υἱῶν
ΔΙΑΚΟΡΙ(Α)ΝΟΟΥΘΙΚΟΥ ἔτει ρλϛ'.

With the opening words of this building-inscription we may compare *P.A.E.S.* A. 2, 177 (= Wadd. 2053) εὐ<χ>τυχῶς ἐκοδομήθη ὁ πύργος, and the concluding line of Wadd. 2381. The inflexion and spelling of οἰκοδομέω and its parts caused ancient engravers peculiar difficulty : see, *e.g.*, Wadd. 2436 ἠκωδώμεσεν, *P.A.E.S.* A. 2, 25 οἰκωδώμεισαν.

What follows υἱῶν I cannot determine. A personal name in the genitive would seem most likely, though not absolutely necessary, and I had thought that ΔΙΑΚΟ might stand for διακό(νου) with the name following in l. 7 : I am not, however, convinced that this is a Christian inscription, and its comparatively early date tells against this interpretation. A possible alternative is to read διὰ Κορίνθου? οἰκ(οδόμ)ου. The builder is often named in such inscriptions and the word οἰκοδόμος is sometimes abbreviated (*e.g.* Wadd. 2022 *a*, 2091, 2235, 2299), though never, so far as I am aware, by contraction (see note on No. 4, below).

The year 136 will correspond, if the Arabian calendar is here used, to A.D. 241–2.

2. In the Government Serai. On a slab of white marble, complete except for the left-hand top corner. Plate XXXIV : $\frac{1}{10}$.

[+ Ἀνε]πάη ὁ μακάριος
Ζόναινος ϹΕΡΠΟΓΛ˘
ϹΗΝ τῇ κβ′ μη(νὸς) Ξανθικοῦ
ἰνδ(ικτιῶνος) ζ′, ἔτους τμθ′. +

The name of the deceased recurs in Nos. 15 and 16, in an epitaph of Raheiba (*A.J.A.* 1910, 61 No. 3), beginning + Ἀνεπάε Χάρετος Ζοναίνου, and, in a slightly different spelling, on another stele from the same place (*R.B.* 1905, 256 No. 30 and Plate X : illustrated in *C.R.A.I.* 1904, 300*) which bears the words Σεργίου Ζονένου. The word shows the regular form of the Arabic diminutive.

If the date is reckoned according to the Arabian calendar, the 22nd day of Xanthicus in the year 349 is equivalent to April 12th, A.D. 454. This falls within the seventh indiction, which began on September 1st, A.D. 453.

I leave it to the experts to determine what follows the name Ζόναινος, apparently a patronymic and an abbreviated term denoting profession or status.

3. In a garden near the cemetery. On a slab of limestone, very roughly cut, broken on the left and at the top right-hand corner. Plate XXXIV : $\frac{1}{10}$.

[+ Ἀνε]πάη μακαρ(ία)
- - - όνη, γυνὴ
[τοῦ θε]οσεβ(εστάτου) Σειτίου?
[ἐν μ]ην(ὶ) Δίου, ἰνδ(ικτιῶνος) η′.

I can make nothing of the name contained in l. 3 : Σεργίου is perhaps too bold a conjecture. For the epithet θεοσεβέστατος cf. Wadd. 2089–91 and note on 2089.

4. In the floor of a house near the cemetery. On a marble slab complete on every side. Plate XXXIV : $\frac{1}{10}$.

+ Ἐνθάδε κατ(ετέ)θη ἡ μα(καρία) Νόννα ἡ διάκ(ονος), μη(νὸς) Δαισ(ίου) κγ′, ἰνδ(ικτιῶνος) α′.

For the shortening of words by contraction, *i.e.* by writing only the opening and closing letters, see E. Nachmanson, *Eranos*, x. 101 ff. (cf. G. Rudberg, *ibid.* 71 ff.). Deacons are commemorated in other inscriptions of Bir el Seba (*R.B.* 1905, 252 No. 9 and Plate X : *Rec.* vi. 185 ff.) and Raheiba (*R.B.* 1905, 256 No. 21 = *C.R.A.I.* 1904, 304).

The name Νόννος is found at Salkhad (Wadd. 2009) and at Philadelphia in Lydia (J. Keil u. A. von Premerstein, *Bericht über eine Reise in Lydien*, 76). Νόννα occurs in Central Asia Minor (*C.I.G.* 3989 *b*, 9266, 9269), and an inscription of Bir el Seba records the death of Νόννα Στεφάνου Αἰλησία (*R.B.* 1903, 279, 426), probably the same who is referred to in a Sinaitic text published by Euting and revised by Grégoire (see *Rec.* v. 370, viii. 76 ff.).

If the Arabian calendar is here employed, Daesius 23rd will correspond with June 12th.

5. In the Government Serai.* On a marble slab broken on the right. Roughly cut : 0·35 × 0·28 m. Plate XXXIV.

If we are to regard the initial letters of ll. 1, 2 as purposely deleted, we may restore conjecturally

Ἐντ[αῦθα κεῖτ]αι ἡ π - - Σωσάν[να - -

Σωσάννα, a variant of Σουσάννα, is found in an epitaph of Bir el Seba (*R.B.* 1903, 425 No. 1), as well as in a metrical inscription of Ravenna (*C.I.G.* 9869). Possibly, however, Σωσάν[δρα] should be restored here : Σώσανδρος occurs in two Syrian inscriptions (Wadd. 2684 *a, c*).

6. In a house near the cemetery. A fragment of a limestone slab, 0·20 × 0·18 m. Plate XXXIV.

The first line may contain part of the name Οὐαλέριον, not uncommon in this region (see, *e.g.*, *R.B.* 1905, 251 No. 8). In l. 2 we may have the name Ἄλκιμος, found in an epitaph of Durbah, near Hamath (Wadd. 2640).

7. In the Government Serai. On a slab of white limestone, 0·30 × 0·23 m. Plate XXXIV.

- - - η Σαούδῳ.

Cf. *A.J.A.* 1910, 65 No. 19 (Raheiba) + Σαουδ. Clermont-Ganneau (*ibid.* 427) conjectures that this is an engraver's error for Σαού(λ), " nom propre

---

* Since this article was written, I have noticed that this inscription is published by F. M. Abel in *R.B.* 1909, 105 f. ; the editor suggests the restoration π[αρθένος] in l. 2, and states that the stone was discovered at Khalasa.

T

mieux justifiable." But the name Σαοῦδος is well attested by Wadd. 2070 *d* Ταυρ[ῖ]νος Σαούδου, 2170 Αὖμος Σαούδου, 2516 τὸ μνημῖον Λεοντίου Σαούδου, and reappears in slightly modified' forms in Wadd. 2364 (quoted by R. Brünnow, *Provincia Arabia*, iii. 308) Ὀβαίσατος Σαόδου and 2236 (cf. *Rec.* v. 147 f.), where the two forms Σαούαδος and Σαοῦδος occur side by side with reference to the same man.

8. In the floor of a house near the cemetery. Marble slab, well cut. Plate XXXIV : $\frac{1}{10}$.

> + Ἐνθάδη κατητ(έθη) ὁ μακ(άριος) - - -

If nothing further was written on the stone, we may perhaps regard it as one kept in stock by the mason, who would have filled in the name (and date) after finding a purchaser.

9. In the Government Serai. On a fragment of white marble, 0·18 × 0·22 m. Plate XXXIV.

The mutilated remains of l. 1 probably refer to the month and day of death of the person here commemorated : if so, we may read conjecturally

> - - Δίου ι' [ὥρας τρί ?] της ἰνδ(ικτιῶνος) - +

10. In the floor of a house near the Serai. On a fragment of a marble slab. Plate XXXIV : $\frac{1}{10}$.

> - - τ ἰνδ(ικτιῶνος) ι' - - - [κατ]ετέθ[η],

or possibly

> - - τ ἰνδι[κτιῶνος - - - κατ]ετέθ[η].

KHALASA (ELUSA).

11. On a limestone slab. Plate XXXIV : $\frac{1}{5}$.

> Θάρσι, Οὐάλα, οὐδ[ὶ]ς ἀθά[ν]ατος . μηνὸς Δίστρου ακ', ἔτους τκ'.

This transcription rests upon the copy and a squeeze.

For this type of epitaph see No. 19 (below) and comment. The 21st of Dystrus in the year 320 would be equivalent, if the Arabian calendar is here used, to 7th March, A.D. 426. Οὐάλα I take to be the vocative of Οὐάλης. This name occurs frequently in Syria and elsewhere as the equivalent of the Latin Valens, and then has the genitive Οὐάλεντος, and so on : in other examples, however, it clearly represents some native name, which appears also in the Latin forms Vahalus (*P.A.E.S.* A. 3, 233 = Wadd. 2058) and Vahlis (*P.A.E.S.* A. 4, 536) : see, *e.g.*, Wadd. 2022 *a ἐπὶ προνοίᾳ Σέου Οὐάλου*, 2203 *a* Ῥάεσος Οὐάλου, *P.A.E.S.* A. 3, 358 (and comment), 387, 412. Here the form of the vocative shows that the native name is intended.

12. In the cemetery to the east of the town. On a limestone slab. Plate XXXV : ⅕.

+ Ἀν(ε)πάε μακάριο(ς) Ἰωάννης Ἀβονήου [ἐ](ν) μεν(ὶ) Δησίου ιζ' ἐνδεκ[τ]ιῶνος [ι]β', ἔτους υιδ'.

My reading of line 3 is uncertain. If the calendar here followed is that "of the Arabs," which we know to have been in use at Khalasa (see Nos. 13, 34 and notes), Daesius 17th of the year 414 corresponds to June 6th, A.D. 519. As this date falls within the twelfth Indiction (beginning September 1st, A.D. 518), I have restored ιβ' in place of the β' which stands in the copy.

13. In a graveyard on the Saadi road. On a limestone slab, perfectly preserved. Letters well cut. Plate XXXV : ⅕.

+ Ἀνηπάη ὁ μακάριος Στέφανος Βοήθου ἐτῶν τριάκοντα τριῶν ἐν μεν(ὶ Π)ανήμου ζ' ἑβδόμε, ἰνδ(ικτιῶνος) θ', ἔτους υκς' +

In l. 3 the engraver appears to have written ΠΤ in place of ΙΠ. The repetition of the word ἑβδόμη after the numerical sign ζ' is curious, but not unparalleled. Panemus 7th in the year 426 would correspond to June 26th, A.D. 531, if the calendar here employed were that of the Arabs (see *Rec.* vi. 122 ff.): that this is the case is rendered almost certain by the fact that this date falls within indiction 9, which begins on September 1st, A.D. 530.

14. In a graveyard on the Saadi road. Limestone, well cut : complete except at the top. Plate XXXV : ⅕.

+Ἀνεπάη ὁ μακάριος Ἐρασῖνος ἐ(ν) μεν(ὶ) Δύστρου ιή, ἰνδ(ικτιῶνος) ιγ'.

+Ἀνεπάη ὁ μακάριος Γεόργιος Ἰωάννο(υ) ἐπαγομένον πρότε ἰνδ(ικτιῶνος)

The name Ἐρασῖνος recurs in No. 34 (below). If the Arabian calendar is here used, as seems to be the case in No. 13, Dystrus 18th is March 4th, and the first of the intercalary days (ἐπαγομένων πρώτῃ) is March 17th. In the second epitaph the indiction number is accidentally omitted : probably it too was ιγ' (13) and the two persons commemorated died within a fortnight.

15. The upper part of a slab of limestone. The letters are roughly engraved. Plate XXXV : ⅕.

+ Ἀνεπάε ὁ (μ)ακάριος
Ζόναινος Ὀβέδωνος - - - - ε - - -

The inscription is not easy to decipher, but I seem to see on the squeeze an ϵ as the last letter of l. 1, **PI** at the close of l. 2, **ZO** at the beginning of l. 3. This gives us the name Ζόναινος, which we already know from No. 2 and elsewhere (see note *ad loc.*). Whether the next name is Ἀβέδωνος or Ὀβέδωνος I cannot determine, though the latter is, to judge from the squeeze and the copy, rather more probable. With the former we may compare Ἄβδος, Ἀβδαῖος (Wadd. 2008, 2447, 2603), and the first element in compounds such as Ἀβεδνεσούβης, Ἀβεδράψας, Ἀβδούβαστις, Ἀβδύζμουνος, etc. (*C.I.G.* 9612, 4463, Wadd. 1866 *c*, 2569, 2596, *P.A.E.S.* A. 4, 567, 569), with the latter the second element in Ἀβδοόβδας (*P.A.E.S.* A. 4, 567, 569), Ὀβέδας (*Rec.* vi. 332), Ὄβεδος or Ὄβαιδος (Wadd. 1984 *c*, 1977), and Ὀβόδας (*C.R.A.I.* 1904, 288 ff., *R.B.* 1905, 82 ff.).

If the name is derived from עבד, we should certainly expect it to assume the form Ἄβδων rather than Ἀβέδων.

16, 17. Two adjoining fragments of a limestone slab: the surface is scratched and defaced, and the inscription is in consequence hard to decipher. Plate XXXV : $\frac{1}{5}$.

The stone is difficult to read, and the copy must be corrected in several points by the squeeze. Thus the first letter of l. 1 is clearly **E**, and that of l. 5 **Δ**. The last three letters of this line are unmistakably **ENM**, the fourth of l. 7 is **ⲋ**, but what follows is undecipherable, though I seem to detect on the squeeze a **Y** followed by a tiny fragment of a **Ξ**. With all due reserve, then, I propose the following reading :—

Ἐτελεύτεσε[ν]
ὁ ἐν ἁγίο(ις) μακ[ά]-
ρ(ιος) Ἀλαφα Λ . ΕΑ
. βου Ζοναίνο[υ]
5 διακ(όνου) ἐν μ[ηνὶ Ὑπε]-
ρβερ(εταίου) ιγ′, ἰν[δ(ικτιῶνος) -]
ἔτους νξ′.

The name of the deceased, contained in l. 3, is uncertain : Ἀλαφα seems to me fairly clear, but what follows is puzzling alike in reading and in construction, nor do I know whether Ἀλαφα is a complete name. We may compare Ἀλολεφα in (*J*) above, Ἀλαφιρ in *A.J.A.* 1910, 64 No. 13, Ἀλάφθα in Lidzbarski, *Ephemeris* i. 86, 191, and especially Ἀλαφᾶν (Χαλαφάνης), *ibid.* ii. 338 f. For the name Ζοναίνου (l. 4) see No. 2 and note. Hyperberetaeus 13th in the Arabian calendar is equivalent to September 30th : if I have read aright the first two numerical signs, the year is A.D. 565–6, or one of the nine following years.

18. On a limestone fragment : the inscription is poorly cut, and the surface has flaked away. Plate XXXVI : $\frac{1}{5}$.

$$\Theta\acute{a}[\rho\sigma\iota], \; Ka\sigma\acute{a}\nu\delta\rho\eta, \; [o\mathring{v}]\delta[\grave{\iota}]s \; \mathring{a}\theta\acute{a}\nu a\tau os.$$

For this type of epitaph see No. 19 (below) and note. The text, reconstructed from the copy and a squeeze, is, I think, certain, though I do not understand why $Ka\sigma\acute{a}\nu\delta\rho\eta$ is used in place of $Ka\sigma(\sigma)\acute{a}\nu\delta\rho a$.

19. Limestone. Plate XXXVI : $\frac{1}{5}$.

$$\Theta\acute{a}\rho\sigma\iota, \; Mo\phi\acute{a}\delta\delta\eta.$$

Perhaps the words $o\mathring{v}\delta\epsilon\grave{\iota}s \; \mathring{a}\theta\acute{a}\nu a\tau os$ were added on the stone below. For this type of epitaph see, *e.g.*, Nos. 11, 18 (above), *R.B.* 1905, 251 No. 8, 255 No. 15 (=*C.R.A.I.* 1904, 303), 256 No. 34. $Mo\phi\acute{a}\delta\delta\eta$ must, I take it, be a personal name, but I have not found any parallel to it, or explanation of its meaning.

20. In a cemetery on the Saadi road. On a limestone plaque, on which a large cross is engraved. Plate XXXVI : $\frac{1}{5}$.

$$Ma\rho\acute{\iota}a \; Ka\iota\kappa o\acute{v}\mu o[v].$$

$Ma\rho\acute{\iota}a$ is the commonest woman's name in this district. The name $Ka\acute{\iota}ov\mu os$ (or -μas) is attested by several Greek inscriptions of Syria, *e.g.*, *P.A.E.S.* A. 2, 20 *a*, A. 3, 261, 267, *R.B.* 1903, 274 f. Clermont-Ganneau reads $Ka\iota o\acute{v}\mu as$ in place of $\kappa a\grave{\iota} \; O\mathring{v}\mu as$ in *Bull. Corr. Hell.* 1902, 201 No. 50, and is inclined to correct the **KAIOYNⲰ** of Wadd. 2089 into $Ka\iota o\acute{v}\mu ov$ (*Rec.* v. 368 ff.). We also meet with the names $Ka\acute{\iota}a\mu os$ (Wadd. 2103, 2253 *a*, 2436) or $Ka\ddot{\iota}a\mu os$ (Wadd. 2413 *j*) and $Ka\acute{\epsilon}\mu as$ (*P.A.E.S.* A. 3, 302). Whether $Ka\acute{\iota}a\mu os$ and $Ka\acute{\iota}ov\mu os$ are different names or variant spellings of the same name is doubtful : Clermont-Ganneau regards them as distinct (*Rec.* v. 369) ; the American scholars are divided (*P.A.E.S.* A. 3, 261 note). While leaving the decision to those who have a right to pronounce one, I would call attention to a small piece of evidence, which may or may not be of importance, but has, I think, been overlooked. In Wadd. 2089–91 we have three building-inscriptions from the same place ('Amra in Batanaea), the similarity of which, alike in phraseology and in the names they contain, seems to point to a close connexion between them : 2089 is dated ἐπὶ τοῦ θεοσεβ(εστάτου) Ἡλίου καὶ Καιούνω πρ(εσ)β(υτέρου), 2090 ἐπὶ τῶν θεοσεβ(εστάτων) Δονέσου κ(αὶ) Ἡλίου, 2091 ἐπὶ τὸν θεοσεβ(εστάτων) Καιάνου (so I would write the name instead of Καιανοῦ) καὶ Δονήσου καὶ Ἡλία πρεσβ(υτέρων). I find it hard to resist the inference that the Καιούνω of 2089 and the Καιάνου of 2091 represent one and the same man, and that if Clermont-Ganneau corrects the former to Καιούμου he should correct the latter to Καιάμου. The name קוימא is found also in Syriac (see Payne-Smith, *Thesaurus* ii. 3600) and may be derived from the root קום, denoting strength or permanence (*ibid.* 3523).

21. In the graveyard east of the town. Limestone, 0·20 × 0·14 m. Plate XXXVI.

+ Σέργιος Ἰωάν[νου].

Both names are common in this region.

22. In a graveyard on the Saadi road. On a limestone slab. Plate XXXVI : ⅕.

I cannot read the first line of this inscription. On the right we have, perhaps, the word χαῖρε, below Θεοδωρίς (unless we should read Θεόδωρε or Θεοδώρα), and within the circle A and ω.

23. On a limestone slab, of which the upper left-hand and the lower right-hand corners are broken away. It is covered with a thick deposit, which hides much of the surface. Plate XXXVI : ⅕.

I cannot restore this inscription. In l. 1 we may have the latter part of the word [μν]ήμην, and in l. 4 the beginning of μη[νός] : in l. 5 we certainly have ἰνδ(ικτιῶνος), but the indiction-number is lost.

24. On the lower part of a limestone stele, broken off above, 0·30 × 0·25 m. Plate XXXVI.

The letters ΑΒΡΔΙ I cannot explain.

25. In a cemetery on the Saadi road. On a fragment of limestone, engraved with a large cross. Plate XXXVI : ⅕.

I cannot interpret the extant letters.

26. Limestone plaque, broken into two. Plate XXXVII : ⅕.

Of the inscription I can make nothing.

27. On a fragment of a marble slab. Plate XXXVII : ⅕.

The inscription is too mutilated to be capable of restoration.

RAHEIBA (REHOBOTH).

28. On a limestone slab, complete on the left and below. Plate XXXVII : $\frac{1}{5}$.

+ ’Ανα[πάη ὁ μα]κάρ(ιος) ’Επ - - -

The inscription probably begins thus : the rest is too mutilated to admit of restoration.

29. On the circular top of a limestone stele. Plate XXXVII : $\frac{1}{5}$.

I have not succeeded in deciphering this inscription. It apparently begins + ’Ανεπάε ἡ μακ(αρία), if the sign which follows the α of line 2 is a κ, followed in turn by the sign of abbreviation. Then come the name and patronymic of the deceased (Κασ. ολη Πέφτου ?), and finally the date (μηνὸς ’Απ[ελλαίου ?] ι[γ]΄ ἔτ(ους) - -).

30. Around the circular top of a limestone stele. Plate XXXVII : $\frac{1}{5}$.

The beginning and the end I cannot understand : between come the words :—

- - ὁ μακ(άριος) Στέφ(ανος) καὶ - - -

31. Round the circular top of a limestone stele. Plate XXXVII : $\frac{1}{5}$. Only the words

Παρθένε Θ(ε)ῷ (?)

are legible : the latter may well be part of the adjective θεοσεβής or θεοφιλής.

32. On the lower part of a circular-topped limestone stele. Plate XXXVII : $\frac{1}{5}$.

Beyond the concluding word, ἔτους, preceded by a numeral, I can make nothing of this inscription.

33. On a fragment of a circular plaque of limestone, on which a cross is engraved. Plate XXXVII : $\frac{1}{10}$.

The inscription has been lost save for three letters.

ABDA (EBODA).

34. On a marble slab on the south of the church, 1·50 × 0·55 m. (See Fig. 34.)

+ ’Ανεπάη ὁ μακάριος Ζαχαρίας ’Ερασίνου ἐν μηνὶ Πανέμου δεκάτῃ, ἰνδ(ικτιῶνος) ιδ΄, ἡμέρα Κυριακῇ, ὥραν τρίτη(ν) τῆς νυκτὸς, κατετέθη δὲ ἐνταῦθα τῇ τρίτῃ τοῦ σάμβατος ὥραν ὀγδόην Πανέμω δωδεκάτῃ, ἰνδ(ικτιῶνος) ιδ΄, ἔτους κατὰ Ἐλουσ(ίους) νος΄ι Κ(ύρι)ε <a> ἀνάπαυσον τὴν ψυχὴν αὐτοῦ μετὰ τῶν ἁγίων Σου. ἀμήν.

The name Ἐρασῖνος recurs in No. 14 (above). If the calendar here used is that "of the Arabs," Panemus 10th and 12th of the year 476 will answer to June 29th and July 1st, A.D. 581. The fact that these dates fall within Indiction XIV (which began on September 1st, 580) supports the hypothesis. It is curious to find this calendar here referred to as that κατὰ Ἐλουσίους, a phrase which does not, so far as I am aware, occur elsewhere : Ἐλοῦσα is the ancient name of Khalasa, and we have already seen evidence that the calendar in question was in use there (No. 13 : cf. R.B. 1905, 253 ff).

The precision of the epitaph, which records not only the date, but the day of the week and even the hour, of death and burial, is worth notice. The word σάμβατος has a two-fold peculiarity, the substitution of μβ for ββ (for which many parallels could be quoted) and the derivation from a nominative σάββα in place of σάββατον, of which I know no other examples save the dative plural σάββασι quoted in Sophocles' Lexicon from Macc. i. 2, 38, Meleager 83, and Josephus, Ant. xiii. 12, 4 ; xvi. 6, 2.

35. Graffito on door-jamb of baths, incised in the stone. (See Fig. 39.)

The inscription apparently runs

Κ(ύρι)ε [β]οήθι Στ[εφάν]ου,

and may be complete, though in such texts words like τοῦ δούλου Σου are ordinarily added. The substitution of the genitive for the dative after βοήθει is a very common phenomenon. Cf. A.J.A. 1910, 65 No. 2 (Bir el Seba) Βοήθε [Στεφά]νου, Κύριε, κτλ.

36. Graffito on door-jamb. (See Fig. 41.)

The name Δόμνα is clear : the rest I do not understand. Δόμνος and Δόμνα occur frequently in inscriptions of Syria, e.g., Wadd. 1894, 2413g, 2573, 2642 a, 2683.

I take this opportunity of correcting an error which has crept into the publication of an epitaph from Sbaïta in the Negeb. According to the editors it closes with the words ὁ Θε(ὸ)ς ἀναπαύσῃ δύϊον (R.B. 1905, 257 No. 35 = C.R.A.I. 1904, 304). For **ΔΥΙΟΝ** we should clearly read **ΑΥΤΟΝ** (see R.B. 1905, Plate X) and we thus get a prayer similar to those in R.B. 1905, 250 No. 4 (= C.R.A.I. 1904, 301) Θε(ὸ)ς αὐτὸν ἀναπαύσῃ and R.B. 1903, 425 Κ(ύριο)ς αὐτὴν ἀναπαύσῃ.

INSCRIPTIONS FROM SOUTHERN PALESTINE.

In No. 11 of the Raheiba inscriptions published by N. Schmidt and B. B. Charles (*A.J.A.* 1910, 60 ff.) the final ζε may well stand for ζῇ, while in No. 14 the ευλα may be a fragment of the word εὐλαβέστατος, found, *e.g.*, in Wadd. 2413 *a*.

II. SEMITIC.

The following note on a Nabatean inscription at Khalasa (*see* p. 109) is contributed by Dr. A. Cowley :—

The text, based on a hand copy and a squeeze (Fig. 59), is as follows :—

1. זנה אתרא
2. זי עבד
3. נתירו
4. על חיוהי
5. זי ח[ר]תת
6. מלך
7. נבטו

"This is the place which Nuthairu (?) made for the life of Aretas, King of the Nabateans."

Line 1. אתרא, the last two letters are broken, but are almost certainly to be so restored. As, *e.g.*, in *C.I.S.* ii. 235², the word probably means a chapel or votive pillar.

Line 3. Nuthairu. I cannot find the name. The first letter might be ז , but that would be no better. Or it may be only the left-hand stroke of a letter. The fourth letter might be ד or even ב (?).

Line 4. The usual formula is על חיי פ׳ (cf., *e.g.*, *C.I.S.* ii. 354²).

The inscription is merely votive, like so many of those collected in the *C.I.S.*, and from that point of view does not call for much remark. Its interest lies in the forms of the characters, which are somewhat like those in *C.I.S.* ii. 162, but earlier in style. In fact they belong to an Aramaic alphabet which is only just beginning to develop the peculiarly Nabatean forms. None of the letters is typically Nabatean. Note, *e.g.*, א, ב, י, ל, מ. What then is the date of the inscription, and which is the Aretas to whom it refers? Not Aretas IV., to whose reign (9 B.C. to 39 A.D.) most of the Nabatean inscrip-

FIG. 59.—KHALASA: NABATEAN INSCRIPTION.
(Photo from a squeeze with blackened characters.)

tions in *C.I.S.* belong, since he always has the title רחם עמה "loving his people," and his alphabet is in a much more developed and evidently later style. Nor Aretas III. φιλελλην (85–62 B.C.). We have no inscription belonging certainly to his reign, and we should hardly expect to find one in this corner of Syria, since Aretas III. was fully occupied about Damascus and at Petra. Khalasa is on the high-road about 45 miles south-east of Gaza. Josephus (Ant. xiii, 13, 3) mentions that Aretas II. (ὁ Ἀράβων βασιλεύς) was expected to go to the help of Gaza in 96 B.C., and it seems probable that this inscription is in some way connected with the proposed expedition. Aretas I. (about 169 B.C.) is unlikely on other grounds and also because in 2 Macc. 5[8] he is called τὸν τῶν Ἀράβων τύραννον, which would seem to show that he had not yet assumed the title of king. The early date, 96 B.C., is supported by the forms of the characters; and the fact that they are less developed than those of *C.I.S.* ii. 162 (ascribed to about the same date) may be due to the locality of the inscription, in the south-west of Palestine away from the regular sphere of Nabatean influence. The same local reason no doubt accounts for the use of the common Aramaic היוהי זי ח, זי, זנה instead of the usual Nabatean היי ה, די, דנה.

An inscription in Arabic on a block of yellow limestone broken into three pieces was found lying on the side of the road down the Nagb el Akaba, a few hundred feet above the bridge in Wady el Musri (*see* p. 12). A few characters which were missing have been restored in the transcription. Professor D. S. Margoliouth contributes the following note :—

Inscription of the Sultan Ḳānṣuh al-Ghūri.

(Compare Van Berchem, *Corpus,* p. 594, sqq.)

In Ibn Iyās's list of the buildings, etc., erected by this Sultan (A.D. 1500–1516), we read (iii. 62, last line) : *He repaired the road of 'Akabah and Duwar Ḥakn, and built there a Khān with towers over its gate and set therein storage-places for the deposits of the pilgrims.* The inscription, which was carefully squeezed and copied, is as follows :—

امر بقطع هذا الطريق المبارك مولانا السلطان الملك الاشرف قانصود الغوري عز
نصرد وكان الواقف في هذا الخان المبارك ابراجا لـ(ودائع الحد)جا(جـ)

The cutting of this blessed road was ordered by our master the Sultan al-Malik al-Ashraf Ḳānṣuh al-Ghuri, may his help be strong, who also erected in this blessed khān towers for the deposits of the pilgrims.

The last letters are not quite clear, except for the word meaning *towers*. We are probably safe in supplementing from Ibn Iyās.

The phrase الواقف is ordinarily used somewhat differently.

ILLUSTRATIONS

Plate I

(1) Between Beersheba and Khalasa

(2) Wady el Khalasa

Plate II

(1) Wady Issad, showing Tamarisk hedges of Byzantine fields of Khalasa.

(2) Jebel Araif el Naga from West.

Plate III

(1) Nagb el Akaba

(2) Geziret Faraun

Plate IV

(1) Ain Gharandel

(2) Cairn at Tell el Seram.

Plate V

(1) Tomb at Tell el Seram before excavation.

(2) Same tomb at Tell el Seram after excavation.

Plate VI

(1) Old tomb at Kossaima.

(2) Modern tomb at Kossaima.

Plate VII

(1) Tell el Kasr el Raheiba

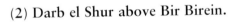

(2) Darb el Shur above Bir Birein.

Plate VIII

(1) Byzantine cistern on Darb el Shur near Bir Birein.

(2) Bir Berein

Plate IX

Darb el Shur below Jebel
Mushrag, where it turns west
for Egypt.

Plate X

Wady Ain Kadeis, looking up the valley over the watering place.

Plate XI

(1) Ai Kadeis: Spring and Rivulet.

(2) Ain Kadeis: The spring.

Plate XII

(1) Ain Kadeis: The wild fig-trees.

(2) Ain Kadeis: A furnished grave.

Plate XIII

Wady Ain el Guderat: The Tell in the valley.

Plate XIV

(1) Wady Ain el Guderat, east.

(2) Wady Ain el Guderat, west.

Plate XV

Ain el Guderat

Plate XVI

(1) Mishrafa

(2) Esbeita

Plate XVII

(1) Esbeita: Reservoirs

(2) Esbeita: Reservoirs

Plate XVIII

(1) Esbeita: North church from its west front.

(2) Esbeita, north church: Fortified postern on S. W. angle.

Plate XIX

(1) Esbeita: Central church and monastery.

(2) Esbeita: South church.

Plate XX

(1) Esbeita: Private house

(2) Esbeita: A wall, showing manner of construction.

Plate XXI

Esbeita: Vaulting and ceiling.

Plate XXII

(1) Esbeita: House with upper storey.

(2) Ebeita: Terrace-wall in a valley.

Plate XXIII

(1) Khoraisha: Rock-cut cistern.

(2) Abda: castle interior from the tower of the south church.

(1) Abda: Tell with graves and upper town.

(2) Abda: Castle from south, seen over ruins of upper town.

(3) Abda: Castle, north gate and tower door.

(4) Abda: Capital from north church.

(1) Abda: Castle, South-east angle.

(2) Abda: Baths, domed room.

Plate XXVI

(1) Beersheba: Font

(2) Beersheba: Statuette

Plate XXVII

(1) Beersheba: Inscription

(2) Beersheba: Byzantine capitals

Plate XXVIII

(1) Raheiba: From a church tower.

(2) Raheiba: Reservoir

Plate XXIX

(1) El Auja: Castle from the church.

(2) El Auja: Church

Plate XXX

(1) Wady Kurnub

Plate XXX

(2) Kurnub: Great dam

Plate XXXI

(1) Kurnub: Town and west government buildings.

Plate XXXI

(2) Kurnub: Capital and voussoirs of west church.

Plate XXXII

(1) Roman blockhouse below Nagb el Safa
(Kurnub-Petra Road).

(2) Nagb el Safa

Plate XXXIII

(1) Rock-cut cistern in Wady Deira.

(2) Typical chalk country in S. desert

Plate XXXIV

Greek Inscriptions I

Plate XXXV

12

13

14

15

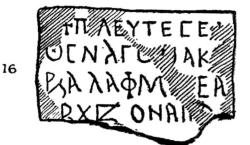

16

17

Greek Inscriptions II

Plate XXXVI

ΘR
ΧΑCΑΝΔΡΗ
ΔΛΕΙΑ
ΝΑΤΟC

18

ΘΑΡCΙΜΟ
ΦΛΔΔΗ

19

ΜΑΡΙΑ
ΚΑΛΟΥΜC

20

+CΕΡΓΙΟC
ΙΩ ΑΝ

21

ΜΛΗΩ
ΒΕΔΑΩΤΙC

22

ΗΜΗΝΤ
ΕΡΜΑΝΧΑ
Α Ο ΕΥΤ
ΜΗ
ΙΝΔC

23

ΑΒΡΔΙ

24

ΗΜΡ ΓΡΑ

25

Greek Inscriptions III

Plate XXXVII

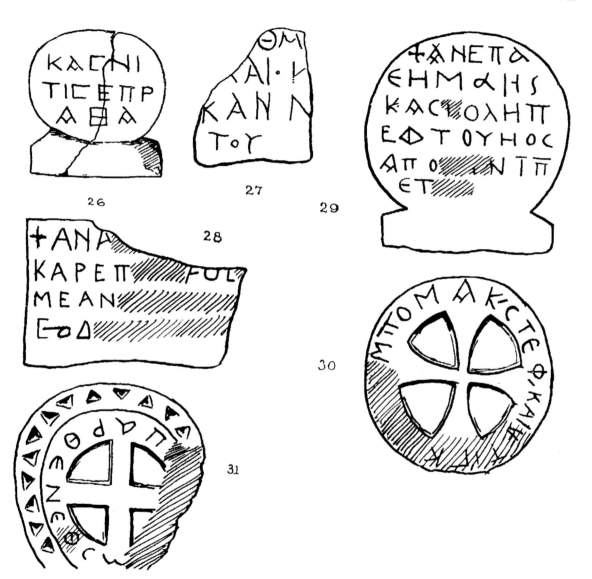

26

27

28

29

30

31

Plate XXXVII

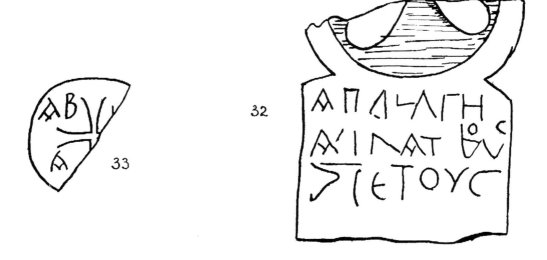

Greek Inscriptions IV(b)

INDEX

PUBLICATIONS OF THE PALESTINE EXPLORATION FUND.

Second-hand Copies of Books and Maps marked "Out of Print" may be had by Application to the Secretary.

BOOKS.

1.—THE QUARTERLY STATEMENT. A Journal of Palestine Research and Discovery. Issued free to Subscribers. Single numbers 2s. 6d. For back numbers apply to the Secretary, 2, Hinde Street, Manchester Square, W. Cases for binding, in yearly vols., in Green or Chocolate, 1s. each.

2.—INDEX TO THE QUARTERLY STATEMENTS, 1869–1892 inclusive. 3s. Index from 1893–1910 inclusive. 5s. (Unbound, 3s. 6d.)

3.—THE SURVEY OF WESTERN PALESTINE. 4to. Seven Volumes and Index, as under: Memoirs, 3 vols. ; Special Papers ; Name Lists ; Jerusalem Volume and Portfolio of Plates ; Fauna and Flora, by Canon TRISTRAM. (*Note.*—"Fauna and Flora," by Canon TRISTRAM, LL.D., D.D., F.R.S., can be purchased separately. Price £3 3s.)

4.—THE SURVEY OF EASTERN PALESTINE. (One Volume.) By Colonel CONDER, LL.D., M.R.A.S., R.E. £3 3s.

5.—ARCHÆOLOGICAL RESEARCHES. (Two Volumes 4to, profusely Illustrated.) By Prof. CLERMONT-GANNEAU, LL.D. Vol. I, Jerusalem and its Vicinity ; Vol. II, Investigations in Southern Palestine. £5 5s.

6.—THE FAUNA AND FLORA OF SINAI, PETRA, AND THE WÂDY 'ARABAH. (One Volume, richly Illustrated.) By H. CHICHESTER HART. £2 2s.

7.—THE GEOLOGY OF PALESTINE AND ARABIA PETRÆA. By Prof. E. HULL, LL.D., F.R.S., F.G.S. Uniform with Nos. 3 to 8. 21s. *Out of print.*

8.—ACROSS THE JORDAN. By G. SCHUMACHER, C.E. 6s. 8vo. *Out of print.*

9.—THE JAULAN. By G. SCHUMACHER. With Map, Plans and Illustrations. 6s.

10.—ABILA, PELLA, AND NORTHERN 'AJLUN. By G. SCHUMACHER. 6s.

11.—LACHISH. By Prof. FLINDERS PETRIE, Litt.D., LL.D. 10s. 6d. *Out of print.*

12.—A MOUND OF MANY CITIES (Lachish). By F. J. BLISS, M.A., Ph.D. With numerous Illustrations. 6s.

13.—EXCAVATIONS AT JERUSALEM, 1894–1897. With Plans and Illustrations. By F. J. BLISS, M.A., Ph.D., and A. C. DICKIE, A.R.I.B.A. 12s. 6d.

14.—EXCAVATIONS IN PALESTINE, 1898–1900. (Profusely Illustrated.) By F. J. BLISS, M.A., Ph.D., R. A. S. MACALISTER, M.A., F.S.A., and Prof. WÜNSCH. 4to. £2 10s.

15.—THIRTY YEARS' WORK : A Memoir of the work of the Society. By Sir WALTER BESANT. 3s. 6d.

16.—JERUSALEM, THE CITY OF HEROD AND SALADIN. By Sir WALTER BESANT and Prof. E. H. PALMER. St. Martin's Library Edition. 2s. cloth, 3s. leather, net.

17.—PALESTINE UNDER THE MOSLEMS. By GUY LE STRANGE. With Map and Illustrations. 16s.

18.—TENT WORK IN PALESTINE. By Colonel CONDER. 6s. *Out of print.*

19.—HETH AND MOAB. By Colonel CONDER. 6s. *Out of print.*

PUBLICATIONS OF THE PALESTINE FUND—*continued.*

20.—JUDAS MACCABÆUS. By Colonel CONDER. 4*s.* 6*d.* *A Reprint.*

21.—THE LATIN KINGDOM OF JERUSALEM, A.D. 1099 to 1291. By Colonel C. R. CONDER. 7*s.* 6*d.*

22.—SYRIAN STONE LORE. By Colonel CONDER. 6*s.* New Edition.

23.—THE TELL AMARNA TABLETS, including the tablet found at Lachish. Translated by Colonel C. R. CONDER. 5*s.* 2nd Edition. *Out of print.*

24.—MOUNT SEIR. By Prof. E. HULL. 6*s.* *Out of print.*

25.—NAMES AND PLACES IN THE OLD AND NEW TESTAMENTS AND APOCRYPHA, with references to Josephus, and identifications. By GEORGE ARMSTRONG. 6*s.* *A Reprint.*

26.—THE BIBLE AND MODERN DISCOVERIES. By HENRY A. HARPER. 7*s.* 6*d.* 5th Edition.

27.—THE CITY AND THE LAND. Seven Lectures on Palestine. Single Lecture, 1*s.* ; the Volume, 3*s.* 6*d.* 2nd Edition.

28.—THE LIFE OF SALADIN. By BEHA ED DIN (A.D. 1137–1193). Translated and Annotated by Colonel CONDER, with a preface and notes by Major-General Sir CHARLES WILSON. 9*s.*

29.—THE ANCIENT CUBIT AND OUR WEIGHTS AND MEASURES. By Lieut.-General Sir CHARLES WARREN, K.C.B. 5*s.* 6*d.*

30.—PAINTED TOMBS AT MARISSA (MARÉSHAH). By the Rev. J. P. PETERS, D.D. (New York), and Dr. HERMANN THIERSCH (Munich). 4to, in cloth, £2 2*s.*

31.—METEOROLOGICAL OBSERVATIONS AT JERUSALEM. With Tables and Diagrams. By JAMES GLAISHER, F.R.S. In paper covers, 2*s.* 6*d.*

32.—GOLGOTHA AND THE HOLY SEPULCHRE. With Plan of Jerusalem and Illustrations. By Major-General Sir CHARLES W. WILSON, K.C.B., K.C.M.G., F.R.S., D.C.L., LL.D., &c. Demy 8vo. Price 6*s.*

33.—AN ARABIC ASTROLOGICAL TREATISE. By a Jerusalem Christian native. Translated and annotated by Miss GLADYS DICKSON. Price 1*s.*

34.—AN OLD HEBREW CALENDAR-INSCRIPTION FROM GEZER.—With facsimile. By Prof. LIDZBARSKI, the Rev. G. B. GRAY, D.D., D.Litt., and Mr. E. J. PILCHER. Reprinted from the *Quarterly Statement*, Jan. 1909. Price 1*s.*

35.—THE EXCAVATION OF GEZER, 1902–5 AND 1907–9. By Prof. R. A. STEWART MACALISTER, M.A., F.S.A. With Illustrations. 3 Vols. 4to. £4 4*s.*

36.—A TABLE OF CHRISTIAN AND THE MOHAMMEDAN ERAS. From July 15th, A.D. 622, the date of the Hejira, to A.D. 1900. By the Rev. J. E. H. HANAUER. (Pamphlet.) Price 7*d.*

37.—PALESTINE PILGRIMS' TEXT SOCIETY'S LIBRARY.—This valuable collection of early descriptions of the Holy Places, and of the topography of Palestine, published by the Palestine Exploration Fund, in 13 vols., royal 8vo, bound in cloth. The complete set, £10 10*s.* A catalogue, giving full details, free on application.

38.—THE ANNUAL Publication giving full reports of Excavations in progress—commencing 1911—price 21*s.* Issued free to all subscribers of 21*s.* and upwards. Contains an account of the excavations at AIN SHEMS (BETH SHEMESH) during 1911, and of investigations carried out at RABBATH AMMON, and PETRA.

39.—ANNUAL No. 2. Double number for the years 1912–13, price 31*s.* 6*d.* Contains a full report of the excavations at AIN SHEMS (BETH SHEMESH) during 1912.

40.—ANNUAL No. 3. Double number for the years 1914–15, price 45*s.* THE WILDERNESS OF ZIN : The complete archæological report of the SURVEY OF THE NEGEB AND N.E. SINAI carried out during 1914.

PUBLICATIONS OF THE PALESTINE FUND—*continued.*

MAPS AND PLANS.

1.—THE GREAT MAP OF WESTERN PALESTINE, with modern names only. (In 26 sheets, with portfolio ; Scale, 1 inch = 1 mile.) £3 3s.

2.—MAP OF PALESTINE, with modern names only. In 20 sheets. Scale, ⅜ of an inch = 1 mile. Including both sides of the Jordan, and extending from Baalbek in the north to Kadesh Barnea in the south. £1 10s. *Out of print.*

3.—MAP OF PALESTINE, with modern names only. In 12 sheets. Scale, ⅜ of an inch = 1 mile. 17s. 6d. *Out of print.*

4.—OLD AND NEW TESTAMENT MAP OF PALESTINE in 20 sheets. Scale, ⅜ of an inch = 1 mile. £1 10s.

5.—OLD AND NEW TESTAMENT MAP OF PALESTINE in 12 sheets. Scale, ⅜ of an inch = 1 mile. 17s. 6d.

6.—MAP OF WESTERN PALESTINE, showing WATER BASINS IN COLOUR, AND 5 VERTICAL SECTIONS. In 6 sheets. Scale, 2¾ miles = 1 inch. 13s. *Out of print.*

7.—THE SECTIONS of the Country north and south, and east and west, on 2 sheets. 2s. (Western Palestine only.)

8.—PLAN OF JERUSALEM (reduced from the Ordnance Survey Plan), showing in red the latest discoveries, with separate list of references. 1s. 6d. ; mounted on cloth, 2s. 6d.

9.—PHOTO-RELIEF MAP OF PALESTINE. Scale, 5 miles to the inch. 6s. 9d., unmounted ; mounted on cloth, roller, and varnished, 10s. 6d. Size mounted, 30 inches by 52 inches.

10.—PHOTO-RELIEF MAP OF PALESTINE (Small). Size, 25 inches by 13 inches. 2s. 9d. unmounted.

11.—NEW MAP OF THE "DESERT OF THE WANDERINGS," from Mount Hor on the East to the Suez Canal on the West, and from Mount Sinai in the South to Beersheba in the North. Compiled by the War Office, and based principally upon the sketch Surveys of the Palestine Exploration Fund. Scale, 4 miles to the inch. In eight sheets. Price 1s. 6d. per sheet. The Complete Map, mounted on linen, and with a few of the scriptural sites inserted in red by hand, 21s.

All maps can be had mounted on rollers for hanging, or on cloth and folded.

MODELS AND CASTS.

1.—RAISED MAP OF PALESTINE. (Constructed from the Surveys of the Palestine Exploration Fund by G. ARMSTRONG.) Scale, ⅜ of an inch = 1 mile (the same as Map No. 4). Casts in fibrous plaster, coloured and framed. £13 13s. The map measures 7 feet 9½ inches by 4 feet 1½ inches.

2.—SMALL RAISED MAP OF PALESTINE. (Constructed by G. ARMSTRONG.) Scale, 6¼ miles to an inch. Casts in fibrous plaster, coloured and framed. £6 6s. The map measures 42 inches by 32 inches.

Both maps are on view at the office of the Fund, 2, Hinde St., Manchester Sq., W.

3.—RAISED CONTOUR MAP OF JERUSALEM AND ENVIRONS. Scale $\frac{1}{2500}$, with the ancient walls discovered on Eastern and Western Hills marked in red. Price £3 3s. Map measures 5 feet by 4 feet 3 inches.

4.—RAISED CONTOUR MAP OF JERUSALEM to smaller scale ($\frac{1}{10000}$) without indication of Ancient Walls. 19 inches by 19 inches. Price 25s.

5.—SEAL OF "HAGGAI, THE SON OF SHEBANIAH." Facsimiles of this Signet, in metal. 1s. each

6.—CASTS OF THE TABLET WITH CUNEIFORM INSCRIPTION FOUND AT LACHISH. 2s. 6d. each.

7.—CASTS OF THE ANCIENT HÆMATITE WEIGHT, brought by Dr. CHAPLIN from Samaria. 2s. 6d. each.

8.—CASTS OF INSCRIBED BEAD, referred to in p. 32, *Quarterly Statement,* 1893. 1s. each.

9.—CASTS OF THE SEAL FOUND ON OPHEL, referred to in p. 181, *Quarterly Statement,* 1897. 2s. 6d. each.

10.—CASTS OF THE SILOAM INSCRIPTION. £1 1s. each, framed.

11.—CASTS OF MOUNT SINAI. Small, Coloured, framed, and names written, 15s. Size, 9½ inches by 9¾ inches. Large, Coloured, framed, and names written, £1 15s. Size, 25 inches by 27 inches. Scale, 6 inches to the mile.

12.—CASTS OF THE INSCRIBED TABLETS FOUND IN THE EXCAVATIONS OF GEZER (*Quarterly Statement,* p. 229, 1904 ; p. 206, 1905). Price 1s. 6d. each.

PHOTOGRAPHS AND SLIDES.

PHOTOGRAPHS. A very large collection, 6½ in. by 8 in., unmounted, 10d. each ; A Catalogue of the Photographs, arranged alphabetically according to the Bible names of places, can be had on application.

Photos, with translations, of the inscription from Herod's Temple, of the Moabite Stone (restored), and of a facsimile of the Siloam Inscription ; also photo of the Jar found at the foundation of the S.E. corner of the wall of the Temple Area, 80 feet below the present surface. Sent to Subscribers for 7d. each, post free.

LANTERN SLIDES of the Bible places mentioned in the Catalogue of Photographs and Special List can be had on application at the Office. A large Assortment. Price 1s. each, uncoloured. 10s. per dozen.

LANTERN SLIDES of the Raised Map. Plain, 1s. 3d. ; coloured, 2s. 9d. each. Post free.

Branch Associations of the Bible Society, all Sunday Schools within the Sunday School Institute, the Sunday School Union, and the Wesleyan Sunday School Institute, will please observe that by a special Resolution of the Committee they are allowed to purchase the books, maps, etc. (by application to the Secretary only), at the reduced price.

Apply to the Secretary, Palestine Exploration Fund, 2, Hinde St., Manchester Sq., W., or, in the U.S.A., to the Hon. Gen. Secretary, 50, Forest Street, Hartford, Conn.

NOTE FOR SUBSCRIBERS.—*Subscribers of a Guinea (or, in America, of $5.0) and upwards can purchase most of the Books or Maps at a considerable reduction upon application to either Secretary, as above.*

HARRISON AND SONS, PRINTERS IN ORDINARY TO HIS MAJESTY, ST. MARTIN'S LANE, LONDON.

APPENDICES

APPENDIX 1

Key

—————— Woolley and
Lawrence

·············· Woolley

-------- Lawrence

**Map from Chapman and Gibson 1996
showing route of survey**

APPENDIX 2

Materials Relating to The Wilderness of Zin Survey
in the P. E. F. Archive

PEF/ZIN and ZIN 2- Two bound volumes of letters and other documents relating to the Survey and the republication of 1936 (bound according to a sort by Jeremy Wilson).

Volume 1 (Zin) contains 100 documents (nos. 1-100) to do with the survey and its publication, 1913-15. Volume 2 (Zin 2) contains 173 documents (nos. 1-173) to do with the republication of the survey in 1936. All items are listed in chronological order.

PEF/LAWRENCE LETTERS 1-11 – Bound volume with 9 letters of Lawrence and 2 of Woolley relating to the publication of *The Wilderness of Zin*.

These letters were apparently separated from the main archive after Lawrence's death in 1935 and were never returned, hence their binding into a different volume. This is confirmed by a note written on the back of a lecture ticket for a talk by Garstang on Jericho, to be given on June 26th, 1936, which reads: 'Survey of Negeb/Wilderness of Zin/1914/Correspondence etc. Newcombe, Woolley, Lawrence'. Many years later was added the note: "Checked 1964 i no (underlined 3 times) correspondence from Lawrence (underlined)." (*Zin Addenda* 5; see below).

There is also a debate as to how many letters written by Lawrence there were originally in the PEF archive. Newcombe refers to19 letters in 1935 (Newcombe 1935, p. 113), but a letter to A. M. Sandston, in Christchurch, New Zealand (dated 11. 9. 1936) states that Newcombe was in error and that there were only eight letters (PEF, Zin *Addenda* 6.2). However, B. Douglas Newton received copies of 10 letters for the Garnett edition on September 11th, 1937 (PEF Zin *Addenda* 5.3). We know that at least two letters are indeed missing (for 24th Sept and Oct. 2nd, 1814; PEF/EC/7, 135-6), and that only nine survive today. It seems that a maximum of ten survived through to 1935, the remainder having already being mislaid. Furthermore, it does seem that the inclusion of two letters by Woolley in this part of the archive could have confused the issue.

PEF/DA/WL/67-122: Drawings, Maps and Plans used in the *Wilderness of Zin*. (Folder labelled 'Maps Plans Sinai Survey 1914 III 1914-15')

This folder contains original artwork and plans from the Survey and prepared for the publication.

PEF/ZIN *Addenda* – A Variety of unbound material relating to the publication of the survey (sorted by Felicity Cobbing and Sam Moorhead):

1-4. 1914/5 Edition text and photographic proofs.

5. Correspondence about Lawrence letters in the PEF with B. D. Newton (1937).

Preparation for Garnett 1938, in which one of the letters was published (p. 188-9, no. 76). Garstang Lecture Card for June 26th, 1936.

6. Correspondence about Lawrence letters in the PEF with A. M. Sandston who was sent typed transcripts (1936).

7.1 28 Newspaper reviews and announcements for the 1936 republication of the *Wilderness of Zin*. [see PEF/Zin 2, 114 for general list of newspapers.]

7.2 Miscellaneous paper cuttings: Lawrence obituaries and memorial service.

PEF Executive Committee Minute Books:

Three Minute Books cover the period of the survey, its publication and republication:

PEF/EC/7 (Dec. 19th, 1911 to June 30th, 1922)
PEF/EC/8 (Sept. 20th, 1922 to July 25th, 1935)
PEF/EC/9 (Sept. 26th, 1935 to November 3rd, 1965)

Wilderness of Zin Survey Map (PEF/M/ZIN *Addenda* 8)

The map presented by Sir Charles Close and Stewart Newcombe on May 18th, 1921 (PEF/EC/7, p 366) is now framed in the PEF archives:
"The Negeb or Desert South of Beersheba", "Surveyed by, and under direction of, Captain S. F. Newcombe R.E. 1913-1914 and printed for The Palestine Exploration Fund by the G.S., G.S., War Office, 1921." [1 inch to 3.95 miles; 1cm to 2.5km]

Wilderness of Zin photographs taken by C. L. Woolley and T. E. Lawrence (PEF/P/W/L)

The archive contains photographs and negatives from the survey. For a comprehensive account of this archive, see Chapman and Gibson 1996.

PEF/ZIN Archaeological Material – A drawer of finds (pottery and flint)

This is to be published in the next volume on the *Wilderness of Zin*.

APPENDIX 3

Selected Archival Material, relating to the Wilderness of Zin
Survey, held at the Palestine Exploration Fund

ZIN 1
Copy of letter (FO 371/1812, fos. 279-80)
To: Under Secretary of State for Foreign Affairs
From: Directorate of Military Operations (M.O.4/Africa/341)
Date: 19th September 1913
Marked "Confidential" and handwritten note: "Submitted by
Colonel Hedley to Committee of Nov. 4, 1913"

The Director of Military Operations presents his compliments to
the Under Secretary of State for Foreign Affairs and begs to refer
to his note of April 18th 1913, No.M.O.4/Africa/153 and Sir A.
Nicolson's reply of May 2nd 1913 (17911/13), on the subject of
obtaining the permission of the Ottoman Government to the
execution of a survey of the area lying between Palestine proper
and the Sinai Peninsula. A party of five officers is at present
employed in completing the survey of the Sinai Peninsula proper,
and they will be able, if permission is granted, to execute a rapid
survey of the area beyond this boundary in the time and with the
money at their disposal. If this area is ever to be surveyed, the
coming winter offers a favourable opportunity such as may not
recur. In Brigadier General Wilson's opinion the circumstances
have changed since last May. The fact that the Balkan war is over
has so modified the situation, as it stood last May, that Brigadier
General Wilson hopes that the objections which were then held to
make it undesirable to approach the Ottoman Government on
this subject, may no longer hold good.

The proposed survey is very desirable from a military point of
view, and is essential for the proper study of the problem
presented by the defence of the north-eastern frontier of Egypt.

Footnotes: See PEF Minute Book 1911-22 (PEC/EC/7), pp. 93-4, for minutes of November 4th, 1913, meeting . See Zin 2 below for further reference to the Balkan War. Mrs. Reider had sent a book on the Balkan War to Lawrence at Carchemish in December 1913 (Garnett 1938, 162, no. 67).

ZIN 2
Copy of Letter
To: No addressee, but apparently the PEF
From: Eyre A. Crowe, for the Secretary of State, Foreign Office
(No. 310. Confidential. 43118/13)
Date: September 25th, 1913

Sir,

With reference to my despatch No. 129 of May 2nd, to Sir G. Lowther, relative to a proposal to complete the survey for military purposes of the region of the Turco-Egyptian frontier, I transmit to you herewith copy of a further communication from the Director of Military Operations on the subject.

   I am myself in no position to judge whether the fact of the termination of the Balkan War is likely, as surmised by Brigadier General Wilson, to make the Turkish Government take a more favourable view of this project than they would have done during its continuance or whether their objections to it would be overcome if the request were put forward, as proposed, through the Palestine Exploration Committee, ostensibly for their own purposes and I should be glad to receive an early expression of your views on the question in its general aspect special reference to the views and suggestions contained in the present communication.

I am, &c.,
(For the Secretary of State),
(Signed) Eyre A. Crowe.

ZIN 5
Original Letter
To: Sir Charles M. Watson, K.C.M.G., C.B., Chairman of the PEF
From: The War Office, Whitehall, S. W.
Date: October 30th, 1913

Dear Sir Charles,

We have just received permission for the "Survey of Palestine Exploration Committee" to extend their work to the Egyptian boundary – The Turkish governments have given permission. The whole of the work must be carried out under the auspices of the P.E.C. [PEF] <u>but we will supply two officers and pay all the expenses.</u> You will perhaps want to send an archaeologist. If you are coming down here we could settle details, or I could come and see you at any time.

Yours sincerely,

W. C. Hedley

Footnote: The PEF Minute Book tells us that Colonel W. C. Hedley, of the Topographical Sector at the War Office, was elected to the Committee of the PEF on October 21st, 1913 (PEF/EC/7, 89 and 92).

ZIN 8
Copy of Letter
To: Under Secretary of State for Foreign Affairs
From: Military Operations Directorate, War Office, S.W. (M.O.4/Africa/341)
Date: 4th November, 1913

The Director of Military Operations presents his compliments to the Under Secretary of State for Foreign Affairs, and, with reference to Sir A. Nicolson's note No. 49258/13, of the 30th October, begs to say that he has been in communication with the Palestine Exploration Fund, of which Sir Charles Watson, K.C.M.G., C.B., is chairman. Sir Charles would be glad if the services of Captain S. F. Newcombe, R. E., could be lent for this survey. Captain Newcombe is now in the Sinai Peninsula, and there will be no difficulty in making his services available. It is thought that he will require the assistance of another officer and two non-commissioned officers, all of whom should be expert topographers. Sir Charles also hopes that it may be possible to secure the services of an archaeologist.

Brig.-General Wilson suggests that a telegram be sent to Lord Kitchener as follows:-

'Turkish Government has given permission for extension of Palestine survey to Turko-Egyptian frontier, the work to be understood as in the interests of Palestine Exploration. Captain Newcombe, now in Sinai, should undertake the work and take one of his officers, the others remaining to complete the Sinai survey. It is considered that Captain Newcombe should start this new work as soon as possible. The area to be done lies west of a straight line from the Dead Sea to Akaba. Captain Newcombe should estimate time and money required. It is proposed to send out two non-commissioned officers, as in the case of the Palestine Survey. It is possible that Palestine Exploration Fund may send out an archaeologist. Suggested that El Arish should be the base for the new work. Full details follow.'

Footnotes: A letter from the Geographical Section, General Staff, War Office, read to the PEF Committee on December 2nd, 1913 (Zin 16 & PEF Minute Book 1911-22 / PEF/EC/7, p. 99) tells us that the team was to be: Captain S. F. Newcombe, R.E., Lieutenant J. P. S. Greig, R.E., Corporal J. Rimmer, R.E. and Lance-Corporal W. W. McDiarmid, R.E. Zin 20 tells us that a Mr. Montagu also joined Newcombe's survey team (also see Zin 37 below).

The PEF was also to receive a grant of £100 from the Royal Geographical Society (Zin 17 and PEF Minute Book 1911-22 / PEF/EC/7, p. 102 for December 16th, 1913).

ZIN 12
Original Letter
To: Sir Charles M. Watson, K.C.M.G., C. B., Chairman of the PEF
From: Frederic G. Kenyon, Director of The British Museum
Date: 21st November, 1913

Dear Sir Charles,

Hogarth [D. G. Hogarth, Director of the Ashmolean Museum] concurs in the idea of lending our men from Jerablus to the PEF survey for about two months from the latter part of December, and suggests that, as the time is short, both should go. Their names are C. L. Woolley and T. E. Lawrence. The former is the senior man, with rather wider experience; the latter is the best at colloquial Arabic, and gets on very well with natives. He has, I think, more of the instincts of an explorer, but is very shy.

Time being short, I have written ahead to Jerablus, to ask them if either or both care to entertain the idea, and to cable their answer. I have warned them that you may have engaged some one else in the interval, or that you may not be able to take both of them. You are therefore quite uncommitted, and can take either, neither or both when their answer comes. Both are good men; Hogarth can tell you more about them, if you wish.

Yours sincerely,

F. G. Kenyon

Footnote: Dr. L. W. King, of the Department of Egyptian and Assyrian Antiquities at the British Museum was to suggest to Sir

Charles Wilson that Woolley and Lawrence should receive £1 a day (Zin 15, letter dated 26th November, 1913). This advice was followed (see Zin 23, below).

[This letter previously published: Wilson 1988, pp. 42-3, no. 72]

ZIN 23
Carbon Copy of Letter
To: C. L. Woolley
From: Sir Charles Watson, K.C.M.G., C.B., Chairman of the PEF
Date December 16th, 1913

Dear Sir,

Sir Frederic Kenyon has informed you of the intended survey of the south country of Palestine, and the Executive Committee are pleased to hear from him that you and Mr. Lawrence are willing to assist in the archaeological exploration of the district. It is proposed that you should each recieve a fee of £1 – 0 – 0. *per diem* and expenses, while engaged on work for the Committee, and they hope that this arrangement will meet your views.

You are no doubt acquainted with the Survey of Western Palestine on the scale of one inch to the mile, which was carried out by the Society in 1872-77, and which has been the basis of exploration in Palestine since it was published. The southern limit of that survey was a line running approximately from west to east, through Gaza and Beersheba, to Masada on the western shore of the Dead Sea.

The country, of which the survey is now to be taken in hand, is that south of the previous survey, up to the line of the Egyptian frontier, which extends from Rafah, on the Mediterranean coast about 20 miles south west to Gaza, in S.S.E. direction, to the head of the Gulf of Akabah. The eastern limit of the new survey will be a line running north through the Arabah, from the Gulf of Akabah to the southern end of the Dead Sea.

This country, notwithstanding its proximity to Palestine and Egypt, is but little known, and, though it has been crossed by travellers in certain parts, is to a great extent unexplored. A favourable opportunity has now presented itself, and Captain Newcombe R.E., with the party of the Royal Engineers, has obtained permission to make a survey of the district. The topographical work will be carried out by Captain Newcombe, but it is of great importance that an examination of the country should be made from the archaeological point of view, as there are many remains of great interest to the Biblical student, and it is for this part of the work that the Committee are desirious of enlisting the services of yourself and Mr. Lawrence.

You will be under the orders of Captain Newcombe, who is to be regarded in every respect as the Chief of the expedition, but the Committee have no doubt that he will do all he can to assist you in your special duties.

Speaking generally, the objects of the expedition are as follows:

1. To produce an accurate map of the country on the scale of half an inch to the mile.
2. To make special plans of important localities, ruins, and other archaeological remains.
3. To take photographs of buildings and other points of interest.
4. To take squeezes and photographs of any inscriptions that may be found.
5. To collect geological specimens, and ancient stone and flint implements.
6. To record carefully all names now in use.

You can understand that it is difficult for the Committee to give any definite instructions as to the mode of carrying out the work, for much will depend on the progress of the survey, but they feel sure that you will understand the spirit of what is required, and will do all you can to collect useful and accurate information.

A sum of £100 is being placed to the credit of the Palestine

Exploration Fund with Messrs. T. Cook and Sons at Jerusalem, who will be informed that you can draw upon it for your expenses, and it is requested that you will keep a careful check on the sums drawn from Messrs Cook, and at once inform the Committee when further amounts are required. As soon as possible after the end each month you should send to this office a return, with general details, of the amount actually expended.

A copy of this letter is being sent to Captain Newcombe, who has been requested to communicate with you, care of Messrs. Cook, Jaffa, and to inform you of his movements. It is understood that he proposes to hire camels and organize his caravan at Gaza, but it is not possible at present to say whether he will have started from that place before you arrive. In that case he will have left information as to his movements with the British Consular Agent at Gaza.

The Committee wish you to know that Yusuf Canaan, who acted as foreman under Professor Macalister at Gezer, and under D. Mackenzie at Beth-Shemesh, is available, and it is for your consideration whether you should like him with you. He is a very useful man and has acquired a considerable knowledge of exploration and of pottery. His rate of pay when employed by the Society is 120 francs monthly. You can hear of him from Professor Porter, of the the Protestant College at Beirut. Dr. Masterman the Hon. Secretary of the Fund in Jerusalem, who has just arrived in England, says that he instructed Prof. Porter to send Yusuf to Jaffa, so as to be ready for work in connection with the present expedition if required, but the Committee do not know whether he has started from Beirut.

The Committee would be obliged if you would acknowledge the receipt of this letter, and express your views as to the proposed exploration. They would also be glad to hear from you about once a fortnight in order that they may know how matters are progressing.

As it is desirable to keep the subscribers to the Palestine Exploration Fund informed of what is being done, the Committee would be obliged if you would send a short article to arrive in

London about March 1st. in time for publication in the Quarterly Statement for April, which might be accompanied by a few photographs, suitable for reproduction as illustrations. On the conclusion of your work a complete report should be furnished, giving all the information that has been obtained, and including name lists in Arabic of all places.

Wishing you and Mr. Lawrence every success in your exploration. Believe me, yours very truly,
Chairman of the Executive Committee

ZIN 37
Copy of an Extract of a Letter (forwarded to Sir Charles Watson, PEF, by Col. W.C. Hedley, 23rd January, 1913 [sic; actually 1914] To: War Office (Col. W. C. Hedley?)
From: Captain S. F. Newcombe, R.E.; Gaza, Palestine
Date: 7th January 1914; second part 10th January 1914

I'm very bored with myself for having taken so long getting a start on this show: and even now not going full steam, as have to visit each party to see that they have got everything they want, even food supplies, and know where to get food, &c., when required. Of course, it isn't as easy as when working in a country where one can employ Government to act as agents for forwarding, &c., when, too, the country is somewhat impassable and much is absolutely uninhabited. However, things are getting along and the first series of ▲ are done by Montagu from El Augi for frontier to Beersheba and by Greig south from Beersheba. After joining up well to PEF work, and in the narrower strip to south, I shan't triangulate much, but will make 2 or 3 really big ▲ from frontier to Mount Hor, where Aaron's tomb is, near Petra, also to Gebel Taba (4200') near Akaba, and one north of Gebel Hor, so that the work will be well tied in by really good balanced and big ▲, should it ever be carried on. The north strip is too wide not to triangulate and also one must join on to PEF (which, by the way, is over 1/2m. too far west).

In 2 or 3 weeks' time Corpl. Rimmer and I move to 30°15' lat. and finish thence to Akaba, while Montagu does 30°15' to 30°45', with McDiarmid's help, and Greig does S.E. from Beersheba thence up Araba to Dead Sea. I must do the rough bit near Akaba so as to see all the country; also it is a bit troublesome being so far from the base that it was up to me to take that on and push it through quickly. I shall then work up to Araba (which must be done before the weather gets too hot and the grazing is good, meeting, I hope, Montagu near Wadi Musa in March); thence we go up Wadi Musa to Mount Hor to observe Sinai gebels to fix it (and see Petra!) I'm calculating to leave the hills east of Beersheba till the end, because they can be done nicely at the end in hot weather and are also least important.

Greig has been ill for a fortnight but is now all right. I go to see him to-morrow, thence to Beersheba to meet Woolley and Lawrence, the archaeologists, who, I'm glad to say, are coming. Naturally, one hasn't much time nor enough knowledge for that part of the business, though after the survey is well through I might devote more time to it, especially if I learn much from them.

The estimate I sent to the Colonel was really too low and I gave myself no room for eventualities. If we finish on that estimate it will only be if everything goes absolutely well. £300 more is about it. I wrote to Nugent last week giving a long yarn of what has happened, but, though I've lost time, it hasn't cost much, and looking back I don't think I could have done otherwise, as my camel contract is good and cheap. We had impossible weather while waiting and Greig was ill for a fortnight. Then the Sheikh of Terabin never turned up at Gaza. I ought to have gone to see him much earlier, but was badly advised. However, things are going quite smoothly now, without being at breakneck speed yet. The map won't be much below Sinai standard, but time won't be wasted on unnecessary detail, if I can help it.

Wish I had another of my T. and Simms *alidades*. I have 2 S.M.E. pattern ones which one of the N.C.O.s has to use, and, though new, they are of very poor value. Badly designed and not well made, the parallel ruler gets loose at once and the base of the telescope has side play, not being strong enough. The telescope is very good but has an inverted field, and the N.C.O., of course, took the useless vertical arc off the first day; but its box is its worst fault, as, when new, there is 1/4" play between lid and box (only being closed by a strap, hence any amount of dust can get in; the leather straps are sewn on with cord, which will soon go. My box, however, is both easy to carry and very easy and quick to open; also won't get worn and keeps dust out.

Footplate of telescope should have three screws, not 2, as in S.M.E. pattern.

[Newcombe includes a sketch of the footplate]

[3 paragraphs about an expedition to Nile-Congo frontier omitted]

10.1.14.

[one paragraph about Nile-Congo expedition omitted]

Woolley and Laurence [sic] have turned up: quite nice fellows; they have been working at Kharkamish, near the Euphrates, for some years for the British Museum. I've come to Beersheba to meet them and leave to-morrow for Khalasa. Two days awful sandstorm, which stops all work; fearfully annoying, but, fortunately, I couldn't have done much, being at Beersheba fixing up Woolley and Laurence. I presume their expenses have nothing to do with me.

PEF maps reduced to 1/2" not yet received, so have no edges to join to.

(Sd.) Stewart F. Newcombe.

ZIN 47
Original Letter
From: Capt. Stewart. F. Newcombe, c/o British Consular Agent,
Gaza, Palestine
To: Sir Charles M. Watson, K.C.M.G., C.B., Chairman of the PEF
Date: February 15th, 1914

Dear Sir Charles Watson,

I have just written a report on events up to date: I am afraid it is
not of much use either scientifically or literary, so please make
whatever use you like of it & abstract whatever you think fit. I
believe I have never written anything except an official report
before for publication.

Lord Kitchener told me that I was to remain under the Army
of Occupation Cairo, so I have sent the report to them, asking the
G.S.O. to forward to you as soon as possible. This I believe is the
correct procedure, as regards anything to be published: & also, by
the way, saves my writing another long report to Cairo!

On the whole, things have gone quite satisfactorily: at the
present moment I am being held up, quite courteously, by the
Kaimmakam at Akaba who says he has no information about us
being allowed to survey in his province; this however will be a
temporary trouble only. Woolley and Lawrence have been most
interesting & I am sure their results will be extremely useful. I
only wish they could have stayed longer. Lawrence has just
reached me from Ain Kadeis & tells me that Woolley has sent you
a fairly long report. Yusuf Kanan was quite useful till they came,
but in much of the country there is nothing for him to do: so he
will probably return North with Woolley.

Yours sincerely,

Stewart F. Newcombe

P.S. I have omitted to thank you for the various PEF journals which have been very interesting: I have lent them to Woolley who I think has found them very useful. Also the book *Kadesh Barnea* [editor's italics] has just reached me in time for Lawrence to study it. Thank you very much for sending it.

Footnote:
The report Newcombe refers to is probably the letter forwarded by W. C. Hedley to the PEF (see Zin 37, above)

ZIN 48/49
Original Letter and Transcript
From: C. Leonard Woolley, Tell Kurnub
To: Sir Charles M. Watson, K.C.M.G, C.B., Chairman of the PEF
Date: February 17th, 1914

Dear Sir,

Your letter of Jan. 22nd has just reached me and I hasten to reply to it. You will, before this reaches you, have received the short article I sent on our work up to the time when we reached Ain Kadeis. We spent nearly a week in that neighbourhood (we had to stop as stores were coming from Egypt) and were rewarded by finding in Wady Ain el Guderat a small fort of early date which we were able to plan and from which I have brought away a lot of potsherds; from Ain Kadeis Mr Lawrence went South, and I have since been at Abda and I am now at Kurnub, both Byzantine Towns of which the latter does not seem to have been remarked before. I know of course that Byzantine sites are late for the interests of the society, but the fact is that there are very few places where traces of earlier occupation exist; the country, at all other points, has been inhabited by nomads only; south of Beersheba there are hardly any old town remains, and the cities of Joshua XV. etc. either lay north of our boundary or were largely mythical, they may have been small collections of tents such as exist today, but just as today there are only three built houses between Beersheba and Akabah so it was throughout history, with the single exception of the Byzantine period, and of a few early forts, of which we have found three dating back to the 2nd. Millennium B.C. and one (at Abda) of the 2nd century B.C. Much of the country is so bad that even the Bedouins move out of it in the summer and come north of Beersheba and its district. You cannot find many traces of nomads, for they leave but few that will last. Indeed I fear that the results of the Survey as a whole can hardly but be a disappointment to the Society at least so far as biblical research is concerned.

In the time at our disposal the only possible course has been to visit the most promising sites and to omit altogether such parts of the the country as are reported by the surveyors to present on the surface little or nothing of interest. The collection of names has also, necessarily, been left to the Surveyors, who are going over the ground in more detail than we are; and it would be impossible for us to enter accurately any considerable number of names on a map that has yet to be made. When things of interest turn up, the site is reported to the surveyor for that district, so that he may locate it, but in accordance with Captain Newcombe's directions we are not attempting to make any list of names as such. A great deal of our work is concerned with Byzantine things simply because they exist, and as we are to examine the archaeology of the country they cannot be omitted.

Mr. Trumbull's book has gone to Captain Newcombe at Akabah, so I have not seen it, I regret this, and must secure it later; but if the rest of it is on a par with his description of Ain Kadeis quoted in "Thirty Years Work," it is the most egregious farrago of lies. It speaks wonders for the Children of Israel that they left Moses alive after he brought them to a place like that.

Up on the north country to which I am now coming I hope to find some early sites, it is on the skirts of the Tell district. But as I have to be in Aleppo by March 1st my time is nearly over.

With best regards.

Yours faithfully,

C Leonard Woolley.

P.S. excuse pencil as I have only indian ink & little of that.

ZIN 56
Original Letter
To: Sir Charles Watson, K.C.M.G., C.B., Chairman of the PEF
From: Colonel W. C. Hedley, Geographical Section, General Staff,
War Office, Whitehall, S. W.
Date: March 10th, 1913

Dear Sir Charles,

I had written note to say that the War Office had no objection to Newcombe's report being published when I noticed that the covering letter from the G. O. C. Egypt was marked "SECRET". I see nothing secret in it but it is hardly possible to publish a document which marked secret by the sender – I am however referring the matter to higher authority and you shall hear again. I forgot if I told you that we have heard from the Foreign Office that the Turks were getting a bit restive about this survey, and have asked that operations should be confined to the province of Gaza. It will not therefore extend down to Akaba, but the southern piece was only a wedge, and not of much importance. I do not know the extent of the province of Gaza but we may be sure that Newcombe will make it extend as far south as possible.

Yours sincerely,

W. C. Hedley

Footnote:
The report in question might in fact be Zin 37 (see above)

ZIN 68
Original Receipt
To: C. L. Woolley
From: T. E. Lawrence, Carchemish
Date: June 1st, 1914

Received of C. Leonard Woolley, the sum of Sixty six pounds (£66-0-0), being the salary due to me for work done on behalf of the Palestine Exploration Fund from December 28th 1913 to March 3rd 1914 inclusive.

T. E. Lawrence
June 1, 1914

Footnote: this is the first correspondence in any form from T. E. Lawrence in the PEF archive. This receipt was sent to the PEF by Woolley in the letter dated July 1st, 1914 (Zin 69).

Lawrence Letter 2
To: Mr. J. D. Crace (PEF)
Date: October 20th 1914.
From: T. E. Lawrence (Oxford – no address given)

Dear Mr. Crace,

I have cut the beginning up as you suggest .... only leaving pages 8 and 9 in Chapter 1 instead of introduction. They deal with Gaza, and go better there, I think.

In the introduction I have cut out four pages, and brought them down to two: you might read them again: you will notice they foreshadow a shortening of Chap V. the Byzantine part. I should be loath to cut down Chaps. 1-4 for they are really rather important ... mostly constructions:... whereas V. deals only with the Christian Greek, which has been all done before nearly as well, and I think about 40 or 50 pages of its 120 could come out. This would relieve you of about 10,000 words ... and so few people like Byzantine things. Also these are bad Byzantine! I think the photographs should each be numbered separately. It was only while arranging them into pairs that I kept a sheet notification.

The shortening of Chap V. would slay about a dozen plans. I will be in town from Wednesday (tomorrow) onwards ... so keep the material by you.

Yours sincerely

T E Lawrence

Postscript at top of first page:

Don't put the introduction into type of course till the last:- or any of it till I have corrected names and numbers

(PEF stamp and LAW/2)

**Lawrence Letter 8
To: Mr. J. D. Crace (PEF)
Date: Sund. (no date); Received Nov. 30th
From: T. E. Lawrence, M. O. 4., W. O.**

Dear Mr. Crace

I drew a map in my spare nights – quite a rough sketch, sufficient for the need – of the part of Sinai which Woolley & I visited: Gaza – Kossaima – Akaba – Dead Sea, and marked on it the names in the book, & two or three old roads we saw. Col. Hedley has passed this as fit for publication, and so I have sent it to Mr. Hogarth, for him to put Darbishire on it to draw it properly. I was afraid to put much detail into it, because then it would have been unsafe to publish it.

This having been approved there is no difficulty further in the way of your publishing our report complete in Jan next. I would recommend you to publish fairly early in the month. Things may happen.

Woolley sails with me on Friday: we have each given up all further part in the book. It is for Mr. Hogarth to do as he pleases with it: so do not send proofs to Egypt.
The enclosed War Office people have assisted publication, & should have free copies.

Yours sincerely,

T E Lawrence

(PEF stamp and LAW/8/1?)

Enclosed list:

Major S. Keffington-Smyth War Office
Captain Russell M. O. I. C. W. O.
and of course Colonel Hedley.
I think also – copy should be sent to
E. M. Dowson Esq. Director Egyptian Survey Dept. Giza, Egypt.
and copies to Mr. Hogarth for Prof. Margoliouth and & Dr. Cowley, & Mr. Tod.

Across page: Large tick and "May 11 1915"

(PEF stamp and LAW/8/2)

Footnote:
It has to be assumed that J. D. Crace ticked Lawrence's list when Annuals were sent out to the people listed on May 11th.

Lawrence Letter 9
To: Mr. J. D. Crace (PEF)
Date: 3 Dec.
From: T. E. Lawrence, M. O. 4.

Dear Mr. Crace

I only got the MSS yesterday from Woolley – and it has been sent on today. I think it is in fairly complete condition .... though we would go tinkering on it or months.
Your 3/8 map of Palestine is being prepared, on two sheets, which suits the W. O. better than six! It is a very pretty map indeed. I go off to Egypt on Tuesday, overland to Marseilles, with Captain Newcombe who is in the W. O. for a few days writing reports, and checking the maps. We are both almost uncomfortably busy, as you guessed.

Woolley goes off on Saturday from London by P. + O. I think these dates are certain: somebody got into a row for delaying our start so long.

The Newcombe map is nearly finished. I'm afraid it can't be sold by you for a few months yet! But it is going to be enormously useful. That survey was a very fortunate stroke.
Addresses of both Woolley & myself will be General Headquarters, British Army [of] Occupation, Cairo. Don't send out proofs, because the Censor would never pass them. Much better Egypt shouldn't know.

Yours sincerely

T E Lawrence

(PEF stamp and LAW/9)

Lawrence Letter 11
To: Mr. D. G. Hogarth
Date: ?late November or early December 1914
From: Leonard Woolley, Old Riffams, Danbury, Essex.

Dear Hogarth

Here is the whole of the Sinai MSS. It would be a good thing if in Ch. III you could add a few words about the pottery fragments (painted) which Lawrence told me you had at the Ashmolean. About the pottery from Gudeirat I wrote from memory all I could but you might care to add to that also. I don't know whether Lawrence arranged for a plate of flints: I hope rather that he did, but it is not a thing of great importance as the text, I think, disposes of the question pretty thoroughly. I put L's name on the title page, which he hadn't done, but of course it ought to be there. * [see below, footnote 1] I've been able to add a bit to the MSS as he left it, & had to rewrite part of his work criticising Prof. Huntington, whom he had rather misrepresented; fortunately I found I had the book here, so was able to put that right. Lawrence tells me you are going to see the book through the press, for which my many thanks.

I wish the Liverpool people would do something about my Deve Huyuk article; but I believe Percy Newberry is at the front! so probably nothing can be done.

Yours

C. Leonard Woolley

Footnotes by T. E. Lawrence (written in red ink)

1. added at foot of the second page

* I must object to this: it wasn't in any respect my book and I would very much rather that my name was not on the title page. TEL

2. after Woolley's signature

Newberry is of the opinion that he sent you the MSS.

(PEF Stamp and LAW/11)

Footnotes:
The first proof of the cover page which only bore C.L. Woolley's name is in the PEF Archive (PEF Zin *Addenda* 3)
Woolley's article on Deve Huyuk was:
C. Leonard Woolley, 'A North Syrian Cemetery of the Persian Period', Annals of Archaeology and Anthropology Vol. VII (Liverpool Institute of Archaeology), 1916, pp. 115-129
Jeremy Wilson suggests this letter dates to October 1914 (Wilson 1988, p. 46, no. 78), but the editor believes that it was written in late November or early December (see Introduction, p. xxxviii-xxxix).

APPENDIX 4

Selected Newspaper Reviews for the *Wilderness of Zin*

The London Guardian (**22 May, 1936**) (Zin *Addenda* 7.1.26)

The Wilderness

It is a sound rule not to review what are, strictly speaking, new editions of old books, giving them the same kind of prominence as really new books. Commendation may be wasted on those who read the first edition; some new book may be ousted which deserves commendation. Yet there is sometimes good excuse for breaking the rule. And there is excuse here, if ever there was. For this book was prepared before the War and seen through the press (by Dr. D. G. Hogarth) when the writers were on active service. They were in 1913 a youngish and a very young scholar, neither of whom had behind him (as each had before him) the support and force of a public reputation. The book was more or less forgotten by the time that both had achieved world-wide reputations, both as oriental savants, and both, in different ways, as literary men who could describe what they had seen; and one, alas! had been cut off untimely in a career that provoked bewildering expectations. The scene, too, of the work described is of perennial interest to all Europeans, and the romance of archaeology, greatly aided by the survivor's work and pen, has a stronger general attraction than ever before. The original publication was as the "Annual" of the Palestine Exploration Fund for 1914-15. The book now has the added distinction of an introduction by Sir Frederic Kenyon. The comments on inscriptions that are reproduced were written by Mr. M. N. Tod, and apparently remain as an original chapter.

The short introduction has its own charm and includes a few kindly criticisms and corrections. Well may Sir Frederic's attitude be almost a fatherly one. In 1913 Sir Leonard Woolley and Colonel T. E. Lawrence were aged 32 and 22 [sic; 24] respectively.

Sir Frederic had sent them out to "dig" for the British Museum at Carchemish in the land of the Hittites. When they were due to come home, he was asked by the Palestine Exploration Fund to let them stay in the East and to help Colonel Newcombe who was surveying for the fund in Southern Palestine. Sir Frederic sent them with his blessing. Neither of them was trained in such things as Greek inscriptions or Byzantine architecture. Neither was properly equipped for the arduous exploration of wide expanses of desert, and as it turned out neither could stay for more than a few weeks. It is astonishing that they covered so much ground as they did and have so much new information to give. They could excavate one grave here, part of one church there, and so on, but could never settle down to a thorough exploration of any whole site. Yet such experience as they had was directed by the wonderful instinct that we now know that both men had born in them, and aided too by a rare sympathy with the Arabs whom they met, with the result that they give us a great quantity of sound learning and original discovery.

The title, *The Wilderness of Zin*, may not convey to readers the extent of the district surveyed, which includes parts of what our old Bible maps used to mark as the Deserts of Shur and of Paran, and Mt. Seir. However, the precise determination of Bible names is a very large and an unsatisfactory task. Our authors on the matter write that:

> Research into local nomenclature is to-day very difficult among the tribesmen; and it is not likely that Moses was more patient and painstaking than a modern surveyor.

This reflection comes from one of several passages in which they dispute with other writers, particularly with the highly imaginative American traveller of the eighties, Mr. H. C. Trumbull, over the headquarters for so long of the Israelites, called in the Pentateuch Kadesh-Barnea, and generally but rashly identified with the modern Ain Kadeis. Every kind of practical consideration is urged here to make the identification untenable, unless the name is used very vaguely for Ain Kadeis and the whole plain of Kossaima to the North-West. Between them one or other of our authors surveyed the country through which the great road, Darb el Shur, from Palestine "went down into Egypt," from Beer-sheba by the ruins of Khalasa, Raheiba and El Auja, and across the Turco-Egyptian boundary; southward along that frontier to Akaba at the head of the Red Sea; northward again up El Araba, leaving Petra to the East, and over the wild country of mountains and wadis in between.

There are 40 plates, mostly photographs taken of the country. To look at them is as instructive in a way as to read the letterpress. Nothing more deadly or depressing could be imagined. They really give the impression of a "god-forsaken" land. Parched rocks, dried watercourses, stony and sandy ground stretching to a pitiless horizon, deserted ruins and inhospitable hills, leave one wondering how the very few miserable beduins [sic] and their wretched animals manage to keep body and soul together in their ragged apologies for tents. A question of general interest is, Was it ever so? We know the theories, applied elsewhere, of climatic changes and of countries depopulated through a diminished rainfall. Our authors declare that they saw no proof whatever of any such change, sudden or slow. The country, they say, never had any settled population to speak of. There is no sign of man at all beyond the second millennium B.C. There is no sign of the land having ever been afforested; in all the ruins of buildings there is not a sign of a piece of timber ever having been used. There is no sign, indeed they say that there is no possibility, of greater areas having been cultivated. It is true that better crops were probably raised because better implements were used and the storage of water better managed. Even so the provision for storage of grain points to the same need to hoard a good crop to carry the people over other rainless seasons. Whenever military posts or monasteries were established (and monks and hermits deliberately sought the most desolate retreats) the first consideration for life was to store water, and traces of elaborate efforts are to be found wherever water could be led to them. Cultivable soil was even more labouriously and jealously terraced than in the familiar rocky parts of Provence and Italy. Unlike the Syria to the North, where the order imposed by the power of Byzantium resulted in a largely increased and settled population so long as that power lasted, the wilderness and solitary places south of Palestine scarcely developed at all because no development was possible. It is a bold theory that a place like Esbeita, which could build, if not fill, three churches, could have existed entirely on stored water, but that is our authors' conclusion. Sir Frederic Kenyon points out that they are a little too sweeping when they go on to say that after the days of the Emperor Heraclius and the Persian campaigns of the Byzantine Empire when the garrisons of the little scattered posts were withdrawn, the organised forces of Mohammedanism wiped out the Christian population, and the few nomads alone struggled to live there as to-day, lacking sufficiency of those first necessaries of life – food, water and shelter – in the grim scene of those photographs.

That is enough to show that this is the most up-to-date book on the subject, apart from its other merits. It also shows that more may be done to carry on the work of Jesuit Fathers, of Royal Engineers (including Lord Kitchener) and others who have deserved well in the past. It is satisfactory, therefore, to know that the PEF and the British School of Archaeology at Jerusalem are planning the completion of the new Survey in the place of the sixty-year-old one. Readers of the Guardian will wish them good luck in the name of the Lord.

Castor.

The Egyptian Gazette, **Alexandria (1 May, 1936)** (Zin Addenda 7.1.21)

The Wilderness of Zin

The Wilderness of Zin was first published in 1915 by the Palestine Exploration Fund, and is an account – a hurriedly written one – of an archaeological expedition undertaken by Sir L. Woolley and Col. T. E. Lawrence through the wild, unexplored country that lies south of Beersheba. It is said now that there was some special significance in the fitting up of the expedition which started at the end of 1913, as the object was not so much the studying of the various Byzantine towns, but was organised rather with a view to mapping and obtaining some knowledge of this unknown stretch of country which would no doubt figure in the war that was impending. Captain (now Colonel) Newcombe was hard at work mapping in the Wadi Araba to the south and arousing the suspicions of the Turk in Akaba, and Lawrence and Woolley were entrusted with a hurried survey of the area to the north. Whether there is any truth in these rumours only those "in the know" can tell, but one must be grateful to the organization that inspired the expedition, for it has provided us today with another specimen of Lawrence's work.

The book was completed in a hurry in 1914 after the War had broken out and proof-reading and the seeing of the volume through the press was undertaken by Mr. D. G. Hogarth, as both Lawrence and Woolley had been called to Egypt for special service. The book, as its title denotes, is a description illustrated by plans, maps and photographs of the archaeological remains in the area of Zin, which comprises Southern Palestine and Eastern Sinai, and is also a most concise topographical record of the country.

With a joint authorship it is difficult to detect how much of the book is the work of Lawrence and how much that of Woolley, for the quality of writing throughout is of a very high order, with the easy attractive style of *The Seven Pillars of Wisdom*.

The book deals with the plateau country south of Beersheba, and gives a full description of the deserted Byzantine towns of Esbeita, Raheiba, and Khalasa. The expedition then crossed over into Sinai in the vicinity of Auja and spent some days studying the traces of Roman occupation in the area. Here they parted, and Woolley crossed over the border again at Ain Gedeirat to visit Kurnub and Abda south of Beersheba, whilst Lawrence journeyed south to meet Colonel Newcombe near Akaba.

The book is chiefly remarkable for the fact that, though the two authors were only engaged for a short six weeks making their survey, they have nevertheless compiled a most conclusive and accurate account of the whole of this very wide area. Lawrence particularly shows his very remarkable clarity of vision and powers of deduction in his all too short description of Eastern Sinai and the Darb el Shur – the ancient road to Egypt:

"The wearying monotony of senseless rounded hills and unmeaning valleys makes this southern desert of Syria one of the most inhospitable of all deserts – one which, since the Mohammedan invasion, has been the unenvied resort of defeated tribes too weak to face the strenuous life of the greater deserts."

He saw that Sinai has never had a prosperous past, and attributes rightly the signs of cultivation and intensive cultivation in the Kossiema and Auja areas to the fact that the main road to Egypt ran through this district: and the caravans coming from the ports of Suez and Tor with the merchandise of the East required halting-places where supplies, water and forage could be obtained.

In his account of Ain Kadeis his puckish humour comes out, and he scarifies a Mr. H. C. Trumbull, an American, who in 1882 gave this Ain a typical American "write-up" in flowing journalism and was therefore responsible for the identification of this dirty little waterhole with the Kadesh Barnea of the Bible.

A pleasing side to the book is the tribute to Colonel Newcombe for the work he had done in southern Palestine and the unfailing help he rendered to this expedition. Colonel Newcombe has so successfully "hidden his light under a bushel" that only those conversant with his work and activities in the past are aware of how much he achieved in the days prior to the War and exactly how far he was responsible for the success of the Arab revolt in 1917 and 1918.

It is interesting to note that an Archaeological Survey of the whole of Palestine is being planned to commence shortly which will follow to a large extent the methods adopted by the English Royal Commission on Ancient and Historical Monuments. This great work will be carried out jointly by the Palestine Exploration Fund and the British School of Archaeology in Jerusalem, and will, when completed, furnish a concise record of all the ancient and mediaeval sites of Palestine. It will bring up to date, revise and amplify in the light of modern knowledge the old Survey which was made over 60 years ago, when the services of Lieut. H. H. Kitchener (the late Field. Marshall. Viscount Kitchener) and officers of the Royal Engineers were employed by the Fund.

C. S. Jarvis

Footnote (by R.L. Chapman III):
'Major Claude Scudamore Jarvis, CMG, OBE., (1879-1952) was a soldier, administrator and orientalist who served in South Africa at the turn of the century and later in France, Egypt and Palestine during the First World War. In 1918 he joined the Egyptian Frontier Administration and succeeded Lieutenant-Colonel W. F. Stirling as Governor of Sinai in 1922. In the following thirteen years he acquired an extensive knowledge of Arabic and Bedouin customs and established a reputation for settling tribal disputes. He wrote a number of books about his experiences in the Middle East including two that have a Lawrence interest: Three Deserts and Arab Command: the Biography of Lieutenant-Colonel F. G. Peake Pasha. Although

his meeting with Lawrence was very brief, he was familiar with those connected with the Arab Revolt and with the terrain over which they operated' (P. Kerrigan, 'Notes on the Article and Contributors', *The Journal of the T.E. Lawrene Society, Vol. VIII:I, pp.4-5,* 1998:4). In 1938 Jarvis was awarded the Royal Society for Asian Affairs' Lawrence of Arabia Memorial Medal for Services in the Develpoment of Sinai (Wilson, J. and Wilson, N. 2000 'Lawrence of Arabia Factfile', www.castle-hill-press. com/teweb/life/memmed).

The Montreal Gazette (**9 May, 1936**) (Zin Addenda 7.1.24)

"They Have Their Day And Cease to Be"

This handsome book is more for the scholar than the general reader but admirers of T. E. Lawrence will find it a valuable addition to the ana of that strange and impressive personage. It was written when he was in his early twenties, as an official report, and was published as the Annual of the Palestine Exploration Fund for 1914-15, and apart from its importance archaeologically, it has a real interest in the light it throws on Lawrence's activities just before the outbreak of war and on his character as a painstaking searcher of the tumbled stones of the past. At the same time, the general reader, picking his way through the carefully recorded details, gets something of Lawrence's ability for vivid description, of his dry humor, and gets glimpses, too, in the midst of a weary wilderness, of the colors of romance.

The book is not all Lawrence's, of course, and tribute must be paid to his distinguished colleague Leonard Woolley, and to M. N. Tod, who gives an account of the inscriptions found. Sir Frederick [sic] Kenyon explains how Lawrence and Woolley undertook the explorations, their significance, and the work that has been done in the region since the war. The volume is copiously illustrated with diagrams and has 40 plates, mostly from photographs taken by the two young explorers.

"A blank, my Lord," is the quotation at the head of the chapter "The History of the Southern Desert." The writers speak of "The wear[y]ing monotony of senseless rounded hills and unmeaning valleys" which makes the southern desert of Syria "one of the most inhospitable of all deserts – one which since the Mohammedan invasion, has been an unenvied resort of defeated tribes too weak to face the strenuous life of the greater deserts .... Most of the map is filled with petty hills and small shallow valleys; there are many barren tablelands and a few deep hollows and wide valleys drowned from bank to bank under the great billows of moving sand dunes, and overgrown with colocynth, which emphasises their incurable desolation ..... The climate of Sinai is a trying one. In summer, of course, it is blisteringly hot, and in the winter cold with the unbridled cold of an abandoned country over which the wind can rage in unchecked fury."

It has been argued that the climate was once more attractive and the land less desolate, but the explorers give evidence to show that it was never less a desert than now and that if it flourished with a little more flourish in the Byzantine days, it was because the Byzantines conserved water and improved agricultural methods.

Digging in the ruins of the stone cities – ceilings were flagged, floors paved, and even shelves were stone – they were able to clear up a great many misconceptions about Zin. They show us the trade route from Ceylon and India, over which the caravans passed on the way to Gaza and Greece with their loads of spices, emeralds and silks. They give us news about the Byzantine occupation, about the hermitages in the wilderness, and about the Arab conquest which put a stop to history. They fix for us the wilderness where the Children of Israel wandered for 40 years.

Perhaps the fate of Khalasa – called by the Romans, Elusa – is as good an example as any of man's losing fight against the inhospitable barrens. It was once a great religious centre, with its own god – the morning star, probably called Khalasa, but whether male or female, no one knows; it was great in the days of Byzantium, with its religion, its forts, but many of its stones were taken away by the builders of Gaza, and today it is nothing but a heap of tumbled blocks and stone chippings and bits of broken pottery.

Natal Advertiser, Durban, South Africa (4 May, 1936) (Zin Addenda 7.1.13)

Ruins of An Ancient Race – Old World Highway Examined

Rock and ruins, intermingled with Biblical historical interest, sums up in the briefest terms the story contained in "The Wilderness of Zin," an excellent work of archaeological research written by C. Leonard Woolley and T. E. Lawrence and published by Jonathan Cape, London.

The Wilderness of Zin is found on the map of Palestine. It is bounded by the towns of Gaza and Beersheba on the north, by the Wadi Araba on the east, by the Red Sea on the south and by the approaches to Egypt on the west and it was in fact, as regards a portion of it, the route the ancients trod going to and from Egypt and Mesopotamia and adjacent countries. The book explains the nature of the country, and is the result of a six weeks' expedition in January and February 1914 during which the authors, taking different routes, explored this desert region gathering from it, in spite of its arid nature, plentiful fruits, and many new ideas regarding it. It was first published as the annual report of the Palestine Exploration Fund, and it now takes book form for the first time for the benefit of general readers. Both its value from a scientific point of view and its great public interest entitle it to this promotion.

It introduces the reader to a portion of the earth that has changed little since the time of Moses. It has always been a highway for armies and for commerce and in historical reference it can be found it has always been a wilderness. But it is explained that a wilderness does not necessarily mean a desert, and the Zin region has always been inhabited by people of nomadic instincts, and at long periods by people of more settled ways and of a considerable culture, and it is the remains of this culture that excite the curiosity and spur on the effort of the explorer.

The authors deal widely and precisely with the various ruins of churches, fortifications and private dwellings, and also with wells and tombs, and discuss the excavations and contour of the country and its physical features, and the probabilities of previous beliefs in the light of what they themselves discovered. They must indeed, have had an exceedingly busy six weeks in which not only did they gather material for the present fine work, but also took numerous photographs which are collected in the second half of the book. The pictures supplement the lucid letterpress and together there is presented to the reader a review of the Zin wilderness which cannot fail to give him a grasp of its many remarkable features.

The work has in addition pictures of inscriptions found which the authors discuss, diagrams of the larger towns and churches, an index and a map which is very useful in the following chapter dealing with their separate wanderings in the desert. A knowledge of Arabic and Greek lexicon are desirable adjuncts if the book would be fully absorbed, but there is enough good plain English for the average reader to make the book one of value and interest to him. It is a rich story of a very barren land, and it places in the limelight one of the Noman's-lands [sic] of the present partition of the globe, and it has been well and truly done.

Two photographs from *The Wilderness of Zin* accompany the review (Plate XXV, 1 and 2)

APPENDIX 5

Chronological Chart

1880		Birth of Leonard Woolley
1888		Birth of T. E. Lawrence
1909		Lawrence's walking tour in Syria
1911		Lawrence begins work at Carchemish
1912		Woolley takesover from Hogarth at Carchemish
1913		
	Apr./May:	British Army and Foreign Office wish to survey Sinai
	Summer:	Lawrence brings Dahoum and Hamoudi to Oxford
	Oct. 10th:	Col. Hedley accepts position on PEF Committee
	Oct. 29th:	Turkish Government allow PEF Survey of WOZ
	Nov. 4th:	PEF Committee agree to pursue WOZ survey; Newcombe suggested as the leader of the survey
	Dec. 2nd:	Hedley informs PEF of military personel to be on survey
	Dec. 6th:	Newcombe arrives at Gaza and prepares for survey
	Dec. 11th:	Kenyon informs PEF that Woolley and Lawrence are willing to undertake survey
	Dec. 16th:	Sir Charles Watson sends Woolley PEF instructions for survey; PEF receives £100 from the Royal Geographical Society for the survey.
	Dec. 25th:	Newcombe starts survey

1914

Jan. 1st:	Woolley receives PEF instructions (see 16.12.13) in Aleppo
Jan. 5th:	Woolley, Lawrence (and Dahoum) arrive at Gaza
Jan. 7th:	Woolley and Lawrence set up camp at Beersheba; visit Tell Abu Regaig
Jan. 9th:	They meet Newcombe at Beersheba
Jan. 11th:	Woolley and Lawrence leave Beersheba for Khalasa; based at Khalasa for four days and make visits to Raheiba and Saadi.
Jan. 16th:	Woolley and Lawrence leave Khalasa for Esbeita; visit Mishrafa
Jan. 24th:	Woolley and Lawrence leave Esbeita for El Auja; visit Tell es-Seram
Jan. 27th:	Woolley and Lawrence leave El Auja for 'Ain Kadeis; become separated from baggage camels
Jan. 28th:	Woolley and Lawrence arrive at 'Ain Kadeis and then proceed to government station at Kossaima where they meet rest of the party; visit Muweilleh and 'Ain Kadeis; move camp to Wady 'Ain Guderat; visit *haraba* Khoraisha
Feb. 8th:	Woolley and Lawrence separate. Lawrence and Dahoum go with Newcombe down the 'old road' along Wady Lussan through Kuntilla to Aqaba, then north up Wady Arabah to 'Ain Gharandel.
Feb. 25th:	Lawrence at Petra
Feb. 28th:	Lawrence in Damascus (took train from Ma'an)
Feb. 8th:	Woolley travels up Wady Guderat, over a ridge to a branch of Wady el-'Ain, across

	and northwards along Wadi Khoraisha, to *haraba* Ras el-Aziz.
Feb. 9th:	Woolley travels east to Wadi Hafir, and on to Bir el-Hafir. He continues to Wadi el-Gatun, and then to Wady Ramliya, before reaching Abda.
Feb. 15th:	Woolley leaves Abda, crossing Wady Ramliya and Wady Murra, and then the Nagb el-Gharid, before arrving at Bir Rakhama via the Wady 'Araeigin and Wady el-Jurf
Feb. 16th:	Woolley travels from Bir Rakhma to Kurnub
Feb. 19th:	Woolley leaves Kurnub for Tell es-Seba, from which he visits Tell es-Sawa, Khirbet Wotan, Bir el-Hammam, Tell el-Milah, and Khirbet el-Imshash
Feb. 22nd:	Woolley leaves Beersheba for Gaza and Aleppo
Feb. 26th:	Woolley in Jaffa
Mar. 2nd:	Woolley and Lawrence reunited at Aleppo
Mar. 14th:	Pottery from survey arrives at the PEF
by mid-May:	Newcombe finishes survey
May 19th:	Newcombe with Woolley and Lawrence at Jerablus/Carchemish
June 8th:	Lawrence leaves The Baron Hotel, Aleppo
June:	Lawrence and Woolley return to England (via Turkey)
July 7th:	Woolley and Lawrence attend PEF meeting in London
Aug. 4th:	Outbreak of World War One
Sept. 23rd:	Woolley joins the Territorial Army
Oct. 6th:	Marcus N. Tod recommended to work on

	inscriptions
Oct. 14th:	Woolley gains commission in the Royal Artillery
Oct. 19th:	Lawrence appointed to M.O.4 under Hedley
Oct. 20th:	PEF decide to make *WOZ* Annual for 1914-15.
Oct. 26th:	Lawrence gains commission as second lieutenant
Oct. 29th:	Turkey enters the war
Nov.	Lawrence works on *WOZ* and military projects; Woolley checks *WOZ*
Dec. 1st:	D. G. Hogarth to see *WOZ* through publication
Dec. 3rd:	Lawrence delivers manuscript of *WOZ* to PEF
Dec. 9th:	Lawrence leaves for Egypt
Dec. 12th:	Woolley leaves for Egypt
Dec. 15th:	Lawrence's Sinai Map displayed at PEF; discussion of further payment to Woolley and Lawrence deferred

1915

Apr. 20th:	Printers instructed to produce 1000 copies

1916

Nov. 7th:	Hedley wants to resign from PEF Committee due to pressure of work

1919

May 8th:	Letter written to Lawrence about attending the PEF AGM receives no reply

1920

Sept. 8th:	Thomas Cook & Son Account from *WOZ* survey finally closed

Oct. 20th: Hedley resigns from PEF Committee after leaving the War Office

1921

May 18th: Colonel Newcombe and Sir Charles Close present completed 1914 Negeb map to PEF Committee

1922-33   Woolley at Ur

1935

May 13th: Death of T. E. Lawrence

June 27th: Newcombe suggests that PEF republish WOZ

July 16th: Jonathan Cape offer to republish *WOZ*

July 27th: PEF agree to go with Jonathan Cape if no better offer received

Dec. 5th: PEF agree to present copy of *WOZ* to A. W. Lawrence

1936

Mar 13th: Jonathan Cape Edition of *WOZ* published

1956   Newcombe dies

1960   Woolley dies